CHOSEN

Acknowledgements

I would like to take this space to say thank you to all of those who have poured into my life over the years both physically and spiritually. You are who helped make this book possible.

To My Mother

God saw fit to knit me in your womb. Thank you for not only carrying me but raising me in the fear and admonition of the Lord. You showed me firsthand what it was to be a praying mother. I know the road was not easy but you persevered and birthed strength in me as I looked at you continuing to endure through much adversity. You raised me right. Thank you for always encouraging me to be the woman of God you knew He predestined me to be!

To My Spiritual Mother

The Lord knew just what I needed. You may not have carried me in the natural, but you most definitely birthed me in the spiritual. I know without a doubt I would not be walking out this call without your guidance and support. You helped me to understand that I was not crazy but called. Your walk of integrity is rare and is what I endeavor to pattern my prophetic ministry after. You are a woman of prayer and intimacy with God that transcends through the authority and power that you carry. Thank you for being my mom, correcting me where needed, training, grooming, laying hands, and praying for me. You are the one who helped me to embrace my call and for that I am so grateful!

To My Husband

God could not have chosen a better partner for me to journey with. You are such a constant encouragement to not only my walk with Christ but my prophetic journey as well. It is not simple being married to a Prophet, but you make it look so easy! You have prayed and covered me through some of the darkest moments of my life and for that I say thank you. God used you to prophesy this book into existence. You are so much more than just a husband, but a Pastor, counselor, and friend. I love you babe, forever and always.

To My Church Family

Thank you all for your constant support and encouragement. You all have witnessed firsthand God make me into the Prophet I am today. Thank you for believing in and honoring the gift that God has placed on my life. I could not have chosen a better family to be a part of!

To My Children

Thank you for all the sacrifice you have made as mommy and daddy endeavor to do ministry as a family. You may not understand it all now but the seeds we are sowing are for you. It is my prayer that that which we are building will become a firm foundation for you to flourish on in your later years. May the roots of our labor run deep and may it benefit your future!

To You

To those whom God has allowed to speak into my life over the years I want to say thank you. There have been many men and women of God with whom God has used to speak prophetically over my life. Know that your words were not in vain. Your words were seeds that helped to cultivate what you are witnessing today. From a young child, God used men and women to help point me back in the right direction. To confirm the call that He had on my life. Your words brought life to my spiritual womb. There are too many of you to name but you know who you are. Thank you, thank you, thank you!

Dedication

This book is dedicated to God's Chosen Prophets. Those hand selected and set aside for His special purpose and use in these last days. Those who have gone through the refiner's fire being proven and tried. A generation that has been soaking in the secret place like Esther, being prepared for their introduction. For the Lord is raising up a new breed of Prophets. They are going to be washed with the Word, clothed in humility, purity, submitted, understanding authority, leadership, and honor. They will be slow to speak, quick to listen and easy to be entreated. They will have a heavy closet anointing, living, and thriving from God's presence. For there is a dying generation, a world in need and desperate for God. These ones will have a heart that burns for the souls of God's people. This new breed will fear God more than men. Speaking God's truth in love bringing conviction to the heart of men, reconciling them back to God. They will have yes in their belly like Joshua saying, "Lord send me I'll go." They will go where God sends them. And the first will be the last and the last will be first.

TABLE OF CONTENTS

Chosen

Hello, my name is Janell Edmondson, and I am God's chosen vessel, a Prophet of the one and only true and living God. I believe that I can safely assume that if you are reading this book that you are called to be a Prophet or operate in the prophetic as well; but if neither of those two apply to you, I am sure there is something for you to gain by reading this book. So, what does it mean to be chosen? To be chosen simply means you have been set apart by God for a special purpose. He chose to set you apart to do a special work. Not because you were so great, qualified, or experienced, but simply because He chose you!

First, I want to affirm to you today that you have been predestined for this call. Let that sink in. Now I want to bring you through the indicators in your life that confirm that you are truly God's chosen vessel. Let us begin.

From the day you were born, those around you could tell that you were not normal. You may have suffered rejection and abandonment because of this. God's chosen vessels have a mark on them from birth that they may not have known was there, but the enemy did. You have experienced extreme opposition from an early age. You struggled with your identity, confidence, and voice. The more you talk the more you realize that you are not like others. You have been often misunderstood and may have even been labeled crazy. You yourself sometimes feel this way because of the things you have experienced.

You are uncomfortable with being "normal" by the world's standards. Though you try to fit into the mold, it just does not seem to work. You may have had supernatural encounters from youth. Some of which you were not able to identify at first. Sometimes you may not even want to share these experiences because they look so different and do not fit into anything else that you have ever heard or seen from others. What seems strange to others is normal to you. You have an unusual eye. You pick up on the smallest of things that other people may miss. You see God in the little details of everything around you. You see things that you speak manifest around you even if you did not mean for them to. Your words carry an unusual weight and so you must be careful with them.

Like a genetic marker, you can trace back God's influence in your life, relationships, jobs, and even career choice. God was serious about you. So much so that from a child He began to groom you for His purpose. What others got away with you could not get away with no matter how hard you tried. It is as if you had an inner compass that was leading every aspect of your life.

He did not want you to become tainted by the world. Not saying that you are perfect or have always walked the straight and narrow path, but there was a string that God attached to you that would only let you go so far. God had already put His imprint on you like a golden compass that no matter where you went in life, He could always help you navigate your way back. If you have identified any of these in your walk, I want to declare to you today that you are not crazy, a misfit, or any of the above. You are just chosen. A person who is called not only to the prophetic but who has been hand selected as a Chosen vessel of God.

Now I have some questions to ask you. How confident are you in the call that God has placed on your life? Do you feel weak? Do you sometimes feel inadequate? Like where do I start? Can I really hear from God and convey that word accurately? Do I have what it takes to do well what I have seen others do so effortlessly? Or are you one of the ones who have just been told they are a Prophet but have no idea what it entails or if you are really qualified to do the job! Well, if you have answered yes to any of these questions, I want to tell you that you are not alone. As a matter of fact, you are in good company.

There are many prophetic men and women who have sat in the same seat you are sitting in today with feelings of insecurities and inadequacies. I come to help you release some of those fears. God did not choose them because they were so great, well-prepared, smart, or educated. It was not because of who their mother or father was or even because of who they were connected to. He chose them just like He chose you because He knew He could show His power through them. So, repeat after me, "I am chosen by God".

Give Him your yes

I started off by stating my name and the office that I walk in. I can now boldly declare who I am and who God has always called for me to be; but this was not always so. I had some real doubts as well about my ability to be used by God, but as I journeyed with Him, I realized I was not alone. Just take a scroll through the 66 books of the Bible and you will find that there were very few men and women who did not have the same reservations.

Contrary to popular belief, it is not about how much we know, how educated we are, how many prophetic seminars we've attended or books we've read. It's not even about how many accurate prophetic words we have under our belt. Though all these things are good, it's not the most important nor is it a prerequisite for God to move mightily through us.

Then I heard the Lord asking, "Whom should I send as a messenger to this people? Who will go for us?" I said, "Here I am. Send me." And he said, "Yes, go, and say to this people, 'Listen carefully, but do not understand. Watch closely, but learn nothing." Isaiah 6:8-9 NLT

All God needs is your yes. It may seem so simple, but that is the biggest step that you will take on your prophetic journey. This is the start of the making of the Prophet. Just like Isaiah, Moses, David, Gideon, Jeremiah, and even the 12 Apostles. They all had these things in common. Issues and availability. Weaknesses and willingness. They saw the frailty of their humanity and went with God anyhow.

You will never be a perfect Prophet

You may have heard of this popular saying: "God does not call the qualified, but He qualifies the called." This statement is absolutely true, and the Prophet Amos is a perfect example of that.

> *Then Amos answered, and said to Amaziah: "I was no prophet, Nor was I a son of a prophet, But I was a sheepbreeder And a tender of sycamore fruit. Then the Lord took me as I followed the flock, And the Lord said to me, 'Go, prophesy to My people Israel."*
> *Amos 7:14-15 NKJV*

This is one of my favorite scriptures concerning God's Prophets because it so beautifully illustrates what is the most important thing. You see, Amos was no ordinary Prophet. He did not come from a prophetic background which was unusual for the Prophets of this time. I can only imagine how he may have felt about himself and or if he was received by his fellow Prophets due to this fact. Another version of this scriptures says **But Amos replied, "I'm not a professional prophet, and I was never trained to be one."** (NLT). I am sure he may have felt unqualified to do what he was doing or even unprepared. Though he had no formal training to be a Prophet like his counterparts, he did not let that stop him. He offered to God his mouth, and in doing so God used it. This does not take away the necessity for accountability, mentorship, and development. However, God is who calls a Prophet, and it is His ultimate responsibility to train and develop us; but it is in our yielding that we grow. What God really desires is for you to be available in whatever capacity He wants to use you.

Do not stress yourself about your qualifications. That comes with experience. God understands this and He will afford you the opportunity to gain that experience. Also, know that no two Prophet's process will look the same. God will use anything to build that Prophet. Often the very things around you become your building blocks of experience. Whether it be in private on the back of a mountain, with family, or in the pulpit. He used the very sheep David shepherded to prepare him to shepherd His chosen people. He doesn't need your education, expertise, or knowledge, only your yes! As my leader always says, "God is not looking for a perfect vessel, but an available one."

He Chose you

"Because the foolishness of God is wiser than men; and the weakness of God is stronger than men. For ye see your calling, brethren, how that not many wise men after the flesh, not many mighty, not many noble, are called: But God hath chosen the foolish things of the world to confound the wise; and God hath chosen the weak things of the world to confound the things which are mighty;" 1 Corinthians 1:25-27 KJV

The unlikely

If we look carefully throughout Biblical history, we will notice a very unusual thing about God. He has a propensity to choose the most unlikely vessels to do great exploits through. Moses and Jeremiah are just two examples of God's miraculous handiwork done through ordinary individuals. See, they both struggled with their identity and were insecure about their ability to speak for God, but for two totally different reasons. The Prophet Jeremiah was insecure about his age while Moses was insecure about his ability to speak with clarity. Both could be viewed as very valid reasons to feel unqualified as you too may recognize your "shortcomings" and think "Could God really use me?" I am here to tell you, yes He can!

The weak things

You may feel as though you don't have "It." You know, the "It" that others have that causes them to be successful. You don't have the connections or platform. The charisma or eloquent speech. Well again, God does not need any of those things to use you. The Lord called the Apostle Paul to minister salvation to the Gentiles. He had numerous churches he oversaw and even wrote 2/3 of the New Testament. These were all major accomplishments, but even he had some weaknesses that to some would have been counterproductive to the call that was on his life.

In the Book of 2 Corinthians, we see some of those he oversaw had some not-so-nice things to say about him when he wasn't in their presence. They accused him of being weak in the oration department (**2 Corinthians 10**). They even went as far as to say he did better on paper, writing letters, than he did speaking in person. Whew! That was critical! Though it seemed harsh in the moment, their criticism afforded us, the future readers, a glimpse into

Paul's vulnerable places. See, Paul never denied the accusation. He knew he was not the best speaker, but he did not let what others saw as a shortcoming stand in the way of him completing the assignment God gave him. So, neither should you!

God loves to use the overlooked like David, the insecure like Gideon, or the fearful like Elijah. Just look over the life of the men we previously mentioned, and you will see the vast difference between what their *insecurities spoke to them* versus what *God did through them*. We have books of history now that we can read about the life of those whom God chose. God is not afraid of our weaknesses. He is not intimidated by our undeveloped places. He is not turned off by our fears or insecurities. All of these are opportunities for God to show His glory up and out through us.

I want to reintroduce you to yourself. There is more in you than what you can even imagine. I want to prophetically declare over you that God intends to use you in a greater capacity than what you have limited yourself to in your mind. In it He gets all the glory, and no man can boast. As you journey through this book, it is my prayer that you gain greater clarity on your call and the gifts that God has placed in your life. May you gain and grow in and with God as He forms and makes you into the Prophet or prophetic person He has called you to be!

All about the Prophetic

I would like to start this book talking about the basic foundations of prophecy; what it is and what God intended for it to be used for. In the first few chapters, we will be discussing the differences between the Spirit of Prophecy, the Gift of Prophecy, and the Office of the Prophet. We will also discuss the different types of prophetic ministries. If you are new to the prophetic, I hope this brings clarity to the many questions that you may have, and if you are familiar with the prophetic then this will be a refresher for you. We will start this chapter by talking about the source of all *true* prophetic words which is the Spirit of Prophecy. Let's begin!

The Spirit of Prophecy

The Spirit of Prophecy

Contrary to popular belief, prophecy is not as complicated as it may seem. The Spirit of Prophecy in its basic form is the testimony of Jesus Christ. God's Spirit declaring His will through man in the earth.

> *"I am a servant of God, just like you and your brothers and sisters who testify about their faith in Jesus. Worship only God. For the essence of prophecy is to give a clear witness for Jesus." Revelation 19:10 NLT*

We see in the Old Testament where the Spirit of God would move "upon" a man and then they would have the ability to prophesy (**2 Peter 1:21**). This is because the ability to prophesy is not predicated upon human ability but rather the power and ability of the Spirit of God. This word comes from God's heart and is His idea. That is why, in essence, anyone can prophesy. We can see from the life of King Saul two separate occasions where he encountered the Spirit of God "come upon" him and he too prophesied. Let us read into one of his encounters.

> *"When Saul and his servant arrived at Gibeah, they saw a group of prophets coming toward them. Then the Spirit of God came powerfully upon Saul, and he, too, began to prophesy." 1 Samuel 10:10 NLT*

The people around Saul at the time were confused because in those days Prophets came from generational lines; meaning most often if you were a Prophet then your father was a Prophet. In this case, Saul was not from a prophetic background, but because he was in the presence of other Prophets, the Spirit of Prophecy fell upon him and he was able to prophesy. We see this as well in our time where the Spirit of prophecy can fall heavily in a church service and God will speak through whomever He chooses.

Take for instance another example here. In the Book of Numbers, Moses went to anoint 70 leaders to help him serve. As he did so, his Spirit rested upon them, and they had a similar experience.

> *"And the Lord came down in the cloud and spoke to Moses. Then he gave the seventy elders the same Spirit that was upon Moses. And when the Spirit rested upon them, they prophesied. But this never happened again." Numbers 11:25 NLT*

This is the Spirit of prophecy. The Spirit of God moving upon a man and enabling them to declare His Word.

Can you think of an instance where you have witnessed or experienced the Spirit of Prophecy in operation?

The Gift of Prophecy

Now let's venture into the gift of prophecy. The gift of prophecy is one of the 12 spiritual gifts the Apostle Paul mentions in 1st Corinthians 12.

> *"He gives one person the power to perform miracles, and another the ability to prophesy." 1 Corinthians 12:10 NLT*

It is still the Spirit of prophecy but in a gift form. The word gift is translated from the Greek word ***charisma***. The Thayer Bible concordance defines the word gift as a favor with which one receives without any merit of his own; the gift of divine grace; grace of gifts denoting extraordinary powers distinguishing certain Christians and enabling them to serve the Church of Christ. The Strong's concordance defines gifts as a *spiritual endowment*.

As stated before, the gift of prophecy comes without merit, meaning it is irrevocable and is not dependent upon one's lifestyle (**Romans 11:29**). God has given certain individuals this specific gift (ability) to prophesy in order to serve the body of Christ. The purpose of this gift is to *edify*, *exhort* and bring *comfort*, according to 1 Corinthians 14:2.

Let's explore the three functions of the gift of prophecy.

1. **Edify** – Thayer definition: to build; to instruct an improved especially in moral and religious knowledge; to uplift and establish. Promote another's growth in Christian wisdom, piety, happiness, and holiness.

    "He who speaks in a tongue edifies himself, but he who prophesies edifies the church." 1 Corinthians 14:4 NKJV

2. **Exhortation-** Strong Bible concordance defines exhortation as to aid, help, comfort, encourage and beseech or to admonish; a calling near, summons especially for help; consolation which provides comfort.

    "Now Judas and Silas, themselves being prophets also, exhorted and strengthened the brethren with many words." Acts 15:32 NKJV

3. **Comfort** Strong concordance definition: any address whether made or purpose of persuading or arousing and stimulating or a calming and consoling.

    "If therefore the whole church be come together into one place, and all speak with tongues, and there come in those that are unlearned, or unbelievers, will they not say that ye are mad? But if all prophesy, and there come in one that believeth not, or one unlearned, he is convinced of all, he is judged of all: And thus are the secrets of his heart made manifest; and so, falling on his face he will worship God, and report that God is in you of a truth." 1 Corinthians 14:23 KJV

When a person carries the gift of prophecy, they have the ability to speak by the Spirit of God to bring comfort, edification, and exhortation to the body of Christ. They can do this at will, declaring God's Word for these purposes. The gift of Prophecy is very important to the body of Christ. It enables the Spirit of God to speak progressively. Where you see the Spirit of Prophecy moving, there will always be growth, maturity, fresh revelation, and insight. When a church is said to be prophetic, it means that they allow the Spirit of Prophecy to flow freely in the midst. In these types of churches, you can be most certain that there are individuals there who carry the gift of Prophecy and most times the leader will carry it as well.

This gift can be administrated in many ways other than spoken word or preaching. For example, you may have been in a church service and the psalmist began to sing a song and you felt as though the words that he or she was ministering spoke directly to your present situation. Through it you received comfort, peace, and confirmation. This is the gift of Prophecy being used through song. The prophetic gift can also be demonstrated through dance and art as well.

The Office of the Prophet

Prophetic does not equate to Prophet

Having the gift (ability) to prophesy does not mean one is sitting in the Office of the Prophet. This is because prophecy or prophesying is only one aspect of prophetic ministry. Due to this misconception, many people have been given the title of a Prophet when what they truly carry is the Gift of Prophecy. Though the gift is still vital to the body of Christ, God has given a special grace to those who sit in the 5-fold office of the Prophet. It could be very detrimental to an individual to be given the title of a Prophet if they have not also been given the grace to carry the assignment that comes with it. In this next section we will venture into the Office of the Prophet so that you can distinguish the difference.

So, what is the difference between one who carries the Gift of Prophecy and one who holds the Office of a Prophet? Ordination. Prophets have been ordained (*set aside*) by God for His special purpose. Though Apostle Paul tells us that we should covet prophecy (**1 Corinthians 14:39**) which is the gift, one cannot desire to be a Prophet and then become one. Prophets are chosen by God, not men, and He is the one who raises them up.

> *"I will raise up a prophet like you from among their fellow Israelites. I will put my words in his mouth, and he will tell the people everything I command him." Deuteronomy 18:18 NLT*

Vocation is a person's employment or main occupation especially regarded as particularly worthy and requiring great dedication. It can also be defined as one's trade or profession.

Thayer Bible concordance defines **Prophets:** *of men filled with the Spirit of God, who by God's authority and command in words of weight pleads the cause of God and urges salvation of men. In the religious assemblies of the Christians, they were moved by the Holy Spirit to speak, having power to instruct, comfort, encourage, rebuke, convict, and stimulate, their hearers.*

The Office of the Prophet comes with responsibilities that God requires them to carry out. Prophets operate from a Heavenly *seat* that gives them greater authority in the Heavenly Realm. This is their first vocation and *main purpose* for being on Earth. Let's look at the words God spoke to Jeremiah when He first commissioned him into his prophetic ministry.

"The word of the LORD came to me, saying: Before I formed you in the womb I knew you, and before you were born I set you apart and appointed you a prophet to the nations." Jeremiah 1:4-5 NLT

More than Prophesy

There are many misconceptions about the purpose of the Prophet. One of which is that their primary role is to prophesy. But this is not the case at all. This first occurred to me when I heard a prophetic teaching on this concept by a Prophet by the name of Naim Collins. It helped enlighten me further into the real purpose of the Prophet. As God brought me deeper into his prophetic classroom the fullness of this revelation was discovered even the more. Though prophesying is a necessary function, it is just a part of our mandate.

We see from the previously quoted Scripture that being a Prophet was Jeremiah's first vocation; before Jeremiah uttered his first "Word of the Lord," God had already ordained him to be a Prophet. So then, we understand that being a Prophet is not something that you "do" but rather it is who you are. It is who God formed you to be. Everything about you expresses your destiny call. A Prophet's *identity* is not based solely in him or her prophesying. Their whole life speaks something. It is communicating something that Heaven is trying to say. This is the difference between one who has a prophetic anointing and one who walks in the Office of the Prophet.

Being a Prophet is not something that they "do" occasionally. It is the *primary* purpose of their existence. Though they may be gifted in many areas and may even have a secular job, their first vocation is a Prophet; and if you are a Prophet then I am speaking to you. Take a moment and breathe that in. You have been *set-apart* for God's purpose. We must embrace our call; if not, then we will never fulfill the real purpose that God has birthed us into the earth to do.

Types of Prophets

When searching Bible history, we see that there were two types of Prophets. Those who were *born* Prophets like Jeremiah (**Jeremiah 1:4**) and those who God *called* later in life like the Prophet Amos (**Amos 7:14**). No matter whether they were born or called, their purpose remained the same. It is God who predetermines their destiny, and He is the one who raises them up and puts His words in their mouth (**Deuteronomy 18:18**). Now let's dive into some characteristics of a Prophet that distinguishes them from other 5-fold ministry offices.

The Voice of the Prophet

"Elijah replied, If I am a man of God, let fire come down from heaven and destroy you and your fifty men! And again, the fire of God fell from heaven and killed them all." 2 Kings 1:12 NLT

The Prophet's voice carries great **weight** (authority) in the supernatural realm. Some Prophets, depending on their **mantle** (realm of authority), have the ability to command Heaven and the elements. Some biblical examples of these include Elijah and Elisha. This is not limited to the Old Testament as some modern-day Prophets carry this mantle as well. The Prophet Elijah had the ability to command Heaven; first causing it to shut with no rain falling for a season of three and a half years.

"Elijah was as human as we are, and yet when he prayed earnestly that no rain would fall, none fell for three and a half years! Then, when he prayed again, the sky sent down rain and the earth began to yield its crops." James 5:17-18 NLT

The Prophet's voice has the ability to bring life by the Spirit of the Prophet that is within them.

"Then he said to me, Speak a prophetic message to the winds, son of man. Speak a prophetic message and say, This is what the Sovereign Lord says: Come, O breath, from the four winds! Breathe into these dead bodies

so they may live again. So I spoke the message as he commanded me, and breath came into their bodies. They all came to life and stood up on their feet—a great army." Ezekiel 37:9-10 NLT

The power of life and death is in our tongue. This is one of the laws that God has set in place for His creation (**Proverbs 18:21**). Even more so with the voice of the Prophet, and because their voice carries a great weight, they must be careful how they use it. The Prophet Elisha, when being teased by a group of young men, became angry and cursed them. Suddenly a pack of wild bears came and attacked them (**2 Kings 2:23-24**).).

This is the Voice of the Prophet. The ability to manifest things into the Earth realm. When a Prophet speaks life, there is life, but when they speak death, there is death (**Numbers 22:6**). No matter if they realize it or not, their words helped create and form the things that take place around them. This is why it is important for a Prophet's heart to be in the right posture so that when they speak, they do so from God's heart and not from their own selfish desires or emotions.

The Eyes of the Prophet

"Then the Spirit of God came upon him, and this is the message he delivered: This is the message of Balaam son of Beor, the message of the man whose eyes see clearly, the message of one who hears the words of God, who sees a vision from the Almighty, who bows down with eyes wide open." Numbers 24:2-4 NLT

The eyes of the Prophet are open by God, enabling them to see in the Supernatural Realm. In many instances the Lord uses dreams and visions to speak to His Prophets (**Ezekiel 1:1, Jeremiah 1:11, Isaiah 1:1**). This vision is not limited to dreams and open visions, but the ability to see in the unseen realm. The Prophet Elisha carried this gift to see in the Supernatural. When facing an attack from the Aramean army, Elisha's servant began to be fearful. Elisha asked God to give his servant the ability to see as he did.

"Don't be afraid! Elisha told him. For there are more on our side than on theirs! Then Elisha prayed, O Lord, open his eyes and let him see! The Lord opened the young man's eyes, and when he looked up, he saw that the hillside around Elisha was filled with horses and chariots of fire." 2 Kings 6:16-17 NLT

From the eyes of the Prophet Ezekiel, we are given a glimpse into the supernatural world. Ezekiel described in detail Heavenly beings even beholding the Glory of the Lord.

> *"All around him was a glowing halo, like a rainbow shining in the clouds on a rainy day. This is what the glory of the Lord looked like to me. When I saw it, I fell face down on the ground, and I heard someone's voice speaking to me." Ezekiel 1:28 NLT*

It is crucial for the Prophet to be able to see into the supernatural realm. Prophetic words encompass past, present, and future, so it is imperative that their vision is not limited to what they can see in the natural. When a Prophet uses their vision, it enables them to be able to carry the deeper things of God; seeing beyond what the present moment in time is saying and declare into the future.

The Ears of the Prophet

> *"The Lord God hath given me the tongue of the learned, that I should know how to speak a word in season to him that is weary: he wakeneth morning by morning, he wakeneth mine ear to hear as the learned. The Lord God hath opened mine ear, and I was not rebellious, neither turned away back." Isaiah 50:4-5 KJV*

The ears of the Prophet are fine-tuned to be able to hear beyond the natural realm. Thayer Bible concordance definition of **ear**- *is metaphorically the faculty of perceiving with the mind. The facility of understanding and knowing.*

It is their ability to hear the audible voice of the Lord. It is their ability to hear in the Spirit. Though the Lord sometimes uses dreams and visions to speak, there are many Prophets who *hear* more than they *see*. This is because the Lord has chosen for them to perceive more through their ears and hearing His voice audibly. This is what Isaiah experienced when the Lord opened up his ears and he was able to hear the instructions and Word of the Lord.

This gift is not only to hear God's voice, but also to perceive the occurrences that are taking place in the unseen realm. We see where God talked to Samuel in his ear (**1 Samuel 9:15**). In the Book of 1 Kings, the Prophet Elijah discerned, through his hearing, after three and a half years of drought, the sound of the abundance of rain.

"Then Elijah said to Ahab, Go get something to eat and drink, for I hear a mighty rainstorm coming!" 1 Kings 18:41 NLT

It is true that Prophets alone do not carry this ability. It is God who opens the eyes and ears of men, and He does so at His choosing. This is however, to emphasize the ability of the Prophet to hear. This gift enables them to know before, warn and intercede, as we see many of the Prophets in the Bible did.

In the story of the king of Syria in 2 Kings, God gave the Prophet Elisha the ability to hear the very words that the king of Syria spoke in his private chamber. This enabled Elisha to warn the king of Israel ahead of the planned attack.

"The king of Aram became very upset over this. He called his officers together and demanded, Which of you is the traitor? Who has been informing the king of Israel of my plans? It's not us, my Lord the king, one of the officers replied. Elisha, the prophet in Israel, tells the king of Israel even the words you speak in the privacy of your bedroom!" 2 Kings 6:11-12 NLT

The Power of the Prophet

The power of the Prophet is their ability to intervene and intercede on behalf of humanity, invoking the power of God to move in human affairs. In the Book of 1 Samuel, the children of Israel asked God to give them a king to rule over them like the other nations. This displeased not only the Lord, but Samuel as well. Samuel wanted to prove that in fact their request was not in line with God's will, so he asked for God to show them a sign. The Lord heeded to the voice of Samuel by sending rain in a season that rain did not usually fall. This showed that what Samuel was saying was truly of the Lord.

"So, Samuel called to the Lord, and the Lord sent thunder and rain that day. And all the people were terrified of the Lord and of Samuel." 1 Samuel 12:18 NLT

In another incident, the children of Israel asked Samuel to plead to God on their behalf in order to overcome the Philistines. Again, God headed his request (**1 Samuel 7:8-9**).

As much as the children of Israel rebelled against God, Samuel understood his position to them as a Prophet, priest, and judge. He declared unto them that he would continue to intercede for them because failing to do so would be a neglect of his duties and considered a sin. Though we as Christians are all called to intercede on the behalf of others, a true Prophet understands the greater weight of power that they carry and does not take it for granted. Knowing that their ability to plead to God on the behalf of others could not only save lives but is also a part of the mandate given to them by God.

"Don't be afraid, Samuel reassured them. You have certainly done wrong, but make sure now that you worship the Lord with all your heart, and don't turn your back on him. As for me, I will certainly not sin against the Lord by ending my prayers for you. And I will continue to teach you what is good and right." 1 Samuel 12:20, 23 NLT

Power to change God's mind

"Surely the Lord God does nothing, Unless He reveals His secret to His servants the Prophets." Amos 3:7 NKJV

Oftentimes, the Lord would show the Prophet His plan to bring judgment. It was then the Prophet's responsibility to give the warning. Even in this, the Prophet had the ability to plead for mercy on behalf of the people. In some of these instances, the Prophet was even able to *change God's mind*. Let's look at an instance where Moses used his power of negotiation to pacify the anger of God on the behalf of the children of Israel.

"But Moses tried to pacify the Lord his God. "O Lord!" he said. "Why are you so angry with your own people whom you brought from the land of Egypt with such great power and such a strong hand? Why let the Egyptians say, 'Their God rescued them with the evil intention of slaughtering them in the mountains and wiping them from the face of the earth'? Turn away from your fierce anger. Change your mind about this terrible disaster you have threatened against your people! Remember your servants Abraham, Isaac, and Jacob. You bound yourself with an oath to them, saying, 'I will make your descendants as numerous as the stars of heaven. And I will give them all of this land that I have promised to your descendants, and they will possess it forever." So the Lord changed his mind

about the terrible disaster he had threatened to bring on his people."
Exodus 32:11-14 NLT

We see that there was no indication that the people had changed their behavior or had the intent to do so, but because Moses carried the power to negotiate with God, God consented to his prayer, changed His mind, and gave mercy.

Amos was able to change God's mind twice (**Amos 7:1-6**).

"The Sovereign Lord showed me a vision. I saw him preparing to send a vast swarm of locusts over the land. This was after the king's share had been harvested from the fields and as the main crop was coming up. In my vision the locusts ate every green plant in sight. Then I said, "O Sovereign Lord, please forgive us or we will not survive, for Israel is so small." So the Lord relented from this plan. "I will not do it," he said."
Amos 7:1-3 NLT

This very important aspect of the prophetic is one that we should not take for granted. The destruction that God had reserved for the children of Israel would have been most detrimental. Amos understood this and cried from his heart for God's forgiveness. They were certainly deserving of the punishment that God was about to release on them because of the many sins they had committed against the Lord, but because Amos stood in the gap for them, the judgment was withdrawn.

The Heart of the Prophet

"For judgment is without mercy to the one who has shown no mercy. Mercy triumphs over judgment." James 2:13 NKJV

This leads us to the heart of the Prophet. The heart of the Prophet is for the salvation of souls and to see the will of God carried out in the earth. How can one truly use their power to intercede and intervene for the people if they do not have a heart for them? A true Prophet's motive is not rooted in self, but to see the mercies of God extended to others. To see God's purpose fulfilled through His people, nations, or regions. Yes, the Lord uses Prophets to send warnings and to pronounce judgments, but even in a place of judgment their heart always leans toward mercy.

"Lord, I have not abandoned my job as a shepherd for your people. I have not urged you to send disaster. You have heard everything I've said." Jeremiah 17:16 NLT

The Role of the Prophet

Now that we have talked about the office, let's venture into the specific role that the Prophet plays in the body of Christ. As stated before, those who Christ has given these gifts to have also obtained a level of grace to handle and carry out their responsibilities. These are not just titles that are given as a means to separate and to make some look more prestigious than others, but these offices equate to a *duty* that God has given them to fulfill in the body of Christ.

The Role of the Prophet

A **Role** is the function assumed, or part played by a person or thing in a particular situation. Let's explore the role of the Prophet in our present-day Church. I like to look at it as an umbrella. Starting with the top portion which includes the general functions of all the 5-fold ministry offices listed in **Ephesians 4:7**.

Prophetic Umbrella

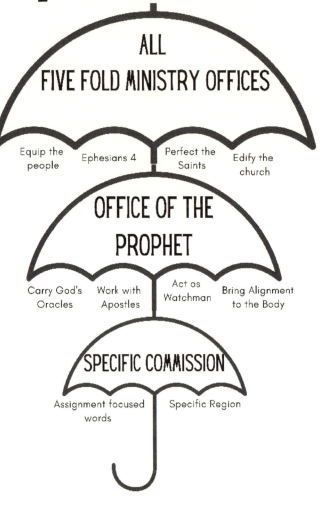

Level 1 - 5-fold Ministry

"Now these are the gifts Christ gave to the church: the apostles, the prophets, the evangelists, and the pastors and teachers. Their responsibility is to equip God's people to do his work and build up the church, the body of Christ. This will continue until we all come to such unity in our faith and knowledge of God's Son that we will be mature in the Lord, measuring up to the full and complete standard of Christ. Then we will no longer be immature like children. We won't be tossed and blown about by every wind of new teaching. We will not be influenced when people try to trick us with lies so clever, they sound like the truth. Instead, we will speak the truth in love, growing in every way more and more like Christ, who is the head of his body, the church." Ephesians 4:11-15 NLT

Jesus Christ has given the body these gifts in order to make the Church ready for His return. These positions require *GREAT DEDICATION.*

Their assignment - Perfect the saints, Equip the people to do the work, to edify (to build). Till we come into the unity of faith, knowledge of the son of God, perfected into the stature of Christ. This is the mandate given to everyone who sits in a the 5-fold ministry office.

Level 2- Office of the Prophet

The next level of the umbrella is more precise, detailing the specific function of the Prophet in the New Testament Church, some of which are similar to that of the Old Testament. Let's explore.

They carry God's oracles

One distinct difference between the gift and the office is Prophets carry God's oracles (*special messages*). Continued Thayer Bible concordance definition of the **Prophet** - *in Greek writings, an interpreter of oracles or of other hidden things; one who, moved by the Spirit of God and hence his organ or spokesman, solemnly declares to men what he has received by inspiration, especially concerning future events, and in particular such as relate to the cause and kingdom of God and to human salvation.*

They are those who God reveals His plans to in order for them to relay the message to the body as a whole. These messages include the ability to *foretell* future events. In the Old Testament, we see where God used Prophets to deliver these divine messages and to speak of His plans or purposes for the world (**Isaiah 24**), nations (**Deuteronomy 6:4**), cities (**Jonah 1:2**), regions (**Isaiah 15:1, Obadiah 1**), peoples (**1 Kings 14:6**), or an individual (**2 Kings 20:1**).

We see this function carried over into the New Testament Church in the Book of Acts when the Prophet Agabus foretold of a famine that would affect the whole earth.

"And in these days, prophets came from Jerusalem to Antioch. Then one of them, named Agabus, stood up and showed by the Spirit that there was going to be a great famine throughout all the world, which also happened in the days of Claudius Caesar." Acts 11:27-28 NLT

During the time of Apostle Paul's missionary work, this same Agabus foretold that Paul would be arrested by the Jews in Jerusalem and then delivered up to the Gentiles. This happened just as he predicted (**Acts 21:11**).

The Apostles and Prophets

"God did not reveal it to previous generations, but now by his Spirit he has revealed it to his holy apostles and prophets." Ephesians 3:5 NLT

The Lord uses Prophets in conjunction with the Apostles to help give direction not only to the local church but also to the body of Christ (**Acts 13:1**). We see this throughout the New Testament where the Apostles and Prophets worked hand in hand. Judas and Silas being two Prophets who were selected to walk alongside Paul and Barnabas on their mission to Antioch.

"And Judas and Silas, being prophets also themselves, exhorted the brethren with many words, and confirmed them." Acts 15:32 KJV

They act as watchman for the body

In ancient times, many cities were built with fortified walls encompassing the entire parameter. Watchtowers, which were raised towers, were set in distinct locations merged into the structure of the wall. The role of the watchman was to stand in these raised towers and "look out, or about" into the distance. They were to watch for impending danger and warn those in the city when they saw something coming by sounding an alarm. This would ensure those who kept watch at the gate (*gatekeepers*) had enough time to secure the city before the danger approached.

"After seven days the Lord gave me a message. He said, Son of man, I have appointed you as a watchman for Israel. Whenever you receive a message from me, warn people immediately." Ezekiel 3:16 NLT

Likewise, the Lord gave Prophets the role of spiritual watchman. They do not watch from physical watch towers, rather they watch from the elevated place of prayer. It is the Prophet's role to stay in a place of constant communion with God so that they can "see" what is taking place in the Spirit and "warn" the bride of impending danger. This is their responsibility. Whether those who hear the warning act upon it or not, they must sound the alarm or else God will hold them responsible.

"If I warn the wicked, saying, 'You are under the penalty of death,' but you fail to deliver the warning, they will die in their sins. And I will hold you responsible for their deaths. If you warn them and they refuse to repent and keep on sinning, they will die in their sins. But you will have saved yourself because you obeyed me." Ezekiel 3:18 NLT

Intercessor

As well as being a watchman for the body of Christ by sending words of warning, the Prophet also acts as an intercessor. An intercessor is a person who intervenes on the behalf of another, especially by prayer. As we stated in the previous chapter, one of the powers of the Prophet is to change God's mind. Prophets are called to intercede for the people they watch over. This is a double call of duty in that the Prophet watches, sounds the alarm, but also intercedes and ensures the well keeping of the people. In doing this, they build back up the hedges and walls and negate the plans of the enemy.

"I looked for someone who might rebuild the wall of righteousness that guards the land. I searched for someone to stand in the gap in the wall so I wouldn't have to destroy the land, but I found no one." Ezekiel 22:30 NLT

Many times, the Lord will even have a Prophet to intercede or *pray into* the word that He calls them to declare. Though God is sovereign, the enemy will still attempt to combat God's will and frustrate His plans. It is important for the Prophet to stay in this position, interceding, decreeing, declaring, and war-faring over God's plan until He releases him, or until they see manifestation.

They bring alignment to the body of Christ

Prophets bring alignment to the body of Christ by bringing words of correction. In the Book of Revelation, the Apostle John, while being exiled on the Island of Patmos, received prophetic words for the seven churches located in Asia Minor (Revelation 2-3). 5 of the 7 churches received words of correction. Let's look at John's letter to the church of Laodicea.

"Write this letter to the angel of the church in Laodicea. This is the message from the one who is the Amen—the faithful and true witness, the beginning[e] of God's new creation: I know all the things you do, that you are neither hot nor cold. I wish that you were one or the other! But since you are like lukewarm water, neither hot nor cold, I will spit you out of my mouth! You say, I am rich. I have everything I want. I don't need a thing! And you don't realize that you are wretched and lying miserable and poor and blind and naked. So I advise you to buy gold from me—gold that has been purified by fire. Then you will be rich. Also buy white garments from me so you will not be shamed by your nakedness, and ointment for your eyes so you will be able to see. I correct and discipline everyone I love. So be diligent and turn from your indifference. Look! I stand at the door and knock. If you hear my voice and open the door, I will come in, and we will share a meal together as friends. Those who are victorious will sit with me on my throne, just as I was victorious and sat with my Father on his throne." Revelation 3:14-21 NLT

This aspect of the prophetic is important because as we see in verse 19 that God corrects or disciplines those who He loves. Without this correction, the body would remain in error and be destined for eternal damnation. It is through God's love and kindness that He gave 5 of the 7 churches of Asia Minor these warnings for them to make the necessary adjustment and escape His judgments.

They give direction to the body by acting as spiritual advisors

"In those days if people wanted a message from God, they would say, "Let's go and ask the seer,," for prophets used to be called seers." 1 Samuel 9:9 NLT

In the Old Testament, Prophets acted as spiritual advisors to both the common people and kings. We see where the people would seek out the Prophet for both great matters such as healing (2 **Kings 4:25**) and also small matters such as finding a lost donkey (**1 Samuel 9:7**). It was also common for kings to seek out the guidance of the Prophet on many different types of matters. They consulted them concerning their health (**2 Kings 8:7; 2 Kings 5**), for guidance in spiritual matters (**2 Kings 22**), and even war strategies (**2 Kings 13:19; 2 Kings 6:9,**). Many of these aspects carried over into the New Testament prophetic ministry.

Sons of Issachar

Some Prophets of today carry the anointing of the sons of Issachar.

"From the tribe of Issachar, there were 200 leaders of the tribe with their relatives. All these men understood the signs of the times and knew the best course for Israel to take." 1 Chronicles 12:32 NLT

The sons of Issachar were warrior men who carried the Spirit of Wisdom. They understood war strategies and instructed Israel on the best action to take. I believe it is important to note that this is not just limited to Prophets; because it is an *anointing*, anyone can operate under this. God uses modern day Prophets in this capacity as it gives them this ability to wisely discern throughout the seasons what the body should do to gain territory in a specific area.

Level 3 - Specific assignment

We can then further distinguish each Prophet by their prophetic ministry. God gives each Prophet a distinct mission. This further differentiates their specific assignment God has placed them in the earth to fulfill. Not every Prophet has been called to the nations. Some Prophets are called to specific *regions* or *peoples*. In the Old Testament, most Prophets were called to prophesy in the region they resided. This is not to say the Lord will not have them intercede for different regions, but it is to say their prophetic words will be *assignment focused*. Let's venture into the different commissions (assignments) that God gave to His Prophets in the Old Testament.

Jeremiah's commission

"Then the Lord reached out and touched my mouth and said, Look, I have put my words in your mouth! Today I appoint you to stand up against nations and kingdoms. Some you must uproot and tear down,

destroy and overthrow. Others you must build up and plant." Jeremiah 1:9-10 NLT

Jeremiah was sent by God to the nations. This was his *who* and *why*. While God sent Jonah and Nahum to prophesy against the city of Nineveh. Amos' and Isaiah's prophetic books carried messages for multiple cities and regions outside of Israel and Judah (**Amos 1, Isaiah 10,13,14**), while Ezekiel's commission was to the children of Israel and his messages were centered around these specific peoples and the regions they occupied.

"Spirit came into me as he spoke, and he set me on my feet. I listened carefully to his words. "Son of man," he said, "I am sending you to the nation of Israel, a rebellious nation that has rebelled against me. They and their ancestors have been rebelling against me to this very day." Ezekiel 2:2-3 NLT

This was the same for a host of other Prophets of the Old Testament such as Hosea, Joel, and Micah whose messages were also centered around Israel. These specific assignments will also define the types of words the Lord will use you to release.

No big "I" and little "You"

It is also important to note that the reason why some Prophets are referred to as *major* or *minor* Prophets is due to the size of their prophetic books. If it could fit on one scroll they were categorized as a minor Prophet, and if their writings were longer, they were considered major Prophets. However nowhere in Scripture do we see God Himself make these distinctions. In God there is no respecter of persons. Every word God gives His Prophets to release is important. There are no big "I's" and little "u's" in the kingdom of God (**Galatians 2:6**). Whether He calls a Prophet to the nations or to a region, to preach to millions or tens, they both play important roles and are vital to the body of Christ.

Commissioned to different platforms

Even the method He chooses for them to release those words will be different and with us coming into the age of social media this part is important. There are a variety of ways the Lord can and will use to get His Word across. Will everyone broadcast through Twitter? No. Will everyone conduct Facebook lives on a regular basis, or YouTube? No. Will every Prophet have a jammed packed itinerary traveling from city to city or across countries? No.

None of these are qualifiers of success. Whatever means the Lord chooses for that Prophet to release his or her words and carry out their ministry will be determined by the purpose that He has set them to fulfill. It will be specific and tailor-made to their call. Therefore, it is important for Prophets not to compare Prophetic Ministries. It would be as foolish as trying to compare apples to oranges. They are both fruit, but they carry different beneficial values.

Common purpose

Even with these many differences, our commonplaces are the who, what, when, where, and why of our prophetic ministry.

Who - Peoples, families, regions, nations, countries, or the elements.

What - The Gospel and prophetic words given to us by Jesus who is the Spirit of Prophecy (**Revelation 19:10, Isaiah 61**).

Where- Wherever He tells us to go (**Jeremiah 1:7**).

When – Always. Being instant, forever ready and prepared to minister (**2 Timothy 4:2**).

Why – To equip the saints, build up the church, until we grow into the full stature of Christ (**Ephesians 4**) .

This should always be the focus of our ministry.

We will talk more about the uniqueness and the peculiarities of each Prophet in the chapter entitled *Prophetic Identity*. But for now, let's venture into the difference between the call and the commission of God.

Janell Edmondson

Commission vs. Call

There is a difference between being called and being commissioned. Many people take the call of God as a license to go and start ministry, but that is not the case at all. On the contrary, the *call* is the invitation to come into the room of *preparation*.

Prepare means to make (something) ready for use or consideration. Jeremiah was ordained to be a Prophet before he was even born. I believe he lived his life as a normal individual until God called him and gave him his commission. Jeremiah was a *born* Prophet. Before he ever uttered a "Word from the Lord" he was already a Prophet. This did not change because he had not prophesied. He was a Prophet because God ordained him to be. It was not until he received his commission from the Lord that he was released to go and start his prophetic ministry.

Let's take Jesus as an example. He knew from a young age that He was born into the earth on an assignment. When He was about twelve years old, He left his parents in order to prepare for this.

"Three days later they finally discovered him in the Temple, sitting among the religious teachers, listening to them and asking questions. All who heard him were amazed at his understanding and his answers." Luke 2:46-47 NLT

Janell Edmondson

Even then, Jesus had not been "officially" released into his ministry. It is not until about 18 years later that He performed His first miracle. So, what happened in the in-between? He used this time to *prepare* himself for what He was *called* to do.

This is the difference between the "call" and the "commission." The call is God bringing you into the *awareness* of your purpose. This is the place where we prepare ourselves to be used by God. The in-between place where the real process begins. The place of refining, purging, and self-development. These areas are very important and create a format of what your ministry will look like. The greater the place of preparation the more solid you will be in your calling. Think of this place as a foundation. The foundation of a building speaks of what the actual building will look like. Architects understand that the foundation is what carries the weight of the rest of the structure. It is what determines the stability of the overall structure. If you want to build a skyscraper, you must dig very deep in order to set a solid and firm foundation.

At the completion of the building, you do not see the details of what went into the foundation. Many times, the foundation itself is not even visible, but I guarantee you if that architect and engineer failed to make the necessary preparations to ensure that the foundation was built properly, that building would become unstable very fast.

This is the same for building a house. Have you ever ridden in a neighborhood that was a fairly new development and the houses were already showing cracks in the sides of the outside walls? This is evidence that the builder did not take their time in building the houses. So it is with our seasons of preparation. It is not a place that we should take lightly.

Though many desire to go and step out and into their prophetic ministry, if you have not been groomed, trained, purged, and prepared when you start to build, you will see cracks and blemishes start to appear in your structure. If you rush into ministry without having a firm foundation, that which you build on top will soon start falling apart. It is not about how fast you go up. It is about the quality of the building process.

"Anyone who listens to my teaching and follows it is wise, like a person who builds a house on solid rock. Though the rain comes in torrents and the floodwaters rise and the winds beat against that house, it won't collapse because it is built on bedrock." Matthew 7:24-25 NLT

God loves us so much that He would not allow us to skip these necessary processes before giving us a Commission. **Commission** is the act of granting certain powers or the authority to carry out a particular task or duty. You could look at it as a driver's license. After you have studied for the test and have enough driving hours under your belt, you are then granted a chance to take the driving test and get your official license. This is the difference between the commission and the call. The commission is God releasing you to go out into your prophetic ministry.

Let us take a look at Jeremiah's commission

"Then the Lord reached out and touched my mouth and said, Look, I have put my words in your mouth! Today I appoint you to stand up against nations and kingdoms. Some you must uproot and tear down, destroy and overthrow. Others you must build up and plant." Jeremiah 1:9-10 NLT

This was God sending Jeremiah out with His stamp of approval. He gave Jeremiah the *authority* to complete his *mission*. It was God's way of validating him, releasing him, and saying he was ready to do the work that He had already predestined him to do.

A vessel that is used by God first needs to be made so that he or she is fit for the master's use. If you try to use a vessel that is in its unfinished state, it will not be able to properly fulfill its purpose. This is not to say that God expects perfection from us to be used by Him, as we will continue to be processed throughout our ministry and the entirety of our walk with Christ. However, it is to say that He knows the point in our process that we are mature enough to properly handle the assignment that He gives us without causing any shame to come to the body of Christ or His name.

So, remember the call of God is His invitation to come and allow Him to work in us and carry out His Kingdom work. There is no need to hurry this process because in the ordained time He will release you into ministry when He knows that you are ready.

Now, let's venture into the different anointing's that each Prophet can carry.

Janell Edmondson

The Prophetic Mantle

You may have heard the term "mantle" used in a prophetic teaching. In the natural, a **mantle** is a loose, sleeveless garment worn over other clothes: cloak; but in the Spirit it *represents an important role or responsibility that passes from one person to another.* The mantle also represents a specific anointing and realm of authority that God gives the Prophet to operate from.

The mantle requires great dedication

The mantle is not just something that a Prophet is automatically born with. It is something that they must pay the price for. Mantels are birth in prayer and in the secret place with God. Operating under a mantle also is not a casual thing, but it comes with an assignment from God. Not all Prophets operate under the *weight* of a mantle. Remember, gifts come without repentance. It is not difficult to operate in gifts and charisma, but in order for you to operate from your mantle, it will require great *dedication.*

Let's explore the example of Elisha. In the Book of 1 Kings, God had instructed Elijah to go and anoint (to smear, consecrate) Elisha to be his successor (1 Kings 19:16). Elijah left from Mount Horeb, found Elisha, and thrust his mantle upon him (1 Kings 19:19). From there he served Elijah until the completion of Elijah's ministry.

> *"When the Lord was about to take Elijah up to heaven in a whirlwind, Elijah and Elisha were traveling from Gilgal. And Elijah said to Elisha, "Stay here, for the Lord has told me to go to Bethel." But Elisha replied, "As surely as the Lord lives and you yourself live, I will never leave you!" So they went down together to Bethel." 2 Kings 2:2 NLT*

Here we see Elijah's time here on Earth was complete, and he was about to be called up to Heaven in a whirlwind. He tried numerous times to get Elisha to stop following him, but Elisha was determined. He was persistent. He had something in mind that he wanted and was not going to give up easy.

> *"When they came to the other side, Elijah said to Elisha, "Tell me what I can do for you before I am taken away." And Elisha replied, "Please let me inherit a double share of your spirit and become your successor." . "You have asked a difficult thing," Elijah replied. "If you see me when I am taken from you, then you will get your request. But if not, then you won't." 2 Kings 2:9-10 NLT*

Elisha greatly desired his predecessor Elijah's mantle and was willing to go the extra mile to receive it. The strange thing about this is that this was something the Lord had already ordained for Elisha to carry (**1 Kings 19:17**). Before he even desired it God predestined him for it, but he still had to be in position in order to receive.

Positioned for the Mantle

Your position is important for you to receive the mantle. The first thrusting of the mantle upon Elisha did not give him the *authority* of the mantle (**1 Kings 19:19**). When the mantle was first thrust upon Elisha, it was an invitation into a place of *submission, training,* and *preparation*. This was the middle period in between the *calling* and the *receiving*. The training before the release.

See, the mantle comes with grooming and maturity. Elisha had to walk through the place of submission, observing Elijah's movements, how he operated, serving the man of God, and most importantly *being in position* in order for him to receive his mantle. It was crucial for him to be in place for him to receive the promotion. Thus, if Elisha had not been in position, he would not have received the mantle.

Price to pay

There is a heavy price one must pay to carry such a great anointing and mantle such as Elijah did. That is because the mantle comes with a great level of expectation. The Bible says to whom much is given much is required (**Luke 12:48**). The heavier level of authority you have, the heavier the level of consecration and accountability the Lord requires of your life.

The Evidence of the Mantle

As Elijah was caught up into Heaven, his mantle fell and Elisha picked it up. From there Elisha travel to the Jordan River, called on the God of Elijah, smote the Jordan and it split just as it did for Elijah (**2 Kings 2:14-15**).

Notice the last miracle that Elijah performed before being *caught up* was the first miracle that Elisha performed. This signified that not only had he been called to be his successor, but that he had the same level of authority and sat in the same realm of operation as Elijah. This was the proof or *evidence* that Elijah's spirit rested upon him. His request of the double portion had been granted. Elisha carried the same anointing, causing not only the Jordan River to split, but also commanding bears (**2 Kings 2:24**), raising a boy from the dead (**1 Kings 17:20**) and many other miracles. This was not the *gifting* that Elisha was operating from but the *evidence* of the mantle of the Prophet.

Different Mantles

It is important to note that not every Prophet carries the same mantle. We see here that Elijah's mantle was one that allowed him to operate as a *Power Prophet*, one who works miracles. Elijah had the ability to command the elements, shut up Heaven, cause water to separate, and heal diseases by God's Word. But there are many Prophets in the Bible who never operated under the gifting of the working of Miracles. This is because there are many types of mantles. There are mantels of *healing* for both spiritual and physical ailments. Mantels of *restoration* bringing people back to a state of wholeness and who God originally intended for them to be, such as the Prophet Isaiah.

"The Spirit of the Sovereign Lord is upon me, for the Lord has anointed me to bring good news to the poor. He has sent me to comfort the brokenhearted and to proclaim that captives will be released, and prisoners will be freed." Isaiah 61:1 NLT

Then there are mantels of *prayer and intercession*; enabling them to engage Heaven on the behalf of men breaking through demonic barriers and strongholds, shifting things in the Spirit realm. Also, mantels of *revelation* unlocking hidden mysteries and the deep things of God, just to name a few. Jesus called John the Baptist the greatest Prophet who ever walked the Earth (**Luke 7:38**), yet it never stated anywhere in the Bible where John the Baptist ever worked a single miracle. Yet he still had a very important task. He was anointed to prepare the way of the Lord, calling the hearts of men to repentance (**Mark 1:3**). There are many other Prophets in the Bible as well who were never referenced to work miracles. So, remember, just because you may not have the ability to work miracles does not mean you are not operating from under the mantle.

Given to serve others

Now let's talk more about what the mantle is for. When Elijah was taken up from the earth, he left his mantle to Elisha. This is because the mantle is made for those here on Earth. The anointing that God places on our lives is given to serve others and not ourselves, and because of this He requires a great level of obedience and submission to His will and cause. One must be able to recognize the purpose of their anointing, their realm of operation, and the jurisdiction that God has given them authority over. Paul talks about these boundaries in 2 Corinthians 10.

"We will not boast about things done outside our area of authority. We will boast only about what has happened within the boundaries of the work God has given us, which includes our working with you." 2 Corinthians 10:13 NLT

As I stated before, not everyone has been given the same kind or level of authority. We each have a specific purpose God has given us to accomplish on Earth.

"Then the Lord told him, Go back the same way you came, and travel to the wilderness of Damascus. When you arrive there, anoint Hazael to be king of Aram. Then anoint Jehu grandson of Nimshi to be king of Israel, and anoint Elisha son of Shaphat from the town of Abel-meholah to replace you as my prophet. Anyone who escapes from Hazael will be killed by Jehu, and those who escape Jehu will be killed by Elisha!" 1 Kings 19:15-17 NLT

The Lord had assignments that He needed to be carried out on Earth. God told Elijah to anoint Hazael to be king of Aram and Jehu king of Israel. Elisha and Jehu were anointed to carry out the assignments that Elijah forfeited. That anointing is directly associated with their assignment. Paul understood this concept and made it clear that he would not try to operate outside the boundaries of authority God had given him. When one tries to operate outside of the anointing that they carry, they will only frustrate the grace of God on their life.

God knows what He has purposed you to do, and what is needed for your assignment. We need not ever compare or desire the anointing of another. God will only give us what He knows we need in order to carry out our specific call. One must know their role, play their part, and most importantly stay in their own lane. In doing this, we will function as a body though we all play different parts, as Paul stated in 1 Corinthians 12. This holds true to not only the anointing that God has placed on your life, but also the gifts that He allows you to function in as well.

Janell Edmondson

Prophetic Identity

Every human on this earth has a specific DNA marker that distinguishes them from others. Even identical twins have different fingerprints. This same concept fits into the way God created His Prophets. Each one of them has what He calls a *prophetic identity*. He too has given them prophetic DNA markers and unique fingerprints. Though they may look similar in function and the way they flow (**prophesy**), no two are the same. This is one reason why the use of comparison in the prophetic is far from wisdom.

Graced to be different

We all have different graces. Just like in the Bible we see each Prophet was cut from a different cloth. We can even look at the Prophets in the Old Testament and see the uniqueness God placed in each one of them. How so? Their encounters with God were all different. How He spoke through them, their personality, even how each one expressed God's prophetic Word in writing was distinct. Let's use Jeremiah as an example. He called Jeremiah and his first encounter was God encouraging him and affirming who he was.

> *"I knew you before I formed you in your mother's womb. Before you were born, I set you apart and appointed you as my prophet to the nations." Jeremiah 1:5 NLT*

Samuel's first encounter was very different. The Lord spoke to Samuel and the first prophetic word He gave him was to pronounce judgment against his very own leader Eli, the one who raised him up in the Lord.

"Then the Lord said to Samuel: "Behold, I will do something in Israel at which both ears of everyone who hears it will tingle. In that day I will perform against Eli all that I have spoken concerning his house, from beginning to end." I Samuel 3:11-12 NKJV

The life of each Prophet was different as well. We can see where He used Ezekiel and Hosea heavily with *types*, meaning that He used their actual life to demonstrate prophetically the message that He was trying to convey to the children of Israel. Everything about them was prophetic. Their marriage and even what they ate all spoke something.

"When the Lord first began speaking to Israel through Hosea, he said to him, "Go and marry a prostitute, so that some of her children will be conceived in prostitution. This will illustrate how Israel has acted like a prostitute by turning against the Lord and worshiping other gods." Hosea 1:2 NLT

Then we can see where God spoke to each Prophet differently. Isaiah received his prophetic words through visions (**Isaiah 1:1**). While God spoke audibly to Samuel (**1 Samuel 9:15**), Daniel had visions and angelic encounters (**Daniel 10:4**), and He spoke to Moses face-to-face as a friend (**Deuteronomy 34:10**).

His relationship and the way He interacted with them was also different. Elijah would get taken up by God in an instance, without notice (**1 Kings 18:12**), while Moses encountered God on top of a mountain and saw His backsides (**Exodus 33:11**). All these differences help to make up our prophetic identity.

Dare to be different

Comparison is our worst enemy. It only limits us because we are trying to measure ourselves based off someone else's mold. It slows us down from reaching our destination because we are always looking at others wondering "why?." Why is my make-up so different? Why do I not receive the same type of words as others? Why do I not flow as others, or why am I not used in the same capacity as He does with others.

Can I just say to you Prophet that all these whys are just a waste of time and a tactic of the enemy to delay and detour your purpose? God made no mistakes about the materials and fabric He used to make you. Questioning God about all the whys will not change a single solitary thing about your make-up. So instead of asking why I am not like someone else, let's ask Him, *"What special purpose have you called me to fulfill that necessitated for me to be so distinct from everyone else around me?"*

Comparison is Unwise

"Oh, don't worry; we wouldn't dare say that we are as wonderful as these other men who tell you how important they are! But they are only comparing themselves with each other, using themselves as the standard of measurement. How ignorant!" 2 *Corinthians 10:12 NLT*

In the Book of 2 Corinthians, the Apostle Paul made it clear that comparing yourself to others is foolish. Why? Because our success is not determined by the achievements of others, but rather our area of authority given to us by God.

Paul knew he could only truly be successful if he was operating in *his* capacity carrying out *his* God given assignment. That's the only comparison we need—between what we are doing and what God has called us to do. This is why we all operate differently. All of our assignments our unique. So, embrace your uniqueness and dare to be different. It is all a part of our prophetic fingerprint. It is what makes you who you are. Now, let me speak to the heart of the Prophet.

When God thought of you, way before you were born, He already purposed you to be a Prophet. He knew that there would be a need to be filled and thus He created you. This call was not something that you stumbled upon or happened because someone prophesied to you and told you that you were a Prophet. No, this call was God ordained, and because of this He considered what would be needed for you to fulfill your purpose. Everything about you is well thought out. The time and dispensation you were born in, your personality, mannerisms; even the region you were born into was all carefully thought out. For you to conform, try to fit in or look like anyone else but who God has created you to be would negate the essence and purpose of why He made you that way in the first place. Trying to adjust to man's idea about you will only hinder you from fulfilling your specific assignment in its totality. Let that sink in. Speak this to yourself. I am different on purpose, for a purpose and God would not have it any other way.

Different Coats

Your coat represents your difference; what distinguishes you from others. We see in the Bible that both Joseph and John the Baptist wore coats. Joseph was made for the palace and his beautiful coat of many colors was a foreshadowing of who God designed him to be. Let's take a closer look at Joseph's coat.

"May my fatherly blessings on you surpass the blessings of my ancestors, reaching to the heights of the eternal hills. May these blessings rest on the head of Joseph, who is a prince among his brothers." Genesis 49:26 NLT

He was called to stand out as a prince among his brethren. Though Joseph's coat showed the love that his father had toward him, it also represented his status and the favor that God placed upon his life. This favor unfortunately also attracted much jealousy.

"Now Israel loved Joseph more than all his children, because he was the son of his old age. Also, he made him a tunic of many colors. But when his brothers saw that their father loved him more than all his brothers, they hated him and could not speak peaceably to him." Genesis 37:3-4 NKJV

He was destined for the Palace, though faced with much difficulty on his way there. God had always purposed him for the position of prestige. Wherever he went, he found favor and was promoted or elevated. From the pit to Potiphar's house all the way to the Palace, God granted him with influence. Even in the prison he was put in a position of authority over all the other prisoners. This was his coat.

It may be like Joseph that God has ordained you to be seated with kings and queens. You may be one who attracts supernatural favor. Even in your difficult places you see yourself being showered with God's grace and provision. This is your coat. You have been called to advise and give instructions to men of great status. Kings, queens, presidents, prime ministers, government officials, and people in high rank and authority.

You have been polished for the master's use. Your anointing is attractive and brings you into great rooms. God has graced your tongue for this position. Your anointing is vibrant and colorful just like Joseph's coat. You carry a charisma that attracts people as well as jealousy. It is your coat; it is what you wear. It is what has been given to you by God.

> *"So, Potiphar gave Joseph complete administrative responsibility over everything he owned. With Joseph there, he didn't worry about a thing—except what kind of food to eat! Joseph was a very handsome and well-built young man." Genesis 39:6 NLT*

Then there are those who carry the coat like John the Baptist. The mantle that he wore was that of camel's hair, wearing a leather belt around his waist. His exterior was a mirror of the messages that he carried. Which was a very (rough) word of repentance and correction.

> *"Prove by the way you live that you have repented of your sins and turned to God. Don't just say to each other, We're safe, for we are descendants of Abraham. That means nothing, for I tell you, God can create children of Abraham from these very stones." Luke 3:8 NLT*

He walked the place of separation and being ostracized. He didn't come to sit at the tables of kings and queens. He didn't come to be accepted of men. His assignment was in the wilderness; to prepare the way of the Lord. You may be one like John, who eats locust and wild honey. This means your diet is specific and distinct.

You can't just eat from anyone's table. You have strong morals and convictions which makes it difficult for some people to walk close to you and still feel comfortable. This may cause you to feel isolated from others at times. You are peculiar. Your heart's cry is for the holiness and righteousness of God. You carry the rod of correction. God gives you words of correction and alignment. Like John the Baptist, you don't seek fame or attention, but you put the spotlight back on Christ and don't mind being in the back as long as God's will is carried out.

"John answered their questions by saying, "I baptize you with water; but someone is coming soon who is greater than I am—so much greater that I'm not even worthy to be his slave and untie the straps of his sandals. He will baptize you with the Holy Spirit and with fire." Luke 3:16 NLT

God has built you this way. You are made for the wilderness. He will send you into rough terrains and regions to speak the truth with authority and power. To uproot, tear down, and build up. You hate wickedness and do not play when it comes to deliverance and spiritual warfare. You teach people how to live holy and right before God. You will turn the hearts of many back to God through the unadulterated truth of His Word. God will use you to demonstrate and show people what God truly requires from us and that is to love God and love one another (**Luke 3:10-11**). You are willing to speak out against unrighteousness and suffer great persecution because of this.

"John also publicly criticized Herod Antipas, the ruler of Galilee, for marrying Herodias, his brother's wife, and for many other wrongs he had done. So Herod put John in prison, adding this sin to his many others." Luke 3:19-20 NLT

This is *your difference*. It is what sets you apart from others. So do not compare your coat to another's because Joseph's assignment was necessary and so was John's. Never covet the coat of another. God has handmade this for you. He knows what you are capable of. He knows the fabric that He made you with. He knows the voice that He placed on the inside of you, and it is Him that will groom and develop you until it fits you perfectly. You do not have to be afraid if your words do not look like others. Or the people He calls you to may not fit the status quo of what the Church looks like. God has given you that coat, so wear your coat and wear it with confidence.

The Purge

In the Bible Prophets were usually born into families, meaning that if there was a Prophet, more than likely their father or mother was one as well (**1 Samuel 10:10**). Rarely did we see in the Old Testament where the Lord raised up men and women who did not come from a prophetic line. Still, there were some exceptions such as Amos, Ezekiel, and Samuel.

Even today we can see that prophetic gifts run in families where you have a line of seers. Ones who dream or have open visions. Some lines may have the ability to see into the supernatural while awake, encountering both demonic and angelic spirits. This is not dependent upon if a person is committed to the ways of God or even in right relationship with God.

For that reason, it is so easy for one who has a prophetic gift to enter over into the Spirit of divination without even being aware. Why is this part important? It is crucial to know the difference between gifting and submitting yourself unto God. Gifts come without repentance. The enemy knows this and if your life is not yielded to the Holy Spirit, living according to His Word, the devil can and will use your gift for his purpose.

The whole vessel

God is so serious about the vessel. No matter how pure of a substance you pour, if the vessel that you are pouring into is not clean, that substance will become contaminated. Likewise, no matter how accurately we hear from God or how "eloquently" we prophesy, if we are not pure within ourselves, that which comes out of us will most certainly be defiled. Before He can put new wine into the vessel, there has to be a purging. So, what does that entail? A greater level of deliverance.

It should be the main focus of any individual who believes he or she is being called into greater realms of the prophetic to come by way of the room of deliverance. It is a prerequisite to ensure longevity as an ambassador in God's kingdom as a Prophet and maintain the ability for God's Spirit to freely flow through you as He desires. One of the things that the Lord placed strongly in my Spirit is that this next generation of Prophets He was grooming differently. No more overnight successes. Being an overnight success causes you to skip the process. Unprocessed vessels will in time bring shame to God's name, and He certainly does not want that. He would use this new remnant to do mighty exploits in the earth like we have not seen in other generations; but in order for Him to be able to use them like He wanted, they had to come through the purge.

Like Esther, having to go and soak herself for one year for just one night with the king (**Esther 2:1**). This process was so clearly represented through this story. The frankincense which represents prayer, the myrrh which is used for cleansing, and the hyssop to fully purify His chosen vessels. This is true for old and new Prophets alike. There are levels of deliverance that you will encounter while entering the room with the Holy Spirit. The methods of deliverance may look different and seem intense at times, but this process is vital. The father is inviting us into the room of deliverance for a total spiritual makeover.

God knows what's in the heart

Let's use the Apostle Peter, for example. He was in ministry with Jesus for three years, even given the ability to cast out devils. Though Peter was able to do many marvelous works, there was still some places in him that needed deliverance.

> *"Simon, Simon, Satan has asked to sift each of you like wheat. But I have pleaded in prayer for you, Simon, that your faith should not fail. So when you have repented and turned to me again, strengthen your brothers." Peter said, "Lord, I am ready to go to prison with you, and even to die with you." But Jesus said, "Peter, let me tell you something. Before the rooster crows tomorrow morning, you will deny three times that you even know me." Luke 22:31-34 NLT*

Peter thought he was "ready," but in reality what Peter had was **zeal**. Though good, zeal and passion alone are not enough to carry out ministry. Though the Spirit is willing the flesh is still weak and is prone to cave under pressure. You will be faced with many circumstances that will shake your faith. The enemy knows this and will strategize against you to get you to fall in your unprocessed places. Yes, you have a call and yes you want to be used by God, but God knows the extent of our human frailty and will never call us into something that He knows we are not ready for. He is a good father.

Purging is a byproduct of conversion and is necessary for this next part of the journey. Though Peter himself could not see the weakness in his flesh, Jesus knew and still wanted to use him; but he needed to go through the place of conversion first. For Peter to go and strengthen his brethren, he himself needed to be stable. There were still some weak areas there that Jesus was trying to help him to identify, but pride would not let Peter see them. Even to the point that he would deny Jesus to protect his own life.

The same goes for us. There are many weak areas in our life that we cannot identify on our own. This is why God will take the Prophet through intense levels of deliverance. He wants to ensure that the gift is not corrupted or mixed in with anything else but the purity of His Spirit and the truth of His Word. Take a moment to reflect. Can you identify an unprocessed area that God is trying to deliver you from?

Purging of the soul

There are many things that could be hidden deep within the soul of a man. If not dealt with, they can spew out into our prophecies. We all have different histories, come from different backgrounds, cultures, and have gone through different experiences. So, depending upon what you have picked up along the way, your purging process will be different. Some things the Lord will attempt to deliver His Prophets from is pride, lust, wrong motives, greed, disobedience, wrong convictions, mindsets, and perspectives. These can all taint our prophetic ministry.

Purging of the heart

> *"What sorrow awaits you teachers of religious law and you Pharisees. Hypocrites! For you are like whitewashed tombs—beautiful on the outside but filled on the inside with dead people's bones and all sorts of impurity." Matthew 23:27 NLT*

What is in you will always at some point come out. That is why He is more concerned about the inside of the vessel than the outside. In these particular scriptures, Jesus was accusing the Jewish leaders of practicing hypocrisy. **Hypocrisy** is not practicing what you preach or living up to the standard you built for others. What Jesus was concerned about more than the outside, what they looked like or how they dressed, was the content of their character.

Lust, greed, and pride all dwell in the heart of a man, and most of the time we are blind to it. This is why Jesus called them the blind guides. They were quick to point out and condemn the faults in others but had a hard time identifying the very same faults in themselves. In turn, they spent very little time working on themselves.

We too must submit ourselves to God and allow the sanctification process to work through us before we can ever go out and preach to others. Does this mean that you must be perfect in order for you to be qualified to preach or prophesy? Certainly not, but we should always strive to perfect the practice of living what we preach. If not, then we will just become not only a hypocritical Christian but a hypocritical Prophet as well.

In the purging process, God will uncover all the deep things that lie hidden in our hearts. Then He will invite you into the room in order to confront and deliver you from them. It is then your choice to come with Him. This is not a place of condemnation as God does not come to condemn us, but rather God refining us to meet the elevation that is on our lives. Remember, you cannot take a people to a place that you yourself have never been before.

<u>Hinderances to the Prophetic</u>

Spirit of Religion

Religion is one of the most dangerous things Prophets can struggle with because it blocks understanding and the revelation of God. Some denominations do not believe in the prophetic. This causes them to reject God's *Rhema* (utterance) Word and only believe in the *Logos* (written) Word. Thus, blocking anything new God has to say. Religion can also breed erroneous teaching, bias, and wrong convictions. Let's continue with Peter as our example.

Long after Jesus died, Peter was out working in ministry calling people to Christ. Yet, he still struggled with the place of religion. However, in Acts, chapter 10, Peter had an encounter with the Lord that would break this Spirit off his life. In this passage Peter was on the roof about to pray when God took him in a trance.

> *"He saw the sky open, and something like a large sheet was let down by its four corners. In the sheet were all sorts of animals, reptiles, and birds. Then a voice said to him, "Get up, Peter; kill and eat them." ."No, Lord," Peter declared. "I have never eaten anything that our Jewish laws have declared impure and unclean." But the voice spoke again: "Do not call something unclean if God has made it clean." The same vision was repeated three times. Then the sheet was suddenly pulled up to heaven."* Acts of the Apostles 10:11-16 NLT

Earlier in this chapter we meet a man named Cornelius who was a God-fearing man but who had not heard about the Gospel of Jesus Christ. He received a visitation from the Lord instructing him to send for a man named Peter who was in another city. God wanted to use Peter to minister the Gospel to him, but there was only one problem: Cornelius was a Roman. Peter's belief was rooted in Jewish laws and traditions. Anyone who was not a Jew was considered a Gentile and deemed unclean. So much so that it was against their law to even associate with such a person.

Jesus died so that all might have access to eternal life and there is no bias in him. This was the interpretation of the vision; that salvation was not just for the Jews but also for the Gentiles. It was necessary for God to break this wrong mindset from off Peter. If it had remained, Peter would continue to be partial in his ministering the Gospel. In this, He opened Peter's eyes to a deeper revelation of who He was and what He came to do.

Religion breeds bias

Let's consider this. If God had not come to Peter, he would not have even considered ministering the Gospel to Cornelius. This is because religion bars us from seeing Christ inside of people that may not look like us or may not look like what we think Christians should look like. Just like Peter, many of us have a distorted view of what Christianity really is. We may have a superiority complex for certain nationalities, denominations, or people groups. But does that really represent God? Certainly not. In God, there is neither Greek, Jew, or any other nationality, male nor female (Galatians 3:28). Peter was blocked from this revelation even though he served Jesus in ministry for years.

In order for a Prophet to fully carry out their call, they too must be free from the Spirit of religion. God can and will send you anywhere He chooses. As *HIS* mouthpiece and messengers in the earth, we do not get to pick who we minister to. We go where we are sent, our mouths speak His words. If our vessels are full of bias, preconceived notions, or prejudice, then the word that He gives us will have to filter through all of that. Just like in the case of Peter, his bias blocked his understanding of the revelation God was releasing to him. Peter was not even aware of this until confronted with it. Many times, we as well are unaware of the Spirit of religion operating in our lives. We must ask God to show us these areas and free us from this Spirit so that what flows out of us is pure and unhindered.

Erroneous teaching leads to erroneous prophecy

Erroneous teaching breeds wrong convictions that could then be impose on others. We saw this in the Early Church where many were teaching the necessity of circumcision which went against Christ perfect work on the cross. Many people insisted that the new Christians should be circumcised. It was a mixture of the Law and the new covenant of Grace. In the Book of Galatians, Paul confronted this erroneous teaching and compelled the Galatians to continue in the teaching that he taught them—graced-based salvation.

"I'll say it again. If you are trying to find favor with God by being circumcised, you must obey every regulation in the whole law of Moses. For if you are trying to make yourselves right with God by keeping the law, you have been cut off from Christ! You have fallen away from God's grace." Galatians 5:3-4 NLT

It may have seemed innocent since circumcision was not a new concept, at least to the Jews, but Paul knew that a little leaven leavens the whole lump (**Galatians 5:9**). This is why the Spirit of religion is so dangerous—it is a mixture of what seems right and what is actually pure. If they would have made circumcision a prerequisite it would have abolished the very foundation of what Christ did. The Jews had been taught circumcision for so long it was difficult for them to break from that age old tradition.

This also transcends to many teachings in modern day Christianity. If not dealt with, your wrong convictions will spew out onto others. Implying on them false burdens and expectations that Christ never required. Causing them to believe they can somehow earn God's grace or Salvation by what they do or omit. Christ died so that we can have access back to God. Our righteousness, however good it may seem will never be enough. The Bible says it is as filthy rags (**Isaiah 64:6**). What He did on the cross was sufficient and we don't need to add anything else to it.

Am I implying that what Christ did allows us to now live anyway we want? No, in fact Jude makes it clear that those who live immoral lives will not inherit the kingdom of God (**Jude 1:4**). Christ died so that we can live the more abundant life and that includes freedom from sin. It is also true that sometimes what we consider sins are just false burdens and wrong convictions camouflaged under the guise of religion. That is why it is important that we come through the purge so that our messages are unadulterated, Bible based, and untainted. Then will be able to bring souls to Christ and edify the body through our prophetic gift.

The Oil

> *"I will praise you as long as I live, lifting up my hands to you in prayer. You satisfy me more than the richest feast. I will praise you with songs of joy. I lie awake thinking of you, meditating on you through the night. Because you are my helper, I sing for joy in the shadow of your wings. I cling to you; your strong right hand holds me securely." Psalm 63:4-8 NLT*

The most important part of prophetic ministry is what I call the oil. The oil is comprised of 3 things: prayer, the Word of God, and worship. These are our landmarks, our foundation upon which we build upon. If I could divide it by number, I would conclude that operating in the prophetic is 20 percent of what people see (operating in your gift, prophesying) and 80 percent of what happens in the secret place. Your personal relationship with God.

What we do behind closed doors does matter and will definitely show up in the flow of our anointing and the way we operate. Don't be fooled, it is not in your gift or talent but how deeply you live in the place of intimacy with God that causes you to flourish on the outside.

Building an altar

Let's start with building an altar, which is prayer. Prayer is what births a Prophet. It is the entrance into hearing accurately from God, the door into the prophetic realm. Prayer fine-tunes your hearing and is what allows you to receive God's mysteries. Without a consistent prayer life, there is no way for you to truly know what God is saying. How else can we perceive if we are truly hearing from God lest we know His voice through prayer. A prayerless Prophet is a dull Prophet. Dull of hearing and sight. Without prayer, you ultimately lose your sensitivity to the things of the Spirit. The Lord spoke in the Book of Jeremiah concerning prayerless Prophets.

> *"Have any of these prophets been in the Lord's presence to hear what he is really saying? Has even one of them cared enough to listen? I have not sent these prophets, yet they run around claiming to speak for me. I have given them no message, yet they go on prophesying. If they had stood before me and listened to me, they would have spoken my words, and they would have turned my people from their evil ways and deeds." Jeremiah 23:18, 21-22 NLT*

We are messengers, and in order to receive His counsel, we must sit in His presence, and this happens in the secret place. The place we build communication. It is the highest point in the Spirit realm. This is our spiritual seat. It is where we delegate and operate from. Just like the watchtower, our prayer is where we watch from. We must watch as well as pray. As I stated before, it is a door into the prophetic. Any attempts to enter another way than prayer is illegal. Without prayer you are destined to depend on your gift and enter into divination. So, if you feel as though you are stagnated, not birthing, check your prayer life.

The enemy knows the importance of prayer and will fight the Prophet tooth and nail to keep them from being consistent. This is why we must make prayer a priority. God himself will give the Prophet a set prayer time. You may notice at first that you wake up the same time in the middle of the night or in the early morning. This is the Holy Spirit prompting you and revealing to you your set prayer watch. We must remain consistent in this, building an altar before God that does not shift based off our circumstances or how we feel. In this prayer becomes our oxygen in which we thrive on. A wise man who happens to be my uncle once told me this: More prayer more power, less prayer less power, no prayer no power.

> *"Then he answered and spake unto me, saying, "This is the word of the Lord unto Zerubbabel, saying, Not by might, nor by power, but by my spirit, saith the Lord of hosts." Zechariah 4:6 KJV*

If you find yourself being inconsistent in prayer, I encourage you to get a prayer partner. Someone who can hold you accountable to your set watch time and encourage you to remain faithful. It may be someone at your church who is more mature than you are that could even help you in your prayer journey. It may be difficult at first, and most definitely will be a sacrifice, but if you keep at it , it will get easier. Grace is there to complete every assignment that God gives you.

The Word is our Spiritual metal detector

Now let's talk about the Word. Prophets must have a healthy diet of God's Word to operate the prophetic in a mature manner. Just like we need prayer to know God's voice, we need the Word to know His character. The Word of God is a compilation of God's nature. By it we can judge what He would or would not do based off what He has done. It is the final authority in our lives and must be what we use to judge any matter. It is like our spiritual metal detector, discerning between what is true and false. No one is above deception. It is easy to go off into error. The Word brings an illumination to what we see and sense in the prophetic.

Through thy precepts I get understanding: therefore I hate every false way. Thy word is a lamp unto my feet, and a light unto my path. Psalm 119:104-105 KJV

Prophets in the Old Testament would often quote Scripture in their prophecies. Likewise, we see authors of the New Testament refer to Scripture when elaborating on a topic they are teaching their readers (**Romans 9:28; 1 Corinthians 2:16**). Even Jesus quoted Scripture (**Matthew 22:32**). Why? because Scripture is foundational. It is like a building block. Most times when the Lord is putting a Word in my Spirit, I will always seek for a confirming Scripture through His Word. You can never go wrong when you prophesy Scripture while keeping it in its proper context.

Different spirits

We must remember that not all prophetic words originate from the Spirit of Prophecy. The Apostle John warned us and told us that we must test the spirits to see if they are of God and how to do so.

"Beloved, believe not every Spirit, but try the spirits whether they are of God: because many false prophets are gone out into the world. Hereby know ye the Spirit of God: Every spirit that confesseth that Jesus Christ is come in the flesh is of God: And every spirit that confesseth not that Jesus Christ is come in the flesh is not of God: and this is that spirit of antichrist, whereof ye have heard that it should come; and even now already is it in the world." 1 John 4:1-3 KJV

The spirit of the Antichrist which breeds the spirit of the False Prophet is already active in this world. There have been many words and prophetic decrees that have been released in the world that were not God's idea. That is why it is imperative for us to know God's Word in order for us to know His character and understand His will. In this we can judge correctly what He would and would not say or do. We will discuss the topic of judging prophetic words in a later chapter entitled *The False Prophet*.

The Lord will never go against His Word. If we see someone prophesying something that goes against the Word of God, then by default we know it is false. Likewise, if we feel led to Prophesy something that goes against the Word of God, then we should automatically determine that spirit to be false. This is why knowing God's Word in depth is so important for a Prophet.

When Jesus was led into the wilderness to be tempted by the devil, He used the Word to defeat him. Satan knew the Word and tried to use it to get Jesus to fall. But Jesus knew how to rightly divide the Word of truth. When tempted to throw Himself off a high building, He did not fall into the devil's trap because He understood God's character through the Word.

"Then the devil took him to Jerusalem, to the highest point of the Temple, and said, "If you are the Son of God, jump off! For the Scriptures say, 'He will order his angels to protect and guard you. And they will hold you up with their hands so you won't even hurt your foot on a stone.'" Jesus responded, "The Scriptures also say, 'You must not test the Lord your God."" Luke 4:9-12 NLT

What you don't know can hurt you. Just like the enemy came to temp Jesus, he will come to temp you into going against God's will. If one is not skilled in the Word of God, then they do not have a firm foundation to stand on and will begin to rely on intuition and hunches, rather than the truth that is revealed through His Word.

It feeds us

The Word is our bread, what feeds our spiritual babies helping them to grow. The Lord will use His Word to confirm or bring understanding to what He is speaking to our spirits. This is why private self-study is so important. So do not just eat when you need to feed others. We must eat for ourselves first. In this the Word will be so embedded in our hearts, it will just flow out without effort. Nothing worse than hearing a Prophet with no foundation. We become charismatic with no depth of revelation. Have you ever heard a sermon that preached you happy but was totally contradictory to God's Word? Misquoted Scripture used out of context in order to fulfill the desire of the people. This is what happens when we try to build others without building ourselves first.

<u>Place of Humility in Worship</u>

Worship is the last part of the oil. But contrary to what you may assume, it is more than just a song or high note but an acknowledgement that God is the greatest, He is Lord of all. Nothing goes before Him; nothing is above Him. No one is more worthy of our gratitude or reverence than Him. Worship brings us into a place of humility. It is the place that we come to grips with our human frailty. We acknowledge Him as the single source of strength, knowledge, insight, and capability. We boldly proclaim, "Without you I am nothing, without you I can do nothing." In worship we become small. Pride has no place here. This is where we grow by humbling ourselves before Him with a pure heart. Let's look at this vision the Apostle John had about heaven while exiled on the island of Patmos.

"Twenty-four thrones surrounded him, and twenty-four elders sat on them. They were all clothed in white and had gold crowns on their heads. Whenever the living beings give glory and honor and thanks to the one sitting on the throne (the one who lives forever and ever), the twenty-four elders fall down and worship the one sitting on the throne (the one who lives forever and ever). And they lay their crowns before the throne and say, You are worthy, O Lord our God, to receive glory and honor and

power. For you created all things, and they exist because you created what you pleased." Revelation 4:4, 9-11 NLT

What I love about this Scripture is that each one of the 24 was an Elder, meaning they held a high position. We do not know exactly what entitled them to be in that place, but their title separated them from the others. Each one of them had a throne and crown, yet all of those facts were insignificant in the sight of the king. They all recognized that though they were in high rank in heaven there was someone higher than them all, who alone was worthy of their worship.

Likewise, we must recognize that no matter how gifted we are, the authority we operate in the Spirit, the anointing that we carry, or even how much we are esteemed by men, we will never be so great that we need not to worship God. Those who have no worship life will most definitely become puffed up in pride and their gifting's. This place of worship, casting our crowns before the king is a safeguard against haughtiness.

Though I note worship as the last part of the oil, it is actually what precedes you entering into the presence of God. It is the key to the door we talked about earlier. Before we even consider entering in prayer or even intercession, we must come by the way of worship. It is a sweet aroma to the father's nostrils. It is what we owe Him. What I have found in worship is almost indescribable. There is a peace that surpasses human understanding. David says it like this

"Thou wilt shew me the path of life: in thy presence is fulness of joy; at thy right hand there are pleasures for evermore." Psalm 16:11 KJV

When you need clarity, go to worship. Peace? Go into worship. Need an encounter with God start with worship. So, before we ever endeavor to master anything that is contained in the pages of this book, we must first master the oil.

Though the oil has much to do with our relationship with God and keeping our gifts sharp and oil pure, God uses it to help us as well. In this place God will correct you when you need correction. Redirect you when you are off. Fill you when you are empty and refresh you when you encounter seasons of drought. Prophetic ministry is no easy task, and you will most definitely encounter some rough seasons but if you can maintain this place of the oil

God can always fill, heal, and restore you with whatever you need. Make it your endeavor to always keep your oil running!

Consecration

What is consecration?

Consecration means to be "set apart" for the service of a deity; and in this context to be set apart for God's special use. Fasting is often associated with consecration. Though similar in context, as it is a set apart time whereby you abstain from food or certain things to seek God on a more intimate level, is different from consecration. Unlike fasting we do not "come down" from our consecration. It is a lifestyle dedicated to God.

> *"And so, dear brothers and sisters, I plead with you to give your bodies to God because of all he has done for you. Let them be a living and holy sacrifice—the kind he will find acceptable. This is truly the way to worship him. Don't copy the behavior and customs of this world, but let God transform you into a new person by changing the way you think. Then you will learn to know God's will for you, which is good and pleasing and perfect." Romans 12:1-2 NLT*

As Christ followers we are all expected to live a life of Holiness; uncontaminated from worldly mindsets and behaviors, but apart from that there is another level of accountability that God holds each individual to. Even more so those who serve in a five-fold ministry role.

This is a personal place of conviction to certain things and the revealing of truths that is given to you by God. What God may hold you to, may not be the same as what He holds another to. Likewise, what He expects from your leader He may not expect from you. This is because God sets the consecration for your life. Many times, we will try and give God what we think

He requires of us. Some people give him less, while others go to extremes giving him things He never asked for.

Consecration is not a list of religious rules to follow in order to stay in Gods good graces, but rather a set of boundaries God sets for our lives to protect us and the gift of God He has placed in us. Consecration involves all three aspects of yourself: mind body and Spirit. In this sense, it causes us to come into a deeper place of discipline, acknowledging God on a greater level and not just during certain times of the year. Including Him in every aspect of our lives.

So now we will not wonder aimlessly on social media and watching tv for hours on end with no restriction or sensitivity to the things we watch. We will be careful what we expose our eye and ear gates to. Now we will watch the things we put in our body because we understand that it is God's temple, and we must take care of it. We will watch our conversations every day, being careful not to gossip, backbite or be busy bodies in others business because we know God hears our conversation EVERYDAY and not just when we fast.

<u>Set Apart</u>

When the children of Israel came out of Egypt God established the Aaronic priesthood. He chose the sons of Aaron and the tribe of Levi to be "Set Apart" for His special use. This however was not by coincidence. In the Book of Exodus, God called Moses up to the Mt. Sanai to receive the ten commandments. When he came down, to his surprise many of the children of Israel had used their jewelry to build an idol. The infamous golden calf (**Exodus 32**). God's anger was kindled against them. He was determined to destroy them all. However, Moses interceded on their behalf and God changed His mind. Moses then called them to make a decision, familiar idol worship or the true living God. The sons of Levi joined with Moses in serving the Lord and God then gave this command.

"Moses told them, "This is what the Lord, the God of Israel, says: Each of you, take your swords and go back and forth from one end of the camp to the other. Kill everyone—even your brothers, friends, and neighbors.." The Levites obeyed Moses' command, and about 3,000 people died that day. Then Moses told the Levites, "Today you have ordained yourselves for the service of the Lord, for you obeyed him even though it

meant killing your own sons and brothers. Today you have earned a blessing." Exodus 32:27-29 NLT

The tribe of Levi had a very hard decision. One that involved killing even those they loved, but it was one they were willing to make. In this single act, they showed their dedication to the Lord and God in turn honored them. Aaron sons would serve along with the Levites as priest. Taking care of the tabernacle and in charge of the offerings. These were His chosen set of people to perform these specific duties.

Honored by God

"But in a great house there are not only vessels of gold and of silver, but also of wood and of earth; and some to honour, and some to dishonour. 21 If a man therefore purge himself from these, he shall be a vessel unto honour, sanctified, and meet for the master's use, and prepared unto every good work." 2 Timothy 2:20-21 KJV

God honors those who honor Him. In 2 Timothy Paul was admonishing Timothy to stay pure, separated from the world system and youthful lust. To not be afraid to be set apart. In this he would remain and honorable vessel. Sometimes honoring God means forsaking relationships and friends. It sometimes means being separated from those who we love the most for the sake of not falling back into sin. Forsaking the things and way of life we are so use to. When we choose to walk the straight path God sets before us, God bestows unto us greater wisdom, revelation, and anointing. He also knows that He can trust us with more weightier assignments such as in the case of the sons of Levi.

The Call comes with Consecration

"Then the Lord said to Moses, "Bring Aaron and his sons, along with their sacred garments, the anointing oil, the bull for the sin offering, the two rams, and the basket of bread made without yeast, and call the entire community of Israel together at the entrance of the Tabernacle." Leviticus 8:1-3 NLT

God told Moses to consecrate Aaron and his sons for the dedication of the tabernacle. See, what many may assume God requires from them is a time of periodic fasting and denial of oneself. While this is an absolutely important aspect of Christianity, in the case of Aaron's sons and the Levites,

God was requiring something much more consistent. What Moses was about to present to them was a lifestyle adjustment. That meant their WHOLE life was set apart for the service of God. How they dressed, what they ate, where they lived, every aspect of their life governed by God because of their assignment (**Exodus 28**). This was a pattern that God set for the entire line of Aaron. These requirements came from God, not man. This is what He expected for their life.

God elevated the tribe of Levi amongst the rest of their brethren. They served in the tabernacle; the place God chose for His Spirit to rest among the children of Israel. The high priest would go into the inner court, the most holies of holies to make atonement for the people's sins. This was where the Ark of the covenant was housed. They also had the responsibility to teach the people the statues of God (**Leviticus 10:11**). God in turn gave them special allotments of the sacrifices and tithes for their services. They were given much, and the more God gives you the more he requires from you (**Luke 12:48**).

How present does this speak to us still today. Those who have received revelation from God, sit in leadership positions or teach His Word to others are held to a higher standard because of what they know. Yet and still there are those who want the call but not the consecration. In the Book of 1 Samuel, we are introduced to Eli. He and his sons were serving as priest as they were the descendants of Levi. There was a problem though. Eli's sons were serving as priest but were not willing to submit to the consecration of the priesthood. They did whatever they wanted including taking the best part of the offerings that was meant only to be offered to God. What made matters even worse their father Eli never corrected them. Unfortunately, this did not end well for Eli nor his sons. God judged not only them but brought judgment unto the entire line.

> *"I chose your ancestor Aaron from among all the tribes of Israel to be my priest, to offer sacrifices on my altar, to burn incense, and to wear the priestly vest as he served me. And I assigned the sacrificial offerings to you priests. So why do you scorn my sacrifices and offerings? Why do you give your sons more honor than you give me—for you and they have become fat from the best offerings of my people Israel! "Therefore, the Lord, the God of Israel, says: I promised that your branch of the tribe of Levi would always be my priests. But I will honor those who honor me, and I will despise those who think lightly of me. The time is coming when I will*

put an end to your family, so it will no longer serve as my priests. All the
members of your family will die before their time. None will reach old
age." 1 Samuel 2:28-31 NLT

There were requirements connected to their call as well as consequences. So, now the question is what is it that God is requiring of you?

Be Led by the Spirit

Let's venture into the life of Samson. This was a man consecrated to God. So much so that the Lord had already set Samson apart to be devoted to him before he was even conceived in his mother's womb. In the Book of Judges chapter 13 we meet Samson's mother. At this point she had no children and could not conceive. One day the Angel of the Lord visited her telling her that she would soon be with child. He told her about the plans God had for her future son and the type of life he would live. He also gave her some very important instructions about what she could and could not do while carrying him. See, Samson was predestined to not only be a judge and warrior but also a Nazarite. The word Nazarite means consecrated or devoted one. This meant he could not drink any alcohol, eat grapes, touch anything dead or cut his hair (**Numbers 6**).

Remember, consecration entails your body, mind, and Spirit. The Holy Spirit is the one who directs and instructs us into the ordained consecration God has for us. Just as the Angel of the Lord came to Sampson's mother and instructed her about her son's life, He will instruct you as well. No two assignments or people are the same and so no two consecrations are the same. If we look at the life of Sampson compared to the Levites, we see they both had very peculiar assignments but two totally different consecrations.

Spirit

Don't be surprised as you see the Holy Spirit directing you in strange and unusual ways. Even the littlest details of your life. Ultimately what it will help you to do is learn discipline. How not to only control your flesh but also your spirit.

Some ways that the Holy Spirit will help us discipline our spirit is to set us on a prayer watch. This is a set consistent time that God has ordained for you to pray and spend time with Him. This could be once or multiple times throughout the day. This will not be the same for each individual, but I can guarantee it most certainly will be a sacrifice.

Throughout Scripture we see where Jesus Himself with go off early in the morning leaving His disciples to go and spend time with His father. Right before His death, when in the garden of Gethsemane, He asked His disciples to watch as He prayed. Unfortunately, they were so tired that they fell asleep before Jesus even finished praying. I'm sure that it was probably late at night, and they had a very long day. I'm sure that they could have given many excuses as to why they felt justified in falling asleep, but Jesus left them with none. As a matter of fact, he rebuked them.

"Then he returned to the disciples and found them asleep. He said to Peter, "Couldn't you watch with me even one hour? Keep watch and pray, so that you will not give in to temptation. For the Spirit is willing, but the body is weak!" Matthew 26:40-41 NLT

Let's just be honest, the flesh does not like to be controlled, neither does it like to be inconvenienced. This is why I say that your prayer time will most certainly be a sacrifice. See, when we crucify our flesh, then our spirit can live. When He sees that we are willing to forsake our human needs and come into the appointment of prayer consistently then we earn His trust, and He will begin to reveal His secrets and reward us with greater assignments.

In those early morning hours before the sun rises when everyone else is sleeping, that is when God calls His people out of their slumber to come and search for Him. Don't be afraid to go with Him. In this you are building your Spirit man and putting your flesh under subjection. This goes also for set times a reading your Word and fasting. Allow the Holy Spirit to lead you, He knows what each vessel needs for the assignment.

Body

Your intake and how you take care of your body is also important. Scripture talks repeatedly of how our bodies are the temple of God. When we consider them as much, we not only honor God but also helps us to live a long and healthy life. The Holy Spirit is so wise, and the Lord is so concerned about our whole being. He wants us to be whole in every aspect, even in our health. See, to be able to carry this kingdom assignment and to live a long and prosperous life we must have a healthy body as well as a healthy soul.

As Christians God wants us to bear the fruit of the Spirit one of which is self-control. Food should never have control over us. When we allow our stomachs to lead us in that manner then food ultimately becomes an idol. It can also lead to many health conditions. We can't serve God long if we are sick and battling in our natural bodies.

If you are predisposed to certain hereditary diseases, the Holy Spirit may adjust your diet accordingly. For example, determining when you eat, your sugar, salt or fat intake and implementing exercise. Remember, always be led by the Spirit. He knows what is best for each individual to carry out our God given assignments unhindered. Take a minute to meditate and see where you can identify the nudging of the Holy Spirit concerning your diet and habits. Ask Him for the Spirit of obedience and the grace you need to move into this higher level of consecration.

Mind

> *"The lamp of the body is the eye. Therefore, when your eye is good, your whole body also is full of light. But when your eye is bad, your body also is full of darkness." Luke 11:34*

Just as what you intake into your mouth affects your body, so does what you feed your mind affects your soul. Having a healthy soul is a very important aspect of a Prophet's life. So how do you protect your soul? You do this by guarding the gates that lead to it. Being very careful as to what you allow to enter into your eye and ear gates.

> *"You say, "I am allowed to do anything"—but not everything is good for you. And even though I am allowed to do anything, I must not become a slave to anything." 1 Corinthians 6:12 NLT*

We all have different dispositions and inclinations to certain things depending on what we have encountered in life. Though it may not be a sin persae, it may very well be a weight. Weights are things that could eventually lead you to sin or open doors to past addictions or habits causing you, like Paul stated, to become a slave to it. So, what may be permissible for one may not be permissible for you. Let's think about it. Is there anything in your life that may not necessarily be a sin, but you feel as though you cannot do or live without it?

Janell Edmondson

Some examples of weights could be certain types of TV shows, being involved in certain conversations, the kind of music you listen to, even certain environments or engaging in relationships with certain people could be a hindrance for you. If you feel the nudging of the Holy Spirit leading you to withdraw yourself from watching and listening to certain things or take part in certain activities, obey.

Gentleman

Do not grieve the Holy Spirit. Remember, He is a gentleman. He will press upon your heart, but He will not force Himself upon you. He is a revealer and there are things yet to be discovered about not only you, but demonic assignments that have been set against your life to derail your destiny. While He is uncovering and revealing your main goal is to submit and be obedient. There will be times when we don't understand His ways but trust that he is here to assist you in becoming the version of you God ordained you to be. A new standard for your life. Remember, whoever you yield your members will be your master. You do not want to mix the old you with the new work God is doing in you. You must come to a place where the will of God for your life is more precious than anything in this world.

Don't be afraid to be different

Consecration is not always easy as sometimes it can cause you to feel separated, isolated and may even cause you to be ridiculed. Samson's mother had restrictions placed on her life because of what she was carrying. Her obedience was important to God. What you are carrying is just as important. The gift, talent, purpose and calling you carry is an asset to God's kingdom. So don't be afraid to be different, look strange or be "set apart." It is you staying on consecration that the gift of God can flow through your life unhindered. As long as God is pleased that is all that matters. Let God get the glory from your life.

Benefits of consecration

Though difficult at times being set apart by God comes with many benefits. Firstly, you will always be ready as stated before for God's special use. Secondly our consecration helps us to maintain our deliverance. That means the things that use to be able to find you can't find you that easy when you stay on consecration. You also have less pollutants and distractions clouding your eye and ear gates which makes it easier for you to learn God's voice for yourself. Now you will keep your censors lit with fervent prayer every day, coming into God's Word, and eating every day. Making Him our priority and putting Him first.

Prophetic Accountability

The importance of accountability in the prophetic cannot be overemphasized. I like to say, "Just because you are called by God does not mean the enemy will give you a pass and let you be great." On the contrary your spiritual warfare will intensify, and he will find any way possible to throw you off, and that is why being accountable with your gift is so imperative. I will talk numerous times about accountability throughout this book because this is a place that God has shown me to be very crucial. Accountability will save you from traps, deception, pitfalls and from wandering off the right path.

Accountability is a safeguard

It is like the bumper guards on the side of a bowling alley. As long as you have them up you know the ball is guaranteed not to go into the gutter. Take the guardrails down and your chances become slimmer. Oftentimes, what happens is as we mature, we get comfortable and think we don't need the guardrails anymore. Jesus taught the contrary. He said we should remain humble as children when we walk this walk with Him. We should live with the guard rails up. No matter how mature we get in the prophetic we will always need accountability.

Accountability starts with you

What I have notice in the body, even within the prophetic community, is a misunderstood place of accountability. Accountability is not so much the responsibility of your leaders to check in on you, but it is actually the contrary. You are the one who is responsible to present your thoughts, ideas, prophetic words, and revelation to your spiritual leader in order for them to inspect for inaccuracies or to bring correction.

Janell Edmondson

A lot of what we have seen throughout the body is what my leader calls a "Lone Ranger" mentality especially within the prophetic, leaving many Prophets without a proper covering or someone to be accountable to. This could be for several reasons. One of which is because Prophets hear regularly from God, they assume they can also hear God for themselves. This causes them to not seek for guidance from others, but we must realize that there is safety in counsel.

> *"Without wise leadership, a nation falls; there is safety in having many advisers." Proverbs 11:14 NLT*

Another reason why a Prophet might succumb to the "Lone Ranger" mentality is that they feel being accountable equates to being controlled. This is not only true for the prophetic, but also from many other ministry gifts. Fear of being controlled will cause you to run away from authority and hide from accountability. God is a God of authority and even Jesus submitted Himself unto the will of His father (**John 6:38**). Being accountable also gives us a place to be corrected. Correction is vital for proper growth. Those who feel threatened by correction will only hinder their development.

> *"So, don't bother correcting mockers; they will only hate you. But correct the wise, and they will love you. Instruct the wise, and they will be even wiser. Teach the righteous, and they will learn even more." Proverbs 9:8-9 NLT*

Once a Prophet understands the safety that council provides, they will no longer succumb to this mentality. Remember, God made the body so that we would never be independent from one another. Being able to humbly submit is a sign of maturity and it is in this place that God will elevate you.

> *"So humble yourselves under the mighty power of God, and at the right time he will lift you up in honor." 1 Peter 5:6 NLT*

Live with a guard rails up

This concept of accountability is not only for our prophetic ministry but for our personal lives as well. This is because what we do in our private lives reflects on the church publicly. A Prophet must give their lives over to ensure they don't end up in error. This includes personal relationships.

"The Lord directs the steps of the godly. He delights in every detail of their lives." Psalm 37:23 NLT

It is my firm conviction that every aspect of our lives should be given over to the leadership of God. This includes both private and public affairs. Many have failed in public because they first failed in private. In the Book of 1 Timothy, Paul states the qualifications for one who desires to hold the office of a Deacon or Bishop. Much of these requirements had to do with their personal life.

"This is a trustworthy saying: If someone aspires to be a church leader, he desires an honorable position. So a church leader must be a man whose life is above reproach. He must be faithful to his wife. He must exercise self-control, live wisely, and have a good reputation. He must enjoy having guests in his home, and he must be able to teach. He must not be a heavy drinker or be violent. He must be gentle, not quarrelsome, and not love money. He must manage his own family well, having children who respect and obey him. For if a man cannot manage his own household, how can he take care of God's church?" 1 Timothy 3:1-5 NLT

How we live in private does matter; it has a direct correlation on how we will handle the things of God. It is not enough that we have perfected the art of prophesying, if there is such a thing, but that we submit ourselves in such a way that our private lives are a direct representation of what Christ expects for His body to look like.

Checking prophetic words

People hold Prophets in high regard. Seeing them as ones who hear from and speak for God. It is imperative that the words we speak are vetted for accuracy and released in the proper manner. We must seek counsel before releasing words. Though the prophetic can bring life, an inaccurate or improperly relayed message could bring harm to the hearer. Getting words checked allows you to scan for inaccuracies in interpretation and to ensure it aligns with Scripture. It is a safeguard to you and the people who receive it.

"Let two or three people prophesy, and let the others evaluate what is said." 1 Corinthians 14:29 NLT

The Lord has given the body all five-fold ministry gifts and they work in conjunction to fulfill His purpose. It is important that we all work together in order for our prophetic gifts to be utilized in the proper manner. The Lord has set Apostles in the body of Christ as overseers. They have the ability to see and confirm gifts and callings. He has also given us Pastors, whose job is to watch over our souls and to make sure we are not led astray. The Prophet must remember not only their role but the role of these individuals in order for there not to be any error in the way the word is released.

In matters such as marriages, if a Prophet feels led to release a word, it is my firm belief that one needs to consult with the individuals pastor to confirm the word that they believe God is releasing. God is not the author of confusion, and if a word goes against what has already been spoken by their leader, then we need to weigh that word.

Remember, the prophetic can be both beneficial and detrimental depending on how it is used. There have been instances where people have been thrown off of their prophetic destiny because of affirmations that were given to them by a Prophet. Such as those that affirm an individual leaving one ministry and going to another.

This can also happen if a word is released too soon. Yes, there will be times when the Lord will allow you to see a certain call or gift in an individual, but we must be careful on how we release this information. One must consider, is this individual ready to receive this information, has their leader affirmed this gifting or call. To reiterate, it is not to say that the Lord will not show you these things but we must let everything be done in decency and in order.

School of Prophets

In the Old Testament Prophets traveled together in schools. This is because they were often taught together by a more senior Prophet as was the case with Samuel and Elisha (**1 Samuel 19:20,1 Kings 6**) but also because iron sharpens iron. Being around other Prophets will help you grow and sharpen your gift. There are times where the Lord will use other Prophets to confirm and bring clarity to the words that He has given you. A Prophet must not be afraid or intimidated to submit themselves to a more senior Prophet or fellowship with other Prophets. Communing within prophetic circles will only help you to mature in your calling. If you struggle connecting to other

Prophets or prophetic circles asked the Lord to lead you to voices that can be trusted to help push you further into your prophetic destiny.

Voice Recognition

Are you one on your journey where hearing the voice of God is something you have mixed feelings about? On one hand you are intrigued at the ability of other Prophets to hear the voice of God so accurately, but on the other hand insecure about your own abilities. You may question, how is it that they can hear Him so clearly? If I am a Prophet, why is it that I don't seem to hear Him in the way that others do? You know that you are called to the prophetic, but you struggle to hear God fluently (in a smooth, graceful, and effortless manner). Do you feel unconfident that you will ever be able to hear God's voice in that capacity? Know that you are not alone. There are many that are facing these same questions. This is especially true for those who have just come into the *awareness* of their call or are just beginning to *accept* and walk into the *maturity* of it.

> *"The gatekeeper opens the gate for him, and the sheep recognize his voice and come to him. He calls his own sheep by name and leads them out. After he has gathered his own flock, he walks ahead of them, and they follow him because they know his voice. They won't follow a stranger; they will run from him because they don't know his voice." John 10:3 NLT*

One of the greatest journeys I believe, as a Prophet that the Lord will bring you through is the journey of knowing His voice. The Bible says in the Book of John that God's sheep know His voice and a strange voice they won't follow. It is my experience that when we become saved, we don't automatically know the voice of our Lord. So how do we become sheep that can discern His voice?

What I have come to find out is, just like there are many different languages and dialects around the world, and not everyone speaks the same language in the natural, so it is with hearing God's voice. We must remember that no two Prophets are the same. We have our different personalities and ways of thinking. Some of which are influenced by our culture and that is what makes us all so different. Certain things will affect each one of us differently than they do others. So, with that said the way the Lord conveys information to each of us will be different.

It's like when a baby is born, he does not get to choose the family he is born into nor the language he is first taught. This is similar to our prophetic language. Just like an infant, God will teach us the prophetic language He has predestined for us to speak and understand. Let's take a look through a few Old Testament Prophets.

In this familiar passage we see where the Lord called Jeremiah to be His Prophet. He began to affirm him, telling him who he was and who he was always born to be. At first Jeremiah was very insecure about his ability to fulfill the task the Lord was giving to him. The Lord quickly shifted the focus from Jeremiah's insecurities and begin to ask him what he saw.

> *"Then the Lord said to me, "Look, Jeremiah! What do you see?" And I replied, "I see a branch from an almond tree."[12] And the Lord said, "That's right, and it means that I am watching,[c] and I will certainly carry out all my plans."[13] Then the Lord spoke to me again and asked, "What do you see now?" And I replied, "I see a pot of boiling water, spilling from the north."[14] "Yes," the Lord said, "for terror from the north will boil out on the people of this land. [15] Listen! I am calling the armies of the kingdoms of the north to come to Jerusalem. I, the Lord, have spoken!"Jeremiah 1:11-15 NLT*

See, though Jeremiah was insecure about his ability to speak, as it was with many other Prophets that the Lord had called, this was not God's primary concern. It is God who opens the eyes of man for them to see in the realm of the Spirit. It is also the same God who opens the ears of a man to be able to hear His voice when He speaks to them.

> *"The Lord God has given Me The tongue of the learned, That I should know how to speak A word in season to him who is weary. He awakens Me morning by morning, He awakens My ear to hear as the learned. The Lord God has opened My ear; And I was not rebellious, Nor did I turn away." Isaiah 50:4-5 KJV*

We don't get to choose how He speaks to us

Have you ever heard stories of other Prophets, their ways of hearing God and encounters and covet to have those experiences? I have been guilty of this as well. Unfortunately coveting their prophetic language does not influence God to speak to you in that fashion or give you those types of experiences. Though we may have similar encounters and some Prophets will and can hear the voice of God audibly not everyone will experience His voice in the same manor. This is because He already has a language prepared for you. One that you will learn through prayer, relationship with Him and His Word.

Different forms of communication

One of the first ways God communicated with the Prophet Jeremiah was by way of vision. This can often be the first line of communication for many Prophets. Many of us may have experienced this as early as our childhood. At that time, you may have not recognized that that was God's voice speaking to you. As you come deeper into a place of yielding and sensitivity to the Holy Spirit, you will begin to recognize God's voice more clearly when He speaks. This is why no one should feel insecure about hearing His voice. It is His job to teach you. It is God who trains His chosen Prophets. His voice, His timing, His way. It has been tailor made for you, specifically to His frequency. All He requires us to do is stay alert and pay attention.

Pay attention

God speaks in so many ways and that is why it is important for you to pay attention so that you can learn the way He is speaking to you at any given moment. As He brings you into His classroom, you will begin to see, hear, and experience things that may seem strange to most, but it will become the common place for you.

In these times of teaching, He will prompt you to understand that it was Him speaking. It could be as simple as a repeated pattern that you see on a television, road signs, sounds that seem amplified, open visions that come as clear as reality or those that appear faint as a daydream. Something you hear on the radio where the words just seem to echo out, or a piece of Scripture when reading the Bible that seems to be illuminated and pop off the pages. These are all Gods voice speaking to you.

There are many voices that speak.

When God first brought me through this process, I realized that there were different voices that were not the voice of God. See, there are many voices that speak. There is the voice of God, the voice of the enemy and the voice of our flesh. There are many voices of the flesh that originate from the depths of your soul. These voices in your soul can speak from past pain and trauma. These voices can hold you into a place of fear and intimidation. When one does not discern the difference, they can begin to prophesy from these soulish places. These are all some of the things you must recognize first in order for you to learn His true voice.

"And when he brings out his own sheep, he goes before them; and the sheep follow him, for they know his voice. Yet they will by no means follow a stranger, but will flee from him, for they do not know the voice of strangers." John 10:4-5 NKJV

You may feel as though you struggle to hear God's voice. What I have come to find is that in many times it is not that we cannot hear God but rather we fail to perceive when it is Him speaking. If we are used to being led by our flesh or deceived by the enemy, it is then that we become more familiar with those voices and mistake them as being God's.

Let God's voice lead you

"The Lord is my shepherd; I have all that I need. He lets me rest in green meadows; he leads me beside peaceful streams. He renews my strength. He guides me along right paths, bringing honor to his name." Psalms 23:1-3 NLT

The enemy will often mimic God's voice to try and lead you astray but here is the distinct difference between God's voice and that of the enemy. The voice of the enemy instills fear, anxiety, and confusion which does not lead us to peace but paranoia, distrust, dysfunction, and torment. So how do we discern God's voice. We must first ask this question? Where is the voice *leading me?* What emotions or actions is it producing? Just like a good shepherd God's Spirit leads us not into danger but into safety.

Even when God sends us warnings there should be an underlying sense of peace that comes from the Spirit of God letting us know that it is Him.

The voice that leads us is also the voice we prophecy from. It is easy to prophesy from a place of hurt or suspicion when we don't know His voice. This is why the Lord has to bring His Prophet through voice recognition. Next, we will discuss the different ways God uses in training His Prophets to discern His voice.

Knowing God's Voice through your Leader

"Meanwhile, the boy Samuel served the Lord by assisting Eli. Now in those days messages from the Lord were very rare, and visions were quite uncommon. One night Eli, who was almost blind by now, had gone to bed. The lamp of God had not yet gone out, and Samuel was sleeping in the Tabernacle near the Ark of God. Suddenly the Lord called out, "Samuel!" "Yes?" Samuel replied. "What is it?" He got up and ran to Eli. "Here I am. Did you call me?" "I didn't call you," Eli replied. "Go back to bed." So he did. Then the Lord called out again, "Samuel!" Again Samuel got up and went to Eli. "Here I am. Did you call me?" "I didn't call you, my son," Eli said. "Go back to bed." 1 Samuel 3:1-6 NLT

One of the first ways God will use to teach you His voice is through your leader. We can see with Samuel, where the Lord first revealed Himself to Samuel by way of His audible voice. This was not just any audible voice, however. This voice sounded like the voice of his leader Eli. It was only after Samuel came to Eli several times that Eli recognize that the young lad was hearing the voice of the Lord.

See Eli was learned in hearing the voice of the Lord. God used Eli to confirm to Samuel that it was Him speaking to him and thus was able to give him instructions. As you began to come through to know how to hear the voice of God, many times God will use your leader as a way to learn when He speaks. Often times He will use your leader to confirm something that He was speaking to you about previously. This could be through casual conversation, rebuke, instruction, or prophecy. Have you ever prayed to God about something privately and He brought the answer through your leader? They may not have even known that they were just an answer to your secret prayer.

To many this can seem frustrating because you desire to hear God for yourself. God does it this way not to crippled you or to make you overly dependent, this is simply one of the primary ways He uses to teach his Prophets. His tool to help mature that Prophets ear. They just like Eli, are more learned in God's voice and experienced Him in ways you may never have experienced Him before. This brings a certain level of wisdom and ability to discern.

There are times when the Lord will speak to you through dreams and visions and use your leader in the dream as a symbol of His authority. You see your leader and hear their voice, but it is really God speaking and giving you instructions. These are all the ways God will use those authority figures to teach you, His voice. That is why order is so important. As we see with the story of Samuel, Eli played a very important part in the training of Samuel.

God respects order and authority. As you begin to come into your prophetic journey from crawling to walking you will need that place of security Eli gave Samuel, just as a parent would give their baby. Samuel was able to go to Eli in his place of uncertainty. There are times when the enemy will try to bring confusion to you. God will then use the voice of that leader to bring correction, clarity, and alignment. In the early part of your journey, you may depend very heavily on your leader to be able to discern between the voice of your flesh, the voice of the enemy and the voice of the Lord. This takes a certain level of trust, accountability, and submission.

Even when you mature and grow in your ability to hear God's voice you still will never be without the need of your leader's voice in your life. Why? Though we hear well for others it is often exceedingly difficult to hear God for ourselves. Also, Prophets are used to hearing God's voice regularly and this can easily cause them to fall into the place of pride and independence. Hearing through our leader helps to keep us in a place of humility. When the Lord places His chosen vessel, a shepherd after His own heart to be the set covering over not only your soul but your prophetic ministry, it is important for us to trust their word and guidance. Learn to love God's voice through your leader.

Knowing God's Voice through your Thoughts

Have you ever been sitting, maybe in your quiet time with God and all of a sudden it seemed as though your thoughts just grew a mind of their own? You find yourself thinking about a person or situation and it feels as though you are the one that somehow led yourself down that thought process. Maybe it was prompted by something you saw like a picture or sound that you heard. Whatever it was, you felt like the thought originated with you. Then later you find yourself being confronted with that same hypothetical thought but this time it has made its way into reality. That very thought that you assumed was your own has just come to fruition. You didn't realize that was God's voice speaking to you. This is such a subtle voice of God that it is often overlooked.

Due to the fact that it comes through our thoughts, and it is not aggressive, it can sometimes be neglected. Many people have had encounters with God directing them through their thoughts but failed to recognize it. It could be a as simple as you driving down the street to the store and on your way there you think "They probably don't even have what I need in stock." You brush it off and continue your drive to the store. Then you arrive, and sure enough, what you needed was out of stock. This was just a subtle prompting of His voice trying to save you time. It could speak to you in something a little more meaningful as well.

For example, maybe there is a couple in your ministry who is barren and has been desiring to have kids. When looking through social media, you run across one of their photos. This prompts you to think about their situation. You imagine them finding out they were pregnant and finally receiving their gift from God and having a baby. Maybe you even think about the gender of the baby as well. Then shortly after, the wife calls you and tells you they are finally pregnant. Wow what a surprise! You assumed it was your imagination but in reality, it was God's voice. Seems to be so simple but this is just another way that God speaks.

God uses your thoughts to direct you in intercession as well. He will often put someone in your mind to pray for or check on. Some people use the phrase "The Lord laid you on my heart.." How easy it is to hear His voice when we learn to recognize the way He speaks. This takes time and as you go through your process and experiences you will become keener in discerning between the voice of God and your own thoughts.

Through Dreams and Visions

"For God speaks again and again, though people do not recognize it. He speaks in dreams, in visions of the night, when deep sleep falls on people as they lie in their beds. He whispers in their ears and terrifies them with warnings. He makes them turn from doing wrong; he keeps them from pride. He protects them from the grave, from crossing over the river of death." Job 33:14-18 NLT

Throughout history we have seen where God has spoken to men and women through dreams, though some people don't recognize when it is Him speaking. The Bible is inundated with stories of men and women receiving messages from God by way of dreams and vision. There are instances that God will speak in a dream using His audible voice. Jacob being one example of many (**Genesis 31:11**). Or He will use symbolism like He did with Joseph and the barley stalks when he foretold that his entire family would someday bow down to Him (**Genesis 37:5**). In a dream God can give you warnings as well as instructions. It could be instructions on what job to take or even about what to name an unborn child. It was by way of dream that God warned Joseph to take Mary (Mother of Jesus) and flee into Bethlehem to escape Herod's decree (**Matthew 2:12**).

This is another easily overlooked way that God speaks. Due to the fact that most people dream often, some every night, they may not recognize when their dreams are originating from God. There are times where you may have a dream that seems so random that you may think it came because of something you ate or excessive thoughts. That is why it is important to take our dreams to God and ask Him for direction. This is another form of communication, but it is still God's voice, and we must ask Him for discernment to be able to distinguish when it is Him speaking to us in this way.

Knowing God's Voice through his Word

"All Scripture is inspired by God and is useful to teach us what is true and to make us realize what is wrong in our lives. It corrects us when we are wrong and teaches us to do what is right." 2 Timothy 3:16 NLT

Some people use the acronym **B**asic **I**nstructions **B**efore **L**eaving **E**arth to describe the Bible. I believe there is a Scripture for any problem you may have. Though all Scripture is God inspired and God breathed, not every Scripture may be applicable to a present circumstance that you may be facing. What do I mean by this? If you are facing a situation where your faith is being tested, a Scripture on the dangers of pride may not be of much help to you. That is why it is important to know God's voice through His Word.

Have you ever been reading your Bible and a certain word or phrase seems to jump off the pages? It could be that at first glance it does not correlate to anything you are currently facing. Then maybe hours, days or even weeks later the revelation of what God was trying to relay to you comes to be fully realized. Or have you ever been in a situation where you needed an answer, instructions, or direction? Somehow the Holy Spirit guided you right to the Scripture that gave you the answer that you needed. This is God speaking to you through His Word. Guiding and navigating you through Scripture so you can know His will for your life. Yes, God can use anything to speak but it is ever so important to know His voice through His Word.

God's Audible Voice

"The voice of the Lord is powerful; the voice of the Lord is majestic. The voice of the Lord splits the mighty cedars; the Lord shatters the cedars of Lebanon." Psalm 29:4-5 NLT

We know that God's voice is not limited to sound. He can use images, songs, and even creation to get His message across. But then there are times noted in Scripture where God talked with men using His audible voice. So, what does God's voice sound like? From Scripture God's audible voice did not sound the same to everyone. When Samuel, who was unfamiliar with God's voice, first heard Him he thought it was his Predecessor Eli calling to him (**1 Samuel 3**). Many say that God's voice sounds familiar like someone they always knew. Others describe it as a common voice like that of their thoughts. In an encounter that Elijah had with God on mount Horeb, he described it as a still small voice (**1 Kings 19:12**). The Prophet Ezekiel and the Apostle John had a completely different experience. They described His voice as that of many waters (**Ezekiel 43:2, Revelation 1:15**). In the New Testament it was said to sound like thunder (**John 12:28**). No doubt God still speaks audibly to men. As you begin to experience Him in this way, again you may not recognize it at first. So how to you know when it's Him?

One thing I have learned about God's audible voice is that it is consistent. What do I mean by this? Everything He says is true and credible. When He speaks to you concerning something it will surely come to pass. Sometimes it comes to pass so suddenly you are not even prepared for it. For example, He may say something to you as simple as "The package you been waiting for is on your porch.." You go to open your front door and bam there it is! He may continue to speak to you in this way and as you see each word confirmed you will know that it is Him. This can take a while to get used to and can feel both overwhelming and exhilarating at the same time. Unlike the Holy Spirit that sounds more like an inner voice, God's voice is heard from without. Though subtle at times it is also distinct. The God of all the universe speaking directly to you.

Not everyone will experience God speak to them in an audible way and not every Prophet will receive their prophetic words in this manner. Some Prophets hear God's audible voice regularly and some may only experience this a few times throughout their life. The important part is when He does speak that we recognize that it is Him. Again, this is a process that one must go through as the enemy will often try to mimic God's voice, but don't fret, God is the one who trains His Prophet to know His voice in whatever way that He speaks.

Spiritual Awareness

Spiritual awareness is the ability to see in the spiritual realm through your natural eyes. This is a bit different from the Gift of Discerning of Spirits in that Discerning of Spirits allows a person to perceive a spirit in operation behind an event or action. Spiritual awareness is God opening a man or woman's eyes so that they can visually see what is already taking place in the Spirit.

This is not a new concept by far. The Bible is inundated with men and women who had spiritual encounters after God opened their eyes. Still, for the vast majority of Christians, we remain unmindful to spiritual activity in our everyday lives. It is not to say that we are ignorant of it, but it is as if we unintentionally shut our eyes to what we know is occurring. Due to this fact many are operating out of a carnal mind most of the time, and periodically engage in the spiritual realm when in prayer, a church service, or reading their Word. This is what hinders many people from coming into the deeper things of God, but this was not the case in the beginning.

God is Spirit, we are spirits as well but were made to live in a fleshly body while here on Earth. God always desired for us to engage with the unseen realm. Insensitivity to God pushes us further away and we become so carnally minded that we suppress our Spirit (**Romans 8:5-6**). When we are preoccupied with worldly desires, we lose the sensitivity to what is happening in the unseen realm. That is what the enemy has done to this world, blinded their eyes to the things of the Spirit (**John 12:40**).

Two Worlds

"For through him God created everything in the heavenly realms and on earth. He made the things we can see and the things we can't see— such as thrones, kingdoms, rulers, and authorities in the unseen world. Everything was created through him and for him."
Colossians 1:16 NLT

The spiritual realm is *invisible* which means it cannot be seen with our natural eyes. Yet he repeatedly states that though you cannot see plainly those things with your natural eyes, there is a knowing everyone has, whether you are a Christian or not, that tells us there is more out there than what we can see (**Romans 1:18**).

Think of a cake. You have the layers of the cake and then you have the frosting that makes the cake complete. The layers of the cake represent the dimensions that we can visibly see, and the frosting the dimension we cannot. There is the visible dimension composed of the things that were made throughout the Seven Days Creation in Genesis (**Genesis 1**) and then you have the invisible dimension which contain things that we presume were formed before the visible one. These include angel's, heaven, principalities and so forth. The Prophet Ezekiel scribed about many of his visual encounters with these heavenly beings (Ezekiel 1:4).

Most people only engage in the layers, but what is cake without the frosting? In order to really walk this Christian walk in its fullness you need both. The invisible is the icing, it is what helped make the things we see. It is what holds all things together. That is why it is important for us to always remain cognizant of the other world. Whether you have the ability to physically see it or not. If we don't, we will become carnally minded and cease to fully distinguish the manifestation of physical presentations that are being shaped by spiritual activity (**Ephesians 2:2**).

Things are always happening shifting and moving in the spiritual Realm

"Jacob found a stone to rest his head against and lay down to sleep. As he slept, he dreamed of a stairway that reached from the earth up to heaven. And he saw the angels of God going up and down the stairway."
Genesis 28:11-12 NLT

We see here that Jacobs spiritual eyes were opened, and God allowed him to see what was taking place in the Spirit. Before that point he was unaware of the things that were taking place in the spiritual realm. Like many believers and non-believers alike are unaware of what is taking place in the Spirit Realm. Even with this, these things are still happening every day.

Only God can open our spiritual eyes

Within the Bible we see where God opened the spiritual eyes of men and women. This ability was not something that they always had; though some may have recalled the ability to see spirits both Angelic and demonic from a young age. Many times, we will see those who operate under the anointing of deliverance will have this ability, but unlike the spiritual gifts listed in 1 Corinthians 12, anyone can have spiritual awareness. All we have to do is ask.

"Then Elisha prayed, "O Lord, open his eyes and let him see!" The Lord opened the young man's eyes, and when he looked up, he saw that the hillside around Elisha was filled with horses and chariots of fire." 2 Kings 6:17 NLT

Ask God for Spiritual awareness

In 2 Kings Elisha prayed to God to open his servant spiritual eyes. He needed his servant to see beyond the natural realm so that he would not be afraid. God granted Elisha's request. I believe God created us from the beginning with this ability. I believe it was through the increase of sin and giving ourselves over to the flesh that we have lost it. I believe it is God's desire that all of His children are more aware and sensitive to the things that are happening in the Spirit (**Galatians 5:16**).

Does that mean that you will be able to see demons manifesting or have Angelic encounters? Not necessarily, some people would not be able to handle such types of experiences. He knows each one of us distinctively and takes all of that into consideration. What I do believe will happen at the least is that you will become more sensitive to spiritual activities. It is vital that every believer has this ability no matter what capacity God gives them to operate it from. Ask for God to open your spiritual eyes, ask for spiritual awareness.

Janell Edmondson

The Gifts

Now I would like to speak to you about some of the spiritual gifts that I see are commonly carried by Prophets in the Bible and in the body of Christ today.

"There are different kinds of spiritual gifts, but the same Spirit is the source of them all. There are different kinds of service, but we serve the same Lord. God works in different ways, but it is the same God who does the work in all of us. A spiritual gift is given to each of us so we can help each other." 1 Corinthians 12:4-7 NLT

The gifts of the Spirit are special abilities given by God. We know according to 1 Corinthians 12 that God gives gifts to man severally as He wills to whom He chooses. Depending on your specific assignments and level of operation God may choose to equip you with different gifts, graces, and levels of anointing. In this chapter we will explore some of these gifts and the Prophets in the Bible who operated in them.

Gift of the Word of knowledge

First, we are going to talk about the Revelation gifts which are the Word of Wisdom, Discerning of Spirits and the Word of Knowledge. They are coined the revelation gifts because they all *reveal* something about an individual or situation. In the natural, **Knowledge** are facts, information or skills acquired by a person through experience or education. It can also be defined as the theoretical or practical understanding of a subject; the fact of knowing about something.

The game show Jeopardy celebrates this type of worldly knowledge in that it showcases people who have a vast knowledge about many different subjects from around the world. Their contestants have stored facts in their memory about history, art, music, things that have happened in the past and facts about the present. This knowledge is much different than the gift of the

Spirit that Paul talked about in the Book of 1 Corinthians. Unlike worldly knowledge that must be learned, researched, discovered, or verified; God's Gift of the Word of knowledge is an *instant download* of information that is obtained without research or fore knowledge.

> *"Jesus replied, "You are blessed, Simon son of John, because my Father in heaven has revealed this to you. You did not learn this from any human being." Matthew 16:17 NLT*

As humans, we do not know everything. Though we can be very knowledgeable, it is impossible to carry all information about all things. However, as Christians, we do have an advantage, in that we have been given a gift, one who contains all information and revelation, and His name is the Holy Spirit. So, though I may not know everything, He does.

The Omniscience of God

> *"Thou hast beset me behind and before, and laid thine hand upon me. Such knowledge is too wonderful for me; it is high, I cannot attain unto it." Psalm 139:5-6 KJV*

The Gift of the Word of Knowledge is the **omniscience** of God. Omniscient means *all-knowing*. It is God giving you an instant download from His unlimited knowledge. Have you ever been in a prophetic service and the Prophet or Minister who was speaking was able to give out detailed information about individuals in the crowd such as first or last name, phone number, where they live or even where they worked? This is the gift of knowledge in operation. This gift can entail information about the past, present, or future.

The Gift of the Word of knowledge in the Old Testament

Samuel embodied the Gift of the Word of Knowledge. The Bible says God spoke to Samuel in his ear (**1 Samuel 9:15**). Let's look at one of the key passages that portrayed this gift being demonstrated in the life of Samuel. In this particular passage we will see where Saul sought the Prophet Samuel to inquire the location of his father's lost donkeys.

> *"And don't worry about those donkeys that were lost three days ago, for they have been found. And I am here to tell you that you and your family are the focus of all Israel's hopes." 1 Samuel 9:20 NLT*

Here we see where Samuel used the Gift of the Word of Knowledge to inform Saul about the location of the donkeys. This was a supernatural receiving of information from God to Samuel about a matter that he could not have known from out of his own strength. Those who carry this gift will receive these downloads frequently and is usually associated with a purpose such as them releasing a word to another individual or giving direction.

The Word of knowledge can be driven through the vehicle of prophecy

"Go and get your husband," Jesus told her. "I don't have a husband," the woman replied. Jesus said, "You're right! You don't have a husband— for you have had five husbands, and you aren't even married to the man you're living with now. You certainly spoke the truth!" "Sir," the woman said, "you must be a prophet..." John 4:16-19 NLT

The Gift of the Word of Knowledge is often driven through the vehicle of prophecy. We see this concept being displayed in John 4 when Jesus encountered the Samaritan in the story of the woman at the well. He began to reveal to her sensitive information about her past and present relationships. The woman knew that He could not have known these things from His own self, and that they must have been revealed by the Lord. That word of knowledge that was given caused her to be open to hear more of what He had to say. So likewise, the Lord will use the Gift of the Word of Knowledge in order to "open up" an unbeliever or skeptic, to hear more of what God wants to speak to them.

"So you see that speaking in tongues is a sign, not for believers, but for unbelievers. Prophecy, however, is for the benefit of believers, not unbelievers. Even so, if unbelievers or people who don't understand these things come into your church meeting and hear everyone speaking in an unknown language, they will think you are crazy. But if all of you are prophesying, and unbelievers or people who don't understand these things come into your meeting, they will be convicted of sin and judged by what you say. As they listen, their secret thoughts will be exposed, and they will fall to their knees and worship God, declaring, God is truly here among you." 1 Corinthians 14:22-25 NLT

How to apply the Word of Knowledge using the Word of Wisdom

Unlike other gifts, that we will discuss later in this chapter, The Gift of the Word of Knowledge is an *information only* based gift. Thus, it is often necessary to have a word of wisdom to partner with the Word of Knowledge for it to be effective. Knowledge is the *who, what, when* and *where* but wisdom gives you the *why* or *how to apply*. This is true for most cases but not always. The Lord may show or reveal to you the name of an individual. Surely, He did not have you reveal this information to them just for you to look super prophetic! There has to be a purpose behind it.

As stated before, this gift can be used to cause an individual to "open up" to more you have to say. So one must ask, what is the *more* that He wants to reveal? If He is showing you something about their past or present what word of wisdom, restoration or insight is the Holy Spirit wanting to couple with this knowledge in order to bring this person into a more whole state.

Take this for example. The Lord revealed to you an individual is battling a particular illness. They may have been seeking God concerning this situation on how to move forward. The Holy Spirit could then give you insight and instruct you as to what they need to do next. Maybe God wants to heal them supernaturally or may use you to instruct them to go ahead and seek out professional medical treatment. Or He could disclose to you that an individual suffered some sort of abuse as a child. He may then reveal to you the purpose behind it in order to bring assurance that God understands their pain but also wants them to heal, forgive and move forward with their life. These are just a few examples of the Word of Knowledge and the Word of Wisdom going hand-in-hand.

Word of knowledge can be revealed through many different ways

The Lord can reveal words of knowledge in many different ways. We can see with Samuel; the Bible says that the Lord spoke to him in his ear. This gift can also be revealed by God through dreams, visions and also in prayer.

In the ear

> *"Now the Lord had told Samuel in his ear a day before Saul came, saying,"* 1 Samuel 9:15 KJV

Many times, He will speak directly to you in your ear. Using His audible voice, He will relate to you the information that He wants you to know. You may have experienced this before when meeting new people. God could instantly download to you their name or where they were born. It could be as simple as knowing the age of that person or knowing the gender of a baby that they are carrying. Many Prophets have known God's voice through the hearing of the ear, but this is just one way that God uses to reveal His information.

In dreams and visions

God also uses dreams and Visions to reveal his word of knowledge to you. The Lord can reveal information to you about people that you have yet to meet or situations you have yet to encounter. These revelations are not just for you to know but are usually confirmations of something that He wants you to understand ahead of time so that you can be better prepared.

In prayer

Sometimes God releases things to you in prayer that you would not have known otherwise without research. The purpose of this is to show you the enemies plan, God's plan, or Heaven's agenda and how you can partner with Him for His will to be established in the earth. In this, it is as if you are being downloaded with knowledge that you did not know existed. If this is new to you, it may take some time for you to get used to God speaking to you this way. When He does you must trust that He knows all things. Begin to journal and write down what you hear as you are praying. Whether it is immediate or takes, days, or weeks, He will always confirm His Word.

Knowledge puffs up

"But while knowledge makes us feel important, it is love that strengthens the church." 1 Corinthians 8:1 NLT

When one is wise and full of knowledge it is easy to become proud and look down on others, so it is also with the Gift of the Word of Knowledge. Having access to personal information about people's past, present and future can cause you to become a show-off but that does not edify. Charity builds others up. When getting a word of knowledge or any prophetic word you must ask is the person being helped by the information that you are giving or are they just being mesmerized with our gift. We must know that the Gift of the Word of Knowledge is not just so we can say we know something, but it is a key given to us. Wisdom and revelation helps us to know what we need to do with the key or what door it opens.

How to govern this gift

"A shrewd man is reluctant to display his knowledge [until the proper time], But the heart of [over-confident] fools proclaims foolishness." Proverbs 12:23 AMP

Because the Gift of Discerning of Spirits, Word of Wisdom, and Word of Knowledge all reveals something about a person's life, you need to learn how to steward it properly. One must learn to use discretion when using this gift. **Discretion** is the quality of behaving or speaking in such a way as to avoid causing offense or revealing private information. All the gifts work best when driven through the conduit of love. We see this demonstrated with Jesus from the Scripture we noted above. Before He engaged in conversation with the Samaritan, He sent His disciples away and spoke with her in private. All words are not meant to be shared publicly. We must discern this difference. Be a good Steward over the information God gives you and seek for direction and strategy on how to release these words.

Not just for Prophets

Many people operate in the Gift of the Word of Knowledge, but just because someone carries this gift does not mean ...

1. They are a Prophet
2. They are operating and gaining that information from the Spirit of God.

The revelation gifts are often present in a Prophet but can operate independently through someone who is not a Prophet. This is a common misconception and due to this there are some that have been mislabeled Prophets just because they carry this gift. Remember, the office of the Prophet is not just about a gift but about a role, function, ordination, and commission.

Different Spirits

"Now it happened, as we went to prayer, that a certain slave girl possessed with a spirit of divination met us, who brought her masters much profit by fortune-telling. This girl followed Paul and us, and cried out, saying, "These men are the servants of the Most High God, who proclaim to us the way of salvation." And this she did for many days. But Paul, greatly annoyed, turned and said to the spirit, "I command you in the

name of Jesus Christ to come out of her." And he came out that very hour."
Acts 16:16-18 NKJV

Not everyone who speaks accurately does so by the Spirit of the Lord. Just as the woman in the Book of Acts 16 discerned from a different spirit; so it is so that you can gain knowledge from a different system. Palm readers, psychics, and mediums can all gain access into the spiritual realm to gain information. This does not mean it is from God. Your name, family history, past relationships, and places of employment are all forms of existing information. In this new era, we must ask God for discernment to know what spirit is operating behind these gifts.

Anyone can receive

It is also important to note that anyone can receive these instant downloads from God, but it does not necessarily mean that you have the Gift of the Word of Knowledge. For example, you lose your keys, and you ask the Holy Spirit to help you find your keys. He may *show* you where they are, *lead you* to where they are, or give you an instant download and *tell you* the exact location of where they are. This is the same as when the Holy Spirit brings back to your remembrance passwords, directions, and names. This instant download from the Holy Spirit often involves a present situation and are not frequent and does not necessarily indicate you carry the Gift of the Word of Knowledge.

Gift of the Word of Wisdom

Wisdom is the quality or state of being wise; knowledge of what is true or right coupled with just judgment as to action; sagacity, discernment, or insight. Wisdom in its carnal sense can be summed up in a person's ability to act in judgment through the knowledge they have attained. Wise people learn from their mistakes and the mistakes of others. They observe bad behavior, the outcome of it and choose not to go down that path. They make right decisions based off past experiences. It could also be said that a wise person practices common sense on a consistent basis.

Whereas insanity, which could be said to be the opposite of wisdom, is that you consistently repeat the same mistakes and or bad decisions over again and refuse to make the necessary adjustments. The Book of Proverbs talks heavily about wisdom and its counterpart which is *foolishness*. See, fools act irrationally and largely make decisions based off their emotions; often not thinking about the outcome or consequences of their actions before carrying them out. They live in the moment and not the future. Solomon, who was said to be the wisest man who ever walked the earth, admonished his sons not to live this way but to cherish wisdom.

The fear of the Lord is the beginning of all wisdom

"The fear of the Lord is the beginning of wisdom: and the knowledge of the holy is understanding." Proverbs 9:10 KJV

The Bible says the fear of the Lord is the beginning of wisdom. So, in order to fully understand wisdom, we must first understand the fear of the Lord. The fear of the Lord, unlike natural fear (unpleasant feeling triggered by perception of danger real or unreal), is a deep respect and reverence for God, the things of God, and His Word. You cannot truly have Godly wisdom apart from knowing and reverencing God. So, from this we can understand that one cannot truly fear God, in a healthy way, without knowing Him. Knowing God in His fullness (character, sovereignty, knowing His likes, dislikes, understanding His power, etc.) causes you to have a non-partial view of Him and creates a healthy reverence for Him. That in turn will cause you to desire to walk in His ways and His likeness.

Fear of God results in wisdom, and wisdom results in obedience. One who is wise and fears God will often aspire to obey His commands. So now we see how the Scripture ties together when it says the fear of the Lord is the beginning of all wisdom. Now let us look into the story of Solomon. Solomon desired to carry out God's righteous judgment and ordinances throughout his rule over the Kingdom of Israel. He desired to please God just as his father David did, and to be obedient to Him.

Gift of Wisdom to judge well

Solomon, after being ordained King, was visited by God. He knew that the responsibility of governing all of Israel would be a very challenging task. One that he did not feel equipped to do, nor was it a role that he took lightly. So, with this in mind he asked God for wisdom.

"Give me the wisdom and knowledge to lead them properly, for who could possibly govern this great people of yours." 2 Chronicles 1:10 NLT

God granted his request, but the wisdom Solomon attained from God was different from the Gift of the Word of Wisdom spoken of by Paul in 1 Corinthians 12. A very wise woman who happens to be my Apostle says this about Solomon's wisdom. "Solomon's wisdom was the *gift of wisdom* that allowed him to govern his affairs well, but the *Gift of the Word of Wisdom* is different in that it involves the *revelation* of the divine will of God. When I first heard this teaching, it opened my eyes to a whole new perspective on *carnal wisdom*, the *Gift of Wisdom*, and the *Gift of the Word of Wisdom*.**Carnal wisdom**

See there are many people who have been blessed with the gift of wisdom, both carnal and spiritual. Some who are believers in Christ and some who are not. The list of these could include ancient astronomers and philosophers such as Socrates who once quoted this "Contentment is natural wealth; luxury is artificial poverty." Someone like Socrates would not be considered a follower of Christ but is considered a wise man. But this wisdom is earthly, sensual and based merely on carnal knowledge.

"Because the foolishness of God is wiser than men; and the weakness of God is stronger than men." 1 Corinthians 1:25 KJV

This is where carnal wisdom, the gift of wisdom, and the Gift of the Word of Wisdom differ. The Gift of the Word of Wisdom deals with the supernatural ability to discern and understand the purposes and divine will of God. This gift is not vague but is *specific* to each situation or person. For example, someone you know could be faced with a decision on which university to attend. This person has received two offers, both of which come from very prestigious schools. Both schools offer similar programs, but one is twice as expensive than the other. Unfortunately, the person only has enough financial aid and scholarships to cover the tuition for the less expensive university.

Looking at this carnally, a wise person would say go with the least expensive university because you are saving money, and both schools are reputable. But the Gift of the Word of Wisdom, which is specific to each situation, and is God's supernatural insight says no go to the more expensive college because there is someone there who God needs you to connect with. This person is going to be very important to your future. Along with that, God is going to give you favor with the school and when you graduate you would do so debt-free. See, often because this gift is specific to individuals or situations, it can contradict natural wisdom.

"Let no man deceive himself. If any man among you seemeth to be wise in this world, let him become a fool, that he may be wise. For the wisdom of this world is foolishness with God. For it is written, He taketh the wise in their own craftiness." 1 Corinthians 3:18-19 KJV

God loves to contradict natural wisdom

That is why we must know how to operate this gift correctly. What may be wise for one may not be wise for another, and what may be God's will for one may not be God's will for another.

"Trust in the Lord with all your heart; do not depend on your own understanding. Seek his will in all you do, and he will show you which path to take." Proverbs 3:5-6 NLT

This gift deals heavily with insight which is one of the three site gifts (**insight, foresight, and hindsight**). **Insight** is the ability to have a clear, deep, and sometimes sudden understanding of a complicated problem; power to see into a situation. This insight may go against what seems right in the natural. Let's go and venture into the Book of Jonah.

Jonah was a Prophet of God, received a word from the Lord to go and warn the city of Nineveh to repent or else face God's judgement (**Jonah 1:1-2**). Jonah, however, did not want to take this assignment and decided to go the opposite direction and took a ship going to Tarshish. When on this ship, running from the will of God, a great storm arose and all the men on the ship were very afraid. But Jonah was fast asleep. Then the men cast lots and it fell on Jonah, but he already knew what was happening. He had understanding and was able to give the men instructions on what to do to quiet the storm..

See, Jonah had insight on who brought the storm and why the storm was occurring, which was his disobedience. He also knew what he needed to do for the storm to stop. Though the solution seemed unusual, Jonah knew once he was off the boat the men would no longer be in danger, and if he stayed on it, it could cost all their lives. So, Jonah was thrown off the boat, the storm calmed, and the story goes on.

Wisdom to do uncommon things

We see this also in the Book of Hosea when God instructed him to go and marry a harlot, but in the same Scripture, God gave Hosea insight as to why He was instructing him to do such a strange act.

> *"When the Lord first began speaking to Israel through Hosea, he said to him, "Go and marry a prostitute, so that some of her children will be conceived in prostitution. This will illustrate how Israel has acted like a prostitute by turning against the Lord and worshiping other gods." Hosea 1:2 NLT*

This at first looks like a far from right or righteous thing to do. Hosea being a Prophet of God, going to marry a woman who is not a virgin and who practiced an immoral lifestyle. I believe both the ancient Jewish community in Hosea's time and the Church of today would have protested against a man of God marrying such type of woman. But it was a divine Word of God set for a specific purpose; so, man's opinion did not matter.

See, the revelation behind the act was already given to Hosea. God wanted to use his adulterous wife Gomer to convey the love He had for Israel. That just like Gomer went and defiled herself by sleeping with other men and Hosea redeemed her; God would, in the same way forgive Israel's idolatrous ways and in due time redeem her (**Hosea 3:11**).

Gift for transitions

This Gift of the Word of Wisdom is such an important gift to the body of Christ in that it can help people avoid going the wrong direction when faced with transition and changing of seasons. The Word of Wisdom can help redirect someone who has fallen off get back on the right path. It can also help turn a backslider's life back into alignment with the will of God.

The Word of Wisdom is vital in: Moments of transition, changes in career, transitions in life such as graduating from high school, marriages, starting or restructuring of ministry, after a death of a loved one or traumatic event.

How to govern this gift

Like any gift of the Spirit, this too must be governed properly in order to not do harm. What I have found with both those gifted with wisdom and the Word of Wisdom is that people will gravitate toward the wisdom that they carry. This is not necessarily a bad thing in a sense, but it can easily become misused.

As Prophets, we must understand our role in the body as a mouthpiece of God. The Lord will use us in many different capacities; to give direction, instruction, and warning. This is not uncommon as even the Old Testament Prophets were sought out for council on many occasions (**2 Chronicles 26:5**). Even kings sought out the word of the Prophet before deciding whether to go to war (**1 kings 22:6**). But what I have found with this gift is because of the great revelation and wisdom that person carries (whether Prophet or not), people will begin to rely on their words more than seeking the voice of God for themselves. This is dangerous and is the place where many prophetic calls get displaced.

The role and functions of the New Testament Prophet differ slightly from that of the Old Testament. One difference is because the people in the Old Testament did not have the Holy Spirit living on the inside of them. Before Christ, men did not have direct access to God, but after the New Covenant was given, we now have access. Now God abides in us and we in Him by the way of the Holy Spirit. Still, for many different reasons, some believers still depend heavily on the prophetic voice even in everyday matters.

Do not become a mediator

This is what the Lord admonished me not to do concerning this. He said to me "Do not become their mediator; they already have one and His name is Jesus Christ." As you began to grow and mature in your prophetic call, those around you will recognize that. They may begin to flock to you asking for prayer, direction, and advice.

I have encountered this when someone who felt as though they could not hear from God when they prayed and asked me to pray and hear God for them. Thankfully, the Lord warned me beforehand so I would know how to answer them. I told them God speaks to all of us, but sometimes we do not recognize when it is Him speaking. Instead of praying *for* that person, I prayed *with* them that the Holy Spirit would open their ears and eyes so that they could recognize the way that He was speaking to them. Then they could hear from God for themselves and make the right decision.

See, if I would have consented to what they wanted, I would have hindered their spiritual growth and ability to hear from God. By answering them in that way I reminded them that we are all God's children and have access to Him by way of the Holy Spirit. Whether if they are a Prophet or not, it is a gift of God. This hopefully pushed them to pursue hearing God's voice in a greater way. We must discern keenly how God wants to use this gift through us so that we do not become a hindrance to the body's spiritual growth.

The enemy will use insecurity and identity struggles as a way for us to feel complete by the affirmations of men, bur remember God is the one who affirms us not men. We do not want to create unhealthy attachments to ourselves because of our gifts. This will only create trouble for us in the long run.

Wisdom in counseling

Depending upon your specific role in your local ministry will determine how this gift is used. As stated, before both Old and New Testament Prophets are used by God to council. Those who carry the Gift of the Word of Wisdom too can be used by God to counsel. But with every gift comes responsibility, and with every new responsibility comes training. Though you are a Prophet and carry this gift, it is crucial for you to be *trained to counsel*. Why is this so important? You can detour someone's life by giving them wrong council.

Also, though we are all Prophets, not everyone will carry the same responsibilities in their local body. There are some Prophets who have been given the permission and grace to council in their local ministry. This gives them a bit more freedom in the use of this gift, though they still should be accountable and careful not to cross the line into mediator. Those who operate in this position must always be accountable.

When the Lord gives you a word of wisdom for an individual, couple, or a leader, you must always go back and submit that word to your leader to get checked before releasing it. This is especially true for new Prophets and counseling for major life transitions. You don't want to contradict a word that has already been given. Remember, always be accountable.

Not all words of wisdom need to be released

I am reminded of another experience I had with a couple with whom the Lord allowed me to release a word of wisdom to. I was obedient and release the word, but after I released the word, I saw where that couple began to struggle in faith and begin to make some not so right decisions. After the fact they came back to me wanting to know what they should do.

Fortunately, the Lord had already showed me where they were and gave me instructions to intercede for them. He did not, however, release me to give them another instruction, even though He showed me what they needed to do. See, the Lord needed them to grow in faith and obedience to Him. I instructed them to go back and pray to God for direction. Not too much time later they came back and gave me the word they received from the Lord. It was the same answer that the Lord gave me.

This showed me a few things. One, it is okay to let people learn from their mistakes and to trust that God knows how to redirect and speak to His people. Two, He is Sovereign and though He does use Prophets to direct, He is ultimately in full control. Third, never underestimate the power of prayer and that my prayer is just as potent and powerful as my prophetic word. This was both and eye opening and humbling experience for me.

We must always remember that it was always God's plan to break down that barrier that sin created in order for Him to have a deep personal relationship with His creation. Let us not stand in the way of God and His people. Let us use this gift in the way and capacity He originated it to be used and not go beyond that. Always allowing people to grow in their faith, make mistakes, hear from God for themselves. As my leader always says, "Send them back to God."

Gift of Discerning of Spirits

"To another the working of miracles, to another prophecy,
to another discerning of spirits, to another different kinds of tongues,
to another the interpretation of tongues." 1 Corinthians 10:12 KJV

The Gift of Discernment is the supernatural ability to "know the difference" between that which is good and evil, right, and wrong intent, godly or demonic operation. Often someone who has a strong gift of discernment will say "You did not see that?" or "You did not sense that?." Those around you will oftentimes be unaware to the things that you are picking up or have been given access to in the spiritual realm.

The Gift of Discerning of Spirits vs. Carnal discernment

Your dictionary defines **Discernment** as the ability to notice the fine-point details, the ability to judge something well or the ability to understand and comprehend something. *The Gift of Discerning of Spirits* is different from carnal discernment, as the gift deals with the supernatural operation behind a certain action, event, or spirit in operation within a person.

> *"But solid food belongs to those who are of full age, that is, those who by reason of use have their senses exercised to discern both good and evil." Hebrews 5:14 NKJV*

Secular discernment involves the ability to judge well carnally. On the other hand, the Gift of Discerning of Spirits necessitates one to use their spiritual senses to go beyond what their natural senses can pick up. One can learn or develop natural discernment. I believe both Solomon and Moses carried a heavy level of secular discernment because of the position that they stood in. They had to be able to judge well between matters great and small. But when you have the *gift of discernment* you are not only able to judge between carnal matters, but to see the spirit that is in operation behind any given situation.

Spirits in operation behind the scenes

In the Book of Ephesians chapter 6, Paul reminds us that we do not wrestle against flesh and blood but against these invisible forces (principalities, powers, rulers of darkness,) that sit in high places.

> *"Put on all of God's armor so that you will be able to stand firm against all strategies of the devil. For we are not fighting against flesh-and-blood enemies, but against evil rulers and authorities of the unseen world, against mighty powers in this dark world, and against evil spirits in the heavenly places." Ephesians 6:12 NLT*

All people, both Christian and non-believers alike, face spiritual battles every day. This happens whether they are apt to it or not. They may sense that it is happening but attribute it as coming from a natural source. For example, people that battle with depression may believe that its source is from a hormonal imbalance or something inherited. What they may not recognize is the demonic forces that are working behind the scenes. The Bible correlates depression with a Spirit of heaviness.

"To appoint unto them that mourn in Zion, to give unto them beauty for ashes, the oil of joy for mourning, the garment of praise for the spirit of heaviness." Isaiah 61:3 KJV

Yes, heaviness is a Spirit, and it comes to weigh you down, to keep you in a place of despondency and immobility. Likewise, lunatic spirits are behind many mental ailments like the man at the tomb of Gadarenes (**Luke 8:26**). These illnesses are not just genetic but are rooted in spirits of infirmity, unclean spirits, and disease (**Luke 6:18, Matthew 10:1**). We only recognize the physical manifestation because many of our eyes have not been opened to see in the Spirit. While this is not the case for every sickness, we must ask God for *discernment* to identify what is common and what is not. The difference between what is physical and what is spiritual.

"For though we walk in the flesh, we do not war after the flesh: (For the weapons of our warfare are not carnal, but mighty through God to the pulling down of strong holds." 2 Corinthians 10:3-4 KJV

Some people may be fighting against a spirit of lust in their spouse, but don't realize it and will attempt to fight with carnal weapons and gain no success. I believe many marriages would still be together if we were more spiritually aware and used the right weapons to fight.

Spirits seeking to interfere with our world

These invisible forces of the unseen world seek to control and manipulate the things that occur in the natural world. You may see a controlling boss as if she or he is just acting out of their true character or nature; but this could actually be a power operating against you as a believer to cause you to lose heart or obstruct an advancement that God desires to give you. Daniel experienced a supernatural force seeking to influence what happened in the natural realm.

"Then he said, Don't be afraid, Daniel. Since the first day you began to pray for understanding and to humble yourself before your God, your request has been heard in heaven. I have come in answer to your

prayer. But for twenty-one days the spirit prince of the kingdom of Persia blocked my way. Then Michael, one of the archangels, came to help me, and I left him there with the spirit prince of the kingdom of Persia." Daniel 10:12-13 NLT

Daniel's prayers had been hindered and he was not even aware. Immediately after Daniel prayed, God heard him and sent a messenger angel to deliver Daniel's answer. The Prince of Persia, which was a demonic spirit, resisted the angel. There were principalities at work interfering with the answer to Daniel's prayer, just like there are demonic spirits that interfere in the things that happen in our everyday lives. Those who have the Gift of Discerning of Spirits are able to identify what spirit is operating behind any given idea, motive, plan, or work.

Not everything that "seems" good is God.

Just like when the Apostle Paul encountered a woman who was possessed with a spirit of divination in Acts 16. Paul discerned that though what the woman said was true and sounded good, the spirit that was in operation behind it was demonic. He did not welcome her praises due to this. As a Prophet, it is important for you to govern the gift of discernment well. Darkness is attracted to light. There will be times where you encounter individuals and people who seek to draw themselves close to you, but the influence and motive behind their actions is demonic. This is where the gift of discernment comes into play. We must move beyond the natural realm of our flesh to see what the Spirit of the Lord is saying and revealing through this gift.

The gift of discernment is a revealing of truth that could not be known through your natural ability

Just like in the story where Jesus asked His disciples "Who do you say that I am?" Peter answered Him and said you are the Christ. Jesus then responded and said flesh and blood did not reveal this to you but my father in Heaven (**Matthew 16:15**). There are some things that we will never be able to see or perceive unless the Lord reveals it to us by His Spirit. This is the gift of discernment in operation.

Judging carnally

> *"Beloved, believe not every spirit, but try the spirits whether they are of God: because many false prophets are gone out into the world." 1 John 4:1 KJV*

Not everything that is different is demonic. There have been and will be many moves of God that may seem strange at first, even unorthodox. That does not necessarily mean that it does not originate from God. We must always seek for God to reveal the nature behind a thing.

In the story of Balaam and Balak, we see where Balaam could not see, and because of this he struck his donkey out of ignorance (Numbers 22:22). He could not see that there was the Angel of the Lord standing before him until God opened his eyes. The same goes for us; unless God reveals the Spirit operating behind a thing, we should not be quick to judge it or "strike it down" because it is not something we are familiar with.

How to wield your gift

As stated in Hebrews 5:14, discernment involves the spiritual senses being exercised. I like to think of it like a car that must be operated by a mature believer to be fully functional and avoid mishandling. With any gift that God gives you, you must know how to wield it. Wield means hold and use a tool.

> *"For the word of God is living and powerful, and sharper than any two-edged sword, piercing even to the division of soul and spirit, and of joints and marrow, and is a discerner of the thoughts and intents of the heart." Hebrews 4:12 NKJV*

You do not discern solely by your spirit

Our spirit alone is not enough because it is easy to fluctuate between our soulish realm and operate out of *suspicion*. The Word of God must be a part of your daily regiment in order to operate this gift responsibly. It is what aids in identifying what you are picking up in your spirit. A believer must be skilled in knowledge and understanding of this in order to judge properly. One can discern or pick up something in their spirit and mislabel it if they have not been skillfully trained.

Here are a few things you must consider as one who is not skilled in the gift of discernment.

1. Just because I "pick up" on something in the spirit does not mean I know what it is.

2. Just because I see something does not mean I have the ability to judge it correctly.

3. Just because I sense something on someone does not mean God wants me to reject that person, or what he/she is saying. What do I mean by this? God can use anyone or anything. Just as He used a donkey to speak in the story of Balak and Balaam, God can use an unclean vessel to deliver His Word. We must know how to eat the good and spit out the bones. We must be able to discern the heart of God toward a person even though you have identified that they have a certain struggle.

Things that can be discerned

"Then shall ye return, and discern between the righteous and the wicked, between him that serveth God and him that serveth him not." Malachi 3:18 KJV

There are many different things that can be discerned through your senses. For example, demonic spirits such as lust and perversion. Unclean spirits that manifest in mental mind-disorders, spirits of suicide, schizophrenia, or even rage. Perverted spirits of control that originate from the spirit of Jezebel. You can also discern a lying tongue, wrong motives, anxiety, and fear. Remember that the Gift of Discerning of Spirits is not just about the discerning evil spirits, but you can also discern those that come from the Spirit of God. The Spirit of truth, purity and peace can be discerned through your senses. the presence of angels or the weight of the glory of God. You can also discern shifts that are taking place in the atmosphere, warnings, impending danger, and many other things. Remember, everything or everyone's intention is not bad.

The gift of discernment can be perceived through your five senses

It is important to note that though many people may carry the Gift of Discerning of Spirits, that the Spirit of God does not relay the information to everyone in the same way. As I have conversed with many Prophets and prophetic people, what I have come to find is that the Holy Spirit can speak to each one of us, show us the same thing, but yet we all can perceive it differently.

Janell Edmondson

There are many ways a person could perceive the spirit of perversion through their senses. For example, one might discern the spirit of perversion through their sense of sight. You could see the actual word "perversion" over the person's forehead, or you could see the spirit in its form i.e., an animal or demonic figure. You could even, through your sense of smell, perceive a foul odor.

Is there iniquity in my tongue? cannot my taste discern perverse things? Job 6:30 KJV

These are all examples of how the Holy Spirit can reveal this information to you. As you walk through your prophetic schooling with the Holy Spirit, He will show and teach you how to recognize these spirits through patterns. It could be that when you encounter a certain spirit that you feel a certain way or smell a certain smell and it happens consistently. This is the Holy Spirit getting you to recognize His voice through the gift of discernment.

Some people might experience strange feelings in their natural bodies such as grieving letting you know that you are about to experience a death. Some might pick up feelings that another person has in their body such as a pain or sickness. You may even feel symptoms of pregnancy when encountering someone else who is pregnant. You could even hear sounds in your ear, as Elijah did after the three-year drought where he heard the sound of an abundance of rain (**1 Kings 18:4**). These are all ways you discern through you senses.

Discernment is not superstition

Some people believe that if their hand is itching that it means money is coming to them, or even an eye twitch could be someone gossiping about them. This is called superstition. Though some of these things may sound similar to some old wives tales we may have heard growing up, the gift of discernment is by far not superstition.

See, the gift of discernment can be tracked and is consistent, whereas superstition is not. What do I mean by this? For example, if the Lord chooses to use a butterfly feeling in the middle of your stomach to warn you when you are about to encounter a devastating situation or make a move that He does not want you to, then this will happen consistently. That is how we can track the way God speaks to us through our discernment.

This is unlike superstition, where you may have an itchy hand and only occasionally receive unexpected money. God will use these patterns to teach you when it is Him speaking to you through your senses. It could be that someone around you is suffering with a mental disorder from a mind-boggling spirit. When you are in their presence, you could pick up and almost take on that sense of confusion and discontentment.

As you pay attention and are sensitive to the voice of the Holy Spirit, you will be able to track that this only happens when you are in the presence of people who are fighting with these demonic forces. Whether it be through a gut feeling, a strong or foul odor, a word written in a form of a vision or any other way, you will become skilled at tracking the way God speaks to you through the Gift of Discerning of Spirits. Therefore, it is important for a Prophet to always be on guard because the Holy Spirit will speak to you in so many different ways. If we are too pre-occupied with the cares of life, we will miss the teaching opportunities that He is offering us.

<u>Discerning of Thoughts</u>

Then there is another manifestation of the Gift of Discernment and that is the Discerning of Thoughts. Have you ever known what someone wanted before they told you, or knew how they felt before they voiced it? Have you ever found yourself hearing conversations that you were not in physically? These are all manifestations of the Gift of Discerning of Thoughts. We have talked previously about the Gift of Discerning of Spirits, but there are many other manifestations of the Gift of Discernment. The Gift of Discerning of Thoughts is one of them, which is God *revealing the secrets of the hearts of men.*

Revealer of Secrets

> *"But it was to us that God revealed these things by his Spirit.*
> *For his Spirit searches out everything and shows us God's deep secrets.*
> *11 No one can know a person's thoughts except that person's own*
> *spirit, and no one can know God's thoughts except God's own Spirit."*
> *1 Corinthians 2:10-11 NLT*

This gift is not one that is talked about widely throughout the prophetic community due to many reasons. One reason I believe is because it is seen as taboo or demonic in nature. Another reason is because many times this gift is misinterpreted as something else. Many people associate reading thoughts with witchcraft or fortune-telling. This is far from the gift we are talking about in this chapter. Those who operate in mind reading or fortune telling are operating from a demonic force, a spirit of witchcraft, in an attempt to see and perceive something by *self-will*. If you find yourself attempting to discern the mind of men by self-will, I would admonish you to stop such practices immediately.

It's not what it seems

The Bible says no one knows a person's thought except that person's own spirit, but our thoughts are also open before God.

> *"Even Death and Destruction hold no secrets from the Lord. How much more does he know the human heart!" Proverbs 15:11 NLT*

There is nothing hidden from God, and it is God who reveals these deep secrets to whomever He chooses, not by our ability. This is all done by way of the Holy Spirit. Whether it be to discern motive, a spiritual operation behind an action, or a thought, this is all done through God Spirit operating within us.

Let us use the best example I could think of when it comes to this spiritual gift, which is Jesus! The Bible says that Jesus had the Spirit without measure (**John 3:34**). He was not limited to this natural body when it came to operating from the Spirit. He operated in all the 12 gifts of the Spirit listed in 1 Corinthians 12, and the authors of the four gospels wrote about Jesus's ability to discern the thoughts of men.

> *"But some of the teachers of religious law said to themselves, "That's blasphemy! Does he think he's God?" 4 Jesus knew what they were thinking, so he asked them, "Why do you have such evil thoughts in your hearts?" Matthew 9:3-4 NLT*

In this passage, Jesus healed a lame man and also told him his sins were forgiven. Though those around did not say it out loud, Jesus did not need to hear their voice to discern what they were thinking. Remember, He had the Spirit of God operating through Him without measure. I stated earlier that Discerning of Thoughts can oftentimes be misrepresented because it can manifest in several different ways.

It could be that God allows you to hear the thoughts of those whom you are prophesying to. He could also allow you to hear the heart of someone whom you know, who is close to you relationally but not physically. Meaning you know them personally as a friend, parent, relative, but you are not in direct proximity to them at the time God is allowing you to hear their heart. It could be detailed thoughts that you hear verbatim (exactly how the person thinks them), or it could be broader where God discloses to you how a person feels or a burden that they are carrying. These are all a part of the Revelation (revealing) gifts. Remember, God knows everything (**Proverbs 15:11**) and because He knows everything, it is He who sees the secret hearts of men and chooses to show them to His servants.

The Prophet Elisha showed us this gift in action in the Old Testament. In this passage, Israel was at war with the Arameans. Elisha was able to thwart the plans of their army every time because God allowed him to hear the very conversations the king had in his secret bedchamber.

> *"The king of Aram became very upset over this. He called his officers together and demanded, "Which of you is the traitor? Who has been informing the king of Israel of my plans?" "It's not us, my Lord the king," one of the officers replied. "Elisha, the prophet in Israel, tells the king of Israel even the words you speak in the privacy of your bedroom!" 2 Kings 6:11-12 NLT*

This gift is not limited, but God can use many ways to reveal a thing. Many have experienced hearing conversations of people they were not in the room with just like Elisha in 1 Kings chapter 6. There have even been prophetic men and women known to have tapped into phone conversations, as if God 3-way'd them into the call. They have heard verbatim conversations happening in the natural. No need to be afraid of Prophets hacking into your phone calls through spiritual lines. This is not done by their self-will, but rather only occurs if God necessitates them to hear the information that is being spoken.

One who has this gift may often experience these types of encounters. One who is not familiar with this gift may describe it as a deja vu moment when God reveals these secrets to them about an individual; then that person turns around and confirms to them the very thing that the Holy Spirit had showed.

What it is used for

There are many reasons for this gift. He might use it to give someone an encouraging word, thwart the plans of an attempted suicide, or even help heal the heart of someone dealing with hurt or unforgiveness. For example, an individual who you know is encountering a very tough situation on their job. You don't know it at the time, but you begin to hear a voice saying, "I can't take it, I am just going to quit." As you engage in conversation with this individual, you learn of the difficulties they are facing. They may never say it out loud, but the Lord confirms to you that it was them He was speaking to you about. He may then direct you to give them a word of wisdom or knowledge concerning their situation.

Then there are times where you could be in the midst of a conversation and the thought is revealed like the story we previously talked about. For example, you are counseling a married couple and there is a lot of tension, but it seems as though there is a lot that is not being said. This causes you not to be able to come to a resolution. In the mist of the conversation, the Lord may allow you to hear the heart of the matter. There could have been some hurt that occurred but for whatever reason the spouse is hesitant to disclose this information, but God allows you to hear their heart. The Lord allows you to hear what is not being voiced so that you can gently and wisely maneuver through the counseling to bring them to a place of healing.

If you are one who has recognized that you have this gift, know that you are not alone. You need not to be ashamed of what you carry. Though it may seem different, it is a manifestation of God's Spirit, it is biblical and Jesus Himself operated in it. You are not crazy, but gifted. You hear and perceive many things not because you want to, but because God has chosen to share the secrets of man's heart with you.

Be encouraged. God's Spirit has been poured out in the earth, but many have neglected this gift because it has not been taught or has been misunderstood for fear of being misused. Allow God's Spirit to move freely through you as He desires. May the manifestation of His Word and His revelation flow through you without limitation.

Enemies to discernment

Though you may have the gift of discernment, there are some major things that can cause you to not be able to function in this gift properly. I would like to use this section to talk about them. These should be avoided at all costs. The first enemy is gossip.

> *"These six things the Lord hates, Yes, seven are an abomination to Him: A proud look, A lying tongue, Hands that shed innocent blood, A heart that devises wicked plans, Feet that are swift in running to evil, A false witness who speaks lies, And one who sows discord among brethren."* *Proverbs 6:16-19 NKJV*

Gossip is defined as casual or unconstrained conversation or reports about other people, typically involving details that are not confirmed as being true.

We see from the above Scripture that God hates gossip. Gossip clogs your eyes and ears and causes you to have a biased view of a person or situation. When you have received information about something or someone before the Holy Spirit has revealed it to you, you have set yourself up for defeat.

It could very well be that the information that was given to you was false. So, then any information that comes after that now has to counteract the word that you've already heard. Gossip also causes you to have a negative view of individuals sometimes even before you really get to know that person for yourself. Gossip is very dangerous for a Prophet. When you gossip, you not only taint your vessel, but the word that comes out of you also becomes impure. It is very difficult for an individual to prophesy with an impartial view, once they have obtained information that was not revealed to them by the Holy Spirit.

The Lord already discloses to us many confidential and private things. Therefore, gossip can have no benefit to us. That which He wants us to know He will tell us. He knows what we can handle and reveals the information to us in a way that will not cause us to be judgmental but will have respect for that person's privacy and understand the will of God in the matter. God's revelation about a person's personal life is always conveyed through the conduit of love. There is purpose behind why He reveals what He reveals. Whether it be for intercession or for correction.

When engaging in conversations about other individuals, we must first ask ourselves is this something that I need to know. Does this involve confirmation concerning something the Holy Spirit has already revealed to me? Is this a place where the Lord is drawing me into intersession? Many times, people will say they are revealing this information because they want you to help them pray but in reality, neither party intends to do so. You must ask yourself are you a part of the problem or a part of the solution? Am I saying that you will never have conversations where another person or situation will come up? No, but there is a distinct difference between a harmless conversation and gossip.

The Lord knows the intent of the heart and as Prophets we can discern when we have crossed over that fine line of innocent conversation into gossip. We must ask ourselves; would we feel comfortable having this conversation in front of that individual. Would we be okay if the person found out the things that were discussed in the conversation? Would that person be okay with the fact that that information is being disclosed to you? These are all things to consider concerning the distinguishing of gossip and normal conversation. Like my father-in-law always says, "Everybody's business is not everybody's business." This brings us into the next enemy of discernment, which is suspicion.

Suspicion is a feeling that something is likely possible or true without real evidence.

Suspicion, which is rooted from fear or jealousy, will muddy up your spiritual eyes so that you cannot see clearly. Now everything you see becomes a clue to a puzzle that you are trying to figure out, but that puzzle never comes to completion because that information was not given to you by way of the Holy Spirit. See, the Holy Spirit is consistent, and if He gives you a word it will turn out to be true 100% of the time.

For example, someone could have a strong fear of being cheated on. It could be that that person's spouse seems to be acting different then their usual selves. They may see them using their phone more often and feel distant. The person may even have a dream that their spouse is cheating on them. Yes, suspicion and overthinking can cause you to dream false dreams. This person truly believes all of this information is being revealed to them by way of the Holy Spirit. But after time has gone by there is no real evidence of infidelity.

This is because they were not real facts, but *strong feelings* based off something that person perceived. At the end it could have been revealed that that person's spouse was planning them a surprise party or something of the sort. You must be on high alert against this spirit and learn when your mind is trying to navigate you off course into suspicion instead of true discernment. Another enemy to discernment is doubt.

Doubt causes you to ignore or second-guess something that God shows you in order to make yourself feel more comfortable. Have you ever discerned something, but doubted if it was from God because it was not something that you wanted to hear or accept at the time? See, sometimes God will often offend our minds, ideologies, and opinions when He tries to introduce a new truth to us. If we are not humble and open to receive it, it will cause us to reject God's Word. This, in turn, will eventually become an antagonist to our discernment. When you doubt by not accepting the new truth that God is trying to reveal to you, you limit what God will further speak to you about that same matter. It is as if you yourself close the door and lock yourself out of God's revelation.

In the story of Peter and the gentile Cornelius, at first Peter's mind was very offended at that which the Lord was trying to portray to him. The Lord commissioned him not to doubt but go with the men (Gentiles) whom he considered to be unclean.

> *"While Peter thought on the vision, the Spirit said unto him, Behold, three men seek thee. Arise therefore, and get thee down, and go with them, <u>doubting nothing</u>: for I have sent them." Acts 10:19-20 KJV*

He obeyed and when everything was concluded, Peter was able to receive the new revelation and share it with the other disciples. This could happen to you as well. It could be that the Lord begins to reveal to you that someone close to you is about to pass away. You received the revelation through a feeling of mourning. The Holy Spirit reveals to you exactly who the person is that is about to pass away. It could be that you feel as though it is not this person's time to go. Or this person may be very close to you, and you may not be ready to receive the truth. This can cause you to doubt and reject what God is saying. That doubt then hinders you from being able to receive what God wants to say further concerning the situation. It could be that He wants you to warn or prepare the family, or He is allowing you to go through the grieving process first so that when it does happen you are strengthened enough to help others that are mourning.

This is why we must never doubt the things that the Lord shows us even if we don't agree or are not ready to believe. We must always be humble and ready to receive whatever the Lord wants to show us. We should never come to a place to believe that we know it all or have arrived. This will hinder your ability for God to speak to you through the gift of discernment. The next enemy is respecter of person.

> *"These things also belong to the wise. It is not good to have respect of persons in judgment." Proverbs 24:23 KJV*

Respecter of person causes you to turn a blind eye to things you see in those close to you or people you hold in high regard. We will talk more in depth about this subject in the chapter entitled *Testing*.

Not being skilled in the Word of God. The Word of God helps you to identify and name the spirit that is in operation. Everything must line up with the Word. If you feel as though you are discerning something that does not align with the Word of God, that thought, or suggestion should be immediately rejected and cast down (**2 Corinthians 10:5**).

Lack of prayer. Prayer is a spiritual lens that helps you see more clearly and ensure that you have a right perception. Just because I see something does not mean I am seeing it right; prayer will help with that. In prayer, God will bring clarity and give you a deeper revelation to what the spirit has already revealed to you through your discernment.

Lack of worship. Unless you become acquainted with the Spirit of God, you won't know when you are not in his presence. Those with a heavy worship life are very familiar with the presence of God and can discern between false spirits of deception and the true presence of the Living God.

The Gift of Healing

> *"A spiritual gift is given to each of us so we can help each other. To one person the Spirit gives the ability to give wise advice; to another the same Spirit gives a message of special knowledge. The same Spirit gives great faith to another, and to someone else the one Spirit gives the gift of healing." 1 Corinthians 12:7-9 NLT*

Healing is a process of restoration of health from an unbalanced, diseased, damaged, or uncivilized organism. *The Gift of Healing* is the ability to channel the power of God to another individual in order to restore them back to proper health or state of mind. One of the late great giants in the Christian faith Kathryn Cullman embodied this gift. Millions of people came from all over the world to see her gift in action. Though she was well known for performing miracles of healing, she never took the credit for herself. Instead, she always paid homage to the Holy Spirit, the conduit in which her gift flowed. Acknowledging that she was merely a vessel that the Spirit of God chose to use.

How it works

This healing is done without medical intervention and has different forms of manifestation. One of which can manifest through a person's physical body. For example, ailments such as skin diseases, cancers, high blood pressure, diabetes, defected limbs, and so on. Or it could deal with that person's state of mind. Those who carry the Gift of Healing have the authority over the source of many of these ailments, i.e., unclean spirits and spirits of infirmity (**Luke 9:11**). Such as in the case of the woman with the issue of blood or the man at the pool of Bethesda. Or even the man at the tomb of Gadarenes.

"And he cried out with a loud voice and said, "What have I to do with You, Jesus, Son of the Most High God? I implore You by God that You do not torment me." For He said to him, "Come out of the man, unclean spirit!" Mark 5:7-8 NKJV

He was possessed by unclean spirits that caused mental torment. Jesus cast the spirits out, healed him and the man came back to his original state of mind.

Many ways of healing

We also see the Gifts of Healing can be demonstrated in many ways. As we see with Jesus, who had the fullness of the spirit without measure, He demonstrated the Gift of Healing in some very common and unique ways. To some He spoke healing, for some He laid hands, to some He spit in the dirt, some He simply asked will thou be made whole. There are some things that Jesus said that only come by way of fasting and prayer. Then there are times where their faith in Him caused healing to manifest in their lives, like in the case with Jairus daughter.

"But when Jesus heard what had happened, he said to Jairus, "Don't be afraid. Just have faith, and she will be healed." Luke 8:50 NLT

Hindrances to healing

"When Jesus had finished telling these stories and illustrations, he left that part of the country. He returned to Nazareth, his hometown. When he taught there in the synagogue, everyone was amazed and said, "Where does he get this wisdom and the power to do miracles?" Then they scoffed, "He's just the carpenter's son, and we know Mary, his mother, and his brothers—James, Joseph, Simon, and Judas. All his sisters live right here among us. Where did he learn all these things?" And they were deeply offended and refused to believe in him. Then Jesus told them, "A prophet is honored everywhere except in his own hometown and among his own family." And so he did only a few miracles there because of their unbelief. Matthew 13:53-58 NLT

Just because someone has the Gift of Healing does not mean healing will manifest on every occasion. We see from the previous Scripture that *faith is necessary* on both sides for this gift to function properly. There are some people that do not have the faith to believe that God can heal them. In this case the believing individual could not force healing on the unbelieving person.

The Gift of Healing used as an evangelistic tool

"Now when he was in Jerusalem at the Passover, in the feast day, many believed in his name, when they saw the miracles which he did." John 2:23 KJV

The Gift of Healing, like many other gifts that God has given to the body, is a way to bring unbelievers to Christ. We see that the Gospel was always preached alongside the demonstration of miracles. The Lord knows that many people's hearts are not open to receive the Gospel without the evidence. This is not true for all cases, such as John the Baptist, with whom many came to repentance by the preaching of the Word alone. But there are still some people who will not believe without proof. Some people cannot see beyond the natural realm, so the supernatural gifting's, signs, wonders, and miracles act as evidence to support the claim of the Gospel.

Why do we have this gift?

> *"Jesus saw the huge crowd as he stepped from the boat, and he had compassion on them and healed their sick." Matthew 14:14 NLT*

God has compassion on His people and desires to see them healed and set free. Jesus came to give us life more abundantly. In his death, He freed us from the weight of sin. But He didn't stop there. Just as John stated when he told them he wished above all that they would prosper and be in good health even as their soul prospered (**3 John 1:2**).

The abundant life that God intended for us to have transcends beyond our soul to the natural man. He wants his people to be free from sickness, diseases, and ailments. It is true that not everyone who seeks God for supernatural healing receives it. They are many variables in the operation of this gift and even in our great faith God is still sovereign and knows what His perfect will is for every one of His people.

Dreams and Visions

> *"And it shall come to pass afterward, that I will pour out my spirit upon all flesh; and your sons and your daughters shall prophesy, your old men shall dream dreams, your young men shall see visions:" Joel 2:28 KJV*

The Gift of Dreams and Visions is a gift of Holy Spirit as stated in Joel 2:28 whereby God reveals his plans, mysteries, and warnings to man. Those who carry this gift are often called *dreamers*. It is important to note that not all Prophets are dreamers and not all dreamers are Prophets. It is a gift of the spirit given to whomever He wills (**1 Corinthians 12:11**).

One who has a Gift of Dreams and Visions is marked by having frequent Spirit given dreams. God on a regular basis reveals past, present, or future events to them through the dream realm. This realm of sight is open to them and becomes their normal way of communication. It is confirmed that these dreams are given by God by the manifestation of that which they dream coming to pass in the natural.

The distinct difference between what we call dreams and visions are the state of consciousness of the person that is having them. Dreams are visions that we have while we are asleep, while open visions happen while we are awake. All men have the ability to dream. Though it is true some people dream more often than others, it can be said that everyone experiences dreams at least once in their life. We are Spirit beings that have a soul and live in a body. Our physical man goes into a place of rest while we sleep but our subconscious mind does not. This is a place where our dreams are experienced.

God uses dreams to speak to his creation

"For God speaks again and again, though people do not recognize it. He speaks in dreams, in visions of the night, when deep sleep falls on people as they lie in their beds. He whispers in their ears and terrifies them with warnings. He makes them turn from doing wrong; he keeps them from pride. He protects them from the grave, from crossing over the river of death." Job 33:14-18 NLT

God uses dreams as a way of communicating with man. There are many men and women of God noted in Scripture to have had encounters with God by way of a dream or vision. This is true for *all* his creation. By those who served Him and those who did not. For example, Jacob's first encounter noted in Scripture with God was through a dream (**Genesis 28:10**). Likewise, after the death of his father, King David, Solomon was visited by the Lord in a dream (**1 King 3:5**).

Let's venture into the Book of Genesis where we are presented with a man named Laban who happened to be Jacob's father-in-law. Laban was an Aramean and an idol worshipper who did not serve the true and living God. This did not stop God from speaking to him and making His voice heard. In this passage Jacob had just fled Laban's house, taking his wife and children with him. When Laban heard of it, he was furious and decided to go after them, but the Lord came to him in a dream and warned him not to pursue.

"But the previous night God had appeared to Laban the Aramean in a dream and told him, "I'm warning you—leave Jacob alone!" Genesis 31:24 NLT

We also see in the same book where the Lord spoke to the Egyptian leader Pharaoh and encrypted a warning in a dream about an upcoming famine that was about to hit the region (**Genesis 41**). There have been many instances to where God, through a dream led an unbeliever to Christ or even warned a backslider to come back home to Him. This shows us the limitlessness of the Holy Spirit. That not only those who are *spirit filled* can have *spirit given* dreams. God can and will get his message across to whomever and however He sees fit.

God uses dreams to reveal Himself to His Prophets

"And the Lord said to them, "Now listen to what I say: "If there were prophets among you, I, the Lord, would reveal myself in visions. I would speak to them in dreams. Numbers 12:6 NLT

God will often introduce Himself to his Prophets through the dream realm. Though this is not always the case, we see where many times God will use this as the first line of communication for those who have been called into Prophetic Ministry. It is in these initial meetings that God will affirm that Prophet of his or her calling and teach them His voice. In this, God will open up the Prophet's eyes to His instructions, training them on how to see and interpret his messages through the seer's realm.

Dreams are God's voice

We must remember that though it may not be audible, Dreams and Visions are still God's voice. The purpose is to *reveal* and *communicate*. They are not just for entertainment or to say I *knew* or *saw*. One must understand the importance of the dream they have. God will often warn men through dreams and give them instructions on what to do. We must ask God what He desires to do with the information that He is revealing. We will use the story of Pharaoh and Joseph frequently throughout this chapter in order to understand God's voice through Dreams. In this story the Lord used a dream to preserve their entire region from famine.

"This will happen just as I have described it, for God has revealed to Pharaoh in advance what he is about to do. The next seven years will be a period of great prosperity throughout the land of Egypt. But afterward there will be seven years of famine so great that all the prosperity will be forgotten in Egypt. Famine will destroy the land." Genesis 41:28-30 NLT

Pharaoh recognized God's authoritative voice through the dream that was given to him. He did not hesitate to act on the instructions given by Joseph and because of it not only were the Egyptians and Joseph's family kept, but the surrounding nations as well. We too must recognize God's voice through dreams and act accordingly.

Repetitious Dreams

"As for having two similar dreams, it means that these events have been decreed by God, and he will soon make them happen." Genesis 41:32 NLT

God will often repeat dreams in order to show the urgency of it or to confirm that it is his voice. As He did with Pharaoh. He gave him two separate dreams in the same night. Though He used different symbolism, they both had the same meaning. Sometimes God will give you similar dreams as He did with Pharaoh, or He could give you the exact same dream twice, sometimes multiple times. Oftentimes, we can have the first dream and not take it seriously, God will then repeat that dream as a way to say, "Hey, pay attention, I am speaking to you." Joseph was able to discern the urgency of the double dreams and give Pharaoh a Word of Wisdom.

Purpose is to reveal and communicate

Dreams and Visions are not limited to time and can reveal information about the past (**hindsight**), present (**insight**) or future (**foresight**). God can reveal to you information that has already taken place; when He does this is called *hindsight*. Information revealed about a present situation is called *insight*, and information reveal concerning the future is called *foresight*. The Prophet's eyes and ears must be in tune with the Spirit of God to recognize what He is speaking. Prophets who carry this gift eyes' are constantly receiving information through the seer's realm. When you operate from this realm, God at any given moment can download you with fresh insight, revelation, or instructions.

God's Prophetic messages through visions

God loves to use symbolism to portray his messages, so much so that we see where he would often incorporate dreams and visions into the Prophetic messages he gave to his Prophets. Let's take Jeremiah for example. We see in Scripture where God first came to Jeremiah through the use of his audible voice in what the Bible calls *"The word of the Lord"* (**Jeremiah 1:4**).

Then what seems like immediately after, God began to train Jeremiah's eyes by way of Visions.

> *"Then the Lord said to me, "Look, Jeremiah! What do you see?" And I replied, "I see a branch from an almond tree." And the Lord said, "That's right, and it means that I am watching, and I will certainly carry out all my plans." Jeremiah 1:11-12 NLT*

Visions are just one of the many ways God chooses to speak and reveal his mysteries. The Prophets Isaiah and Amos were noted to have received their prophetic messages this way (**Isaiah 1:1, Amos 7**). As was the case with many other Prophets. Some Prophets are what many may call *visionary* and will receive a large portion if not all of their revelation through this way.

Pay attention

Those who have the Gift of Dreams and Visions can sometimes fall into two spectrums. Those who dream regularly and often ignore their dreams, treating them casually. Or those who dream regularly and obsess over them. Being on either side of this spectrum can become very dangerous. Those who obsess over their dreams can begin to rely on their dreams as the sole way of communication with God. In these cases, if not careful you can make your dreams a type of idol.

Though dreams are God's voice and He uses them to confirm His Word, one does not want to depend solely on them as a spiritual compass. There are many different ways God speaks. The Word of God must be our foundation and what our beliefs and actions are based off of. If your dream goes against God's character, then one must question the origination of that dream. Many people also mistake them hearing from God through dream as confirmation of them being in right standing with God. We see from previously noted Scripture that this is not true. God speaks to his creation whether they are in right standing with Him or not.

Those who ignore their dreams are in just a dangerous position as those who obsess over them. Due to the fact that God sends warnings through dreams, overlooked dreams could cost someone much more than they anticipated. It could be something as simple as averting a bad financial situation or as serious as saving a life. Whatever the purpose is, these types of dreams should never be ignored.

Dreams can help us to make right decisions. Though God is sovereign He does not go beyond our free will. This is why He will warn us in this manner. This is his way of safeguarding us from future events that He may not necessarily want to come to past. If you are one who carries this gift embrace it. You may never hear God's voice audibly or prophesy in the same flow as those who do, but this is just as important. You are a seer and God has chosen to communicate with you through the seer's realm. Do not neglect this gift. Be sure to take heed to the things that God shows you. It is his voice so pay careful attention.

Types of Dreams and Visions

Not all dreams and Visions are created equally. Let's start with dreams. We see where there are different types of dreams one may experience.

Movie like Dreams

Some may experience dreams as if they were watching a movie. These types are for *viewing purposes only*. The Spirit of God is merely revealing to you something but your emotions, and other senses might not necessarily be engaged in the dream (**Genesis 41, Daniel 2**).

Dialogs

Then there are some dreams that allow you to communicate and respond as if you were awake. In these many have been known to actually have a conversation with God (**Genesis 20:3-7**).

Full sensory

Then there are some who *experience* their dreams on a whole different level. In these types of dreams the person's 5 senses are *totally engaged* having the ability to not only see but taste , smell and even feel everything that is happening around them. These types of experiences can be very intense. The individual will often awake feeling exhausted as if they never fell asleep. Depending on what is occurring in this dream, they make wake up suddenly as though a rush of adrenaline just went through their body.

Visions

As stated before, visions are dreams you have while you are awake. Just like dreams, not all visions are the same and there are many types of visions that you can have.

Open Visions

Let's look at the Prophet Ezekiel, in his first encounter with the Lord, he had what many may call an open vision.

> *"On July 31 of my thirtieth year, while I was with the Judean exiles beside the Kebar River in Babylon, the heavens were opened, and I saw visions of God." Ezekiel 1:1 NLT*

In this type of Vision Ezekiel was aware of his surroundings and still had full use of his senses and movements.

> *"All around him was a glowing halo, like a rainbow shining in the clouds on a rainy day. This is what the glory of the Lord looked like to me. When I saw it, I fell face down on the ground, and I heard someone's voice speaking to me. Stand up, son of man, said the voice. I want to speak with you. The Spirit came into me as he spoke, and he set me on my feet. I listened carefully to his words." Ezekiel 1:28, 2:1-2 NLT*

In a trance

Balaam described the type of vision he encountered as a trance.

> *"And Balaam lifted up his eyes, and he saw Israel abiding in his tents according to their tribes; and the spirit of God came upon him. And he took up his parable, and said, Balaam the son of Beor hath said, and the man whose eyes are open hath said: He hath said, which heard the words of God, which saw the vision of the Almighty, falling into a trance, but having his eyes open:" Numbers 24:2-4 KJV*

In these visions one is taken under by the spirit unable to move but still has the use of their sight and hearing.

Away in the spirit

Then there are Visions where God takes you away in the Spirit.

"The Spirit lifted me up and took me away. I went in bitterness and turmoil, but the Lord's hold on me was strong. Then I came to the colony of Judean exiles in Tel-abib, beside the Kebar River. I was overwhelmed and sat among them for seven days." Ezekiel 3:14 NLT

Here Ezekiel describes being taken away in the Spirit, I believe that his body remained, but his spirit was teleported to another location.

God is not limited.

The Spirit of God is not limited and has many ways to reveal information to his people. Some may experience visions where they see images, numbers or even words flash before their eyes. Some may experience visions that seem like a daydream that was not provoked by them. They could be long, lasting several minutes or just a few seconds. All of these are God's way of communicating something to you.

Not all dreams and visions are meant to be uttered (**Revelation10:4**). Some are meant to be revealed at a set time (**Daniel 12:9**). Some are information only. Some are prayer assignments. Some bring clarity. Some give spiritual insight beyond what we can see in the natural. Whatever the purpose is we must always ask what God wants us to do with the information that He is revealing to us. If you are one who carries this gift, I would encourage you to pay close attention to the dreams and visions God gives to you, making sure to write them down and pray over them until you gain clarity on the revelation and until He gives you instructions on what to do.

Interpretation of Dreams

Now that we have learned more about the Gift of Dreams let's dive into the Gift of Interpretation. Those who have this gift have the ability to understand the deep mysteries of God that come by way of dreams. This revelation is given to them by God. Two well noted men in the Bible who had this gift were Joseph and the Prophet Daniel. Throughout their lives, God would frequently use them to interpret dreams. Their stories show us up close how this gift works.

Code maker

It is important to note this gift is used by us, but the revelation comes from God. Just like the Gift of Discerning of Thoughts, it is not something that you can do outside of the Holy Spirit. Let's use Daniel as our first example. In the Book of Daniel chapter 2, the children of Israel had been taken away in exile into Babylon under the rule of King Nebuchadnezzar.

One night the king had a dream that disturbed him, so he called for all the astrologers, wise men, sorcerers, and enchanters to come and interpret his dream. There was one catch though. Not only did they have to interpret the dream, but they had to tell him what happened in the dream as well. We know that no human has the ability to know such things by their own minds. The wise men knew this very well and urged the king to tell him the dream (**Daniel 2:10**). He refused and instead demanded for all of them to be killed for refusing to obey his request.

When Daniel heard this, he implored the king to give him more time to inquire of God about the dream. You see Daniel was in a very hard predicament. Knowing that there was only one source that could help him out of it, he humbled himself before God and asked him to reveal the secret of Nebuchadnezzar's heart. That same night the Lord showed Daniel mercy and revealed to him the dream and the interpretation.

"Daniel replied, "There are no wise men, enchanters, magicians, or fortune-tellers who can reveal the king's secret. But there is a God in heaven who reveals secrets, and he has shown King Nebuchadnezzar what will happen in the future. Now I will tell you your dream and the visions you saw as you lay on your bed." Daniel 2:27-28 NLT

Daniel understood this concept of revelation and its source, that it only comes from God. God is the one who gives the dreams. So, it is only reasonable to understand that he alone can interpret them. We just merely receive his interpretation. Throughout the Bible we see where many other wise women and men of asked God for interpretation of their visions. Alongside Daniel, there is Joseph, the Prophet Zachariah, and the Apostle John just to name a few.

Symbolism in dreams

We know based off Scripture that God loves to use symbols and types in dreams. Although there are times God will use symbolism that we are familiar with, there is no universal language or symbolism for the interpretation of dreams. There are many things that may mean one thing to you and your culture but may represent something totally different to another person. For example, in the dream with Pharaoh he used wheat and cattle to represent the famine that was going to take place (**Genesis 41**). In this story God gave Pharaoh two dreams; using different symbols to represent the same thing. This was something Pharaoh was familiar with as he lived in an agricultural region.

Then there are times you can have the same symbol, but they carry two different meanings as God uses symbolism interchangeably. For example, in Scripture Jesus was depicted as the conquering Lion of Judah (**Revelation 5:5**). The devil also is depicted as a roaring lion seeking whom he may devour (**1Peter 5:8**). Again, in the Garden of Eden the enemy was depicted as a serpent (**Genesis 3:1**). Jesus also was depicted as the serpent on the pole for the healing of the Nations during the time of Moses (**John 3:14**). The Sun, moon and star's original purpose was to tell time and seasons but have also been used to symbolize many different things throughout the Bible. They represented Joseph's family (**Genesis 37:9**), Church Leaders (**Revelation 1:20**) and sickness (**Revelation 8:11**).

So, we see that there are multiple meanings and applications behind symbols. This purpose is not to confuse you but rather for you to become totally dependent on Him for the interpretation. One must always ask God for the meaning and wait for His answer.

No master code

Though we know God has given men these gifts, and gifts come without repentance, it is still the Spirit of God who reveals the interpretation of the dreams and not our own intellect. All gifts flow through the Holy Spirit. There is nothing outside of Him. He is the only one who can give the interpretation. There is no master code to interpreting dreams.

> *"And they said unto him, We have dreamed a dream, and there is no interpreter of it. And Joseph said unto them, Do not interpretations belong to God? tell me them, I pray you." Genesis 40:8 KJV*

Though there is no universal code for dream interpretations, God will build custom patterns in your dreams that will help you interpret what He is saying. Some symbols will be very specific to you based off your experiences.

Therefore, some things will have different meanings to different people depending on their experiences. God will use these symbols in multiple dreams to help you pick up on the pattern.

For example, he may use people from your past or present to represent something to you that will mean the same thing throughout multiple dreams. Maybe you see an old house you use to live in representing an old place or a familiar spirit. A teacher from your past in a dream could represent something new God is trying to teach you. This is where a dream journal comes into play. Writing down your dreams not only helps you to remember them but also aids you into picking up on the patterns faster.

There will be instances where some of your symbols or patterns may mean the same thing to another individual. Upon hearing their dream, you may automatically receive the interpretation. This is where God will build you to help others interpret their dreams.

Though you may see this happen and maybe even often, you must be careful as this is not always the case. A wrongly interpreted dream can be just as detrimental as a false prophecy. There have been many instances where an individual attempted to interpret another's dream based off of their personal dream code and led that person in the wrong direction. Remember, God's knowledge and wisdom is much greater than ours. He is the great and Sovereign one who cannot be confined to a box let alone a dream code. This is why we must always lean into the Holy Spirit, the interpreter of spirit-given dreams.

Seek God

One has to be careful when trying to interpret dreams or visions outside of the originator. When you do, you open yourself up to the spirit of divination. Thus, it is very unwise to try to use books or other resources to help you interpret your dreams. On the island of Patmos, the Apostle John saw and experienced many things but he never assumed to know what they meant (**Revelation 7:14**). When he didn't know or understand he asked, and just like John, if we want to know the interpretation of a dream all we must do is ask. Asking can come in many ways. Whether by prayer or pondering on it. In this you quiet your mind and thoughts, allowing God's Spirit to speak to you.

"This time he told the dream to his father as well as to his brothers, but his father scolded him. "What kind of dream is that?" he asked. "Will your mother and I and your brothers actually come and bow to the ground before you?" But while his brothers were jealous of Joseph, his father wondered what the dreams meant." Genesis 37:10-11 NLT

Many times, when those who carry this gift are asked to interpret someone's dream, this is the first thing they do. They are not depending on their own intellect or past knowledge but rather they open their ears to receive God's voice through the dream.

Revelation comes in different ways

"In a vision during the night, I saw a man sitting on a red horse that was standing among some myrtle trees in a small valley. Behind him were riders on red, brown, and white horses. I asked the angel who was talking with me, "My Lord, what do these horses mean?" "I will show you," the angel replied. The rider standing among the myrtle trees then explained, "They are the ones the Lord has sent out to patrol the earth." Zechariah 1:8-10 NLT

Though we open ourselves up to receive, the interpretation does not always come the same way. It can happen immediately when you hear or recall a dream, as if it were an instant download, or God may bring the revelation to you over time. It may be something you see, hear or experience that brings you into the full understanding of that dream. He may use another individual to interpret it for you like he did with Daniel. Then there are times that the interpretation does not come until the event has happened. So, we must be patient and wait on God to reveal that which is hidden. God will bring the interpretation to you.

Why do we have this gift?

There are many reasons why God has given us the Gift of Dreams and Interpretation. As we stated before, the Lord oftentimes uses dreams to communicate to his creation. God wants to dialog, instruct, give directions, and warn his people. This gift is valuable.

"While Your Majesty was sleeping, you dreamed about coming events. He who reveals secrets has shown you what is going to happen. And it is not because I am wiser than anyone else that I know the secret of your

dream, but because God wants you to understand what was in your heart."
Daniel 2:29-30 NLT.

Though sometimes these dreams are encrypted with secret codes and symbolism it is always God's intent for us to come into the understanding of his mysteries. God granted Daniel's request because He wanted the King to have understanding. In this King Nebuchadnezzar recognized God as being greater than any other deity. Likewise, God allowed Joseph to interpret Pharaoh's dream because He wanted him to be better prepared for the future, and because Pharaoh had understanding he was able to take action. If we don't have an understanding i.e., the interpretation, then we cannot take action. Those who carry this gift help to bring people into comprehension of the message(s) God is trying to relay.

Gift of Foresight

"I am the Lord; that is my name! I will not give my glory to
anyone else, nor share my praise with carved idols. Everything I
prophesied has come true, and now I will prophesy again. I will tell
you the future before it happens." Isaiah 42:8-9 NLT

Foresight is the ability to prophetically see what will happen or be needed in the future. This is a gift from God where He enables you to "see into the future." This can be revealed in many ways, one of which was discussed in a previous chapter as some people receive this information through their dreams. Again, this is not something that you *will* yourself to do but rather God allowing you to peer into mysteries of things to come.

Though prophecy deals with past present and future, most of the prophetic books and Prophets dealt heavily with foresight. The Prophet Elisha had a very strong Gift of Discernment but also operated in the Gift of Foresight. So much so that he was able to accurately see into the future to prepare the people for what was to come.

"Elisha replied, "Listen to this message from the Lord! This is
what the Lord says: By this time tomorrow in the markets of Samaria, six
quarts of choice flour will cost only one piece of silver, and twelve quarts
of barley grain will cost only one piece of silver." 2 Kings 7:1 NLT

In this passage, Elisha declared a Word of the Lord foretelling that there was about to be a shift in the economic condition of that region. This particular region had been in a siege that caused many to be without food. Notice that this was not a prophetic declaration, or Elisha using his prophetic authority to call things into existence. Like in the case where he caused the bears to attack the youth who were mocking him (**2 Kings 2:23**). Nor like his predecessor Elijah did when he declared that there would be no rain for three years (**1 Kings 17:1**). This was a direct Word of the Lord. God allowed him to *see* in order to prepare the people for the upcoming change.

Foresight, which is prophecy, is a gift that God uses to help his people do three things

1. Pray

2. Prepare

3. Prevent

Pray

God will readily show a believer, leader, or Prophet the plan of the enemy in advance so that they can stand in the gap, cover the hedge, and ensure that the will of the Lord be carried out in the earth. As sons of God, we have the authority to petition heaven on our behalf and on the behalf of others.

> *"The people of the land have used oppressions, committed robbery, and mistreated the poor and needy; and they wrongfully oppress the stranger. So I sought for a man among them who would make a wall, and stand in the gap before Me on behalf of the land, that I should not destroy it; but I found no one. Therefore I have poured out My indignation on them; I have consumed them with the fire of My wrath; and I have recompensed their deeds on their own heads, says the Lord GOD." Ezekiel 22:29 NKJV*

In this passage, the children of Israel's own disobedience is what caused God to recompense wrath upon them, but God is merciful and was ready to turn away his anger if he could find a mediator to stand and negotiate with Him. We see this similar narrative with Abraham in his attempt to negotiate with God for Lot and the inhabitants of Sodom and Gomorrah (**Genesis 18:22**). God wants us to engage Him in order to divert destruction.

Prevent

> *"Again, when a righteous person turns from their righteousness and does evil, and I put a stumbling block before them, they will die. Since you did not warn them, they will die for their sin. The righteous things that person did will not be remembered, and I will hold you accountable for their blood." Ezekiel 3:20 KJV*

Every prophetic word is not necessarily set in stone, unable to be changed. Often times God would send a word through a Prophet as a warning beforehand, to prevent the person from walking into an unnecessary situation.

> *"I have also spoken by the prophets, and I have multiplied visions, and used similitudes, by the ministry of the prophets." Hosea 12:10 KJV*

In this text, we see that God had used multiple people to try and warn the children of Israel through dreams, visions, and demonstrations. In most of these cases we see where their warnings were not headed so destruction soon followed, but then there are occasions where that person or peoples repented, and God spared them like in the case of Hezekiah.

In the Book of 2 Kings 20, Hezekiah was warned by the Prophet Isaiah that he was about to die and that he needed to put his house in order, but because he was warned by the Prophet, he was able to act. Immediately Hezekiah turned his face to God and began to pray and ask for mercy. God in turn showed him mercy and extended his life by 15 years. We see this as well in the story of Jonah and the City of Nineveh.

God desires to use his Prophets to divert and prevent destructive occurrences

The Gift of Foresight can help you from walking into some terrible situations. We see throughout the Bible where David and other kings would seek counsel from a Prophet to see if they should engage in war or not, but foresight can also prevent wrong marriages, jobs, career paths and premature moves (going into things that are God ordained but just not the right season). Failing to receive a word of foresight can not only cause you to go through unnecessary situations but also hinder you from receiving the promise.

Janell Edmondson

Believe in the word of the Prophet

We talked earlier about the Prophet Elisha and his prophetic declaration concerning the upcoming shift that would happen in Samaria. Unfortunately, the Kings servant did not believe the word that the Prophet gave. His unbelief did not hinder the word from coming to past just as the Prophet said, but it did disqualify him from receiving the benefits. This man's inability to receive the prophecy caused him not only the ability to enjoy the fruit of it but it also cost him his life.

> *"Then the people went out and plundered the camp of the Arameans. So a seah of the finest flour sold for a shekel, and two seahs of barley sold for a shekel, as the LORD had said. Now the king had put the officer on whose arm he leaned in charge of the gate, and the people trampled him in the gateway, and he died, just as the man of God had foretold when the king came down to his house." 1 Kings 17:16-17 KJV*

What can we learn from this? Inability to heed a word of foresight will only cost you in the end. We must always remember; you don't have to believe the word of foresight for it to come to pass. It is God's Word and none of his words will ever fall to the ground.

Prepare

God also uses the Gift of Foresight to prepare his people for something that they might not necessarily be able to change through prayer. In this case, God will give instructions so that the situation He is foretelling won't hit as hard as it would with someone who is not prepared.

In the Book of 2 Kings 8, Elisha warned the woman whose son he had restored back to life, about the famine that was to come.

> *"Now Elisha had said to the woman whose son he had restored to life, "Go away with your family and stay for a while wherever you can, because the Lord has decreed a famine in the land that will last seven years." The woman proceeded to do as the man of God said. She and her family went away and stayed in the land of the Philistines seven years." 2 Kings 8:1-2 NIV*

The Lord called the famine. This was not something she could pray away or prevent, but because she obeyed Elisha's instruction, she found a place to sojourn in the land of the Philistines for seven years until the famine was over. Foresight, in my opinion, is one of the greatest gifts God has given to the body because it helps prepare you for the future. The Lord could use this gift to prepare a person for the death of a loved one, to save money for a financial situation that would occur, new marriages, jobs, or even changes in ministry.

We see many times throughout Scripture, prophetic words that God gave to warn his people about what He is about to do in the earth. I believe this demonstrates the love of God that He cares so much about his people that even in the strange acts He performs He does not desire us to be caught unprepared.

Janell Edmondson

Honoring the Gifts

*"There are different kinds of spiritual gifts, but the same
Spirit is the source of them all. There are different kinds of service,
but we serve the same Lord. God works in different ways, but it is the
same God who does the work in all of us." 1 Corinthians 12:4-6 NLT*

In this chapter we will talk about honoring our gifts. We will discuss the difference between honor value and appraisal in relation to this topic. **Honor** means to regard with great respect or adoration. **Value** can be defined as the regard that something is held to deserve the importance, worth or usefulness of something. **Appraisal** is the act or instance of assessing something/someone to determine value.

Valuing the gift

The greater the value is placed on something will determine how you treat it. So, what value do you place on your gift? As Prophets and people of God we should value the gifts that God has placed on the inside of us and not neglect them. Think about it, no one leaves a Super Bowl ring on the kitchen table or a Lamborghini sitting out in the sun for days and not cover it. No one would put a cashmere sweater in the washer and dryer machine. If you understand the value of the things I previously listed, then you understand the care that should be involved in handling them. This is how we should treat our gifts as well. Something valuable, that should never be put on the back-shelf lying dormant.

Say to yourself "Just because I am a Prophet does not mean the gifts just flow freely through me." This is where many people get confused and discouraged. They don't understand that there is a process in developing the gifts even though you have already received them. They still need to be cultivated.

How to add value to your gift

So how do you add value to your gifts? Glad you asked! By honoring them. Honoring your gift comes by consistent use of, further education and or extensive study in order to refine it. Think about it; Mozart did not become a famous composer by playing the piano casually, but by constant, intense practice until he mastered his skill.

The more you put in, the greater you build your capacity for more. Like a balloon that is blown up, at first it is very hard to get the air to pass through because it has not been stretch past its original form before. But just keep blowing. The more you do, you will soon see the true capacity of that balloon is revealed. It has been expanded!

Many artists spend countless hours perfecting their skill in voice, dance, acting lessons and so forth. So, when someone calls on them to perform, they cannot just pay them anything. They have set a valuation on their gift. Why are they able to do that? Because they honor it. That artist understands the value of their gift and the work that they put into perfecting it. Now, in no way am I suggesting we place a price on the prophetic call or the word that God gives us because they are for the edification of the body and should be without price. What I am saying is that the more you honor your gift you add value and weight in the kingdom. So, what is your valuation?

"Again, the kingdom of heaven is like treasure hidden in a field, which a man found and hid; and for joy over it he goes and sells all that he has and buys that field. Again, the kingdom of heaven is like a merchant seeking beautiful pearls, who, when he had found one pearl of great price, went and sold all that he had and bought it." Matthew 13:44-46 NKJV

Are the spiritual things of God of greater or lesser value to you? Put them on the scale. Are you willing to put in the work, time, and effort it takes to cultivate and build those gifts?

Prayer births and strengthens prophecy

One very important key that will be reiterated throughout this book is the importance of prayer. What I have found is that prayer helps to birth you in the prophetic and strengthens it. The Lord will often start a Prophet out in the place of prayer, giving them *prayer assignments.* As you pray you gain more insight, and He gives you clarity on how to release the word. As you release those words in obedience, He will then download you with more prayer assignments. This process continues. In your obedience to yield and be consistent you gain trust for weightier assignments.

The more you honor the gift the more you will receive

Another misconception about the prophetic is that honor or value is determined by the opinion of man. Many times, we wait on the affirmation of others as a form of validation of the callings and the gifts of God on our life. If people show attention and see worth in our gifts, then we in turn are more prone to pour into it. This is not a good pattern for ministry because what happens when those around you don't seem to place much value on your gift? Let's take a lesson from Jesus about this topic.

"And they were deeply offended and refused to believe in him. Then Jesus told them, "A prophet is honored everywhere except in his own hometown and among his own family." And so, he did only a few miracles there because of their unbelief." Matthew 13:57-58 NLT

Those closest to Jesus were the very ones who could not benefit from His gifts. It wasn't that Jesus was not called, gifted, anointed, or appointed; it was just that they could not pull from the gift because they did not honor it. I am sure many of us have encountered similar situations, but what was our response? Did we retreat or continue to use the things that God gave us? You must ask yourself this question. Are you letting the opinion of man dictate how you yield your gifts to God? Is not He the one who we should seek approval from? After all, He is the one who gave us the gift. It should be our will to please Him in honoring the gifts that He gives us and not the people around us. Not saying that recognition from our spiritual leaders and mentors is not healthy. They are very important and help to build our confidence, but they should not be the basis or the fuel for us carrying out the assignment that God has given us.

<u>Strength takes effort</u>

A lot of times we believe it is the big noticeable things that strengthen our spiritual muscles and build our gifts, but on the contrary, it is the small, gradual, consistent effort that helps build us over time. Take a muscle builder for example. We see them in their end state but rarely consider how much effort it took for them to get there. They did not start out being able to bench press 200lbs. No, they had to start with the small weights first and then gradually work their way up. As they continued in one weight class, it became easier for them and then they were able to move up to the next weight class because the previous one no longer challenged them. That weight class no longer benefited them. It could not help them grow but only to maintain that same muscle strength. Likewise, it is not the "big prophecy" or the big notable healing that shows that we have arrived, but actually it is the small steps you take every day to build your faith that helps you develop healthy spiritual muscles.

Can you Faith Handle the weight you are trying to achieve?

When David offered to face Goliath and defend Israel from the Philistine's, to many it seemed like David was being pretentious. It was actually quite the contrary, God had built his faith in the secret place. David's faith to defeat Goliath was built on the back side of the mountain. It was not arrogance that they saw but confidence in God. See, David had history with God and having history with God will cause you to grow and increase in your faith to be able to carry greater levels of prophetic impartations and declarations.

Start small

Let's use this hypothetical situation as an example. The Lord may bring to you a situation that one of your sisters or brothers in Christ is facing in your local ministry. It could be concerning their marriage or children. He may start you off with this as a prayer assignment to see his will carried out in their lives. From there God will call you to the declare over their life his will concerning that situation. To you this may seem small but to God these are building blocks to prove, build, and test your faith.

God is a God of wisdom; He will not call you to prophesy to the wind, nations, regions or elements if He knows you do not have the faith to see his promises come to past in the lives of his people. He starts you off first on what may seem to you a much smaller scale. We must always trust the capacity that God has given us and prophesy according to our faith. You would not give a babe a 20 or 50lb weight in the natural. It is the same in the Spirit. Your faith must be able to handle the capacity.

"We have different gifts, according to the grace given to each of us. If your gift is prophesying, then prophesy in accordance with your faith." Romans 12:6 NLT

Do not compare yourself amongst yourselves for this is not wise

All gifts come from God and should be treated with the upmost importance no matter how insignificant it may appear to be. People who are competitive in ministry lack wisdom. God made us all unique differing our gifts to fulfill different purposes, it would be very foolish to look at another brother or sister in Christ and try and measure ourselves against them. God knows the vessel and He knows what He purposed it for. Not all of us are going to look the same or be able to carry the same capacity or weight but as long as that vessel is fulfilling its God given assignment then it is deemed honorable and fit for the master's use.

Different types of Gifts

Dormant gifts

Dormant gifts are those that you don't use because you don't know they are there. These gifts are often identified by a spiritual leader, or you can be led by the Holy Spirit to unlock these hidden gifts. These "unearthed" gifts can be identified and activated through the laying on of hands.

"Therefore I remind you to stir up the gift of God which is in you through the laying on of my hands." 2 Timothy 1:6 NKJV

Through the laying of hands, things you never knew you had in you will be revealed. As it is the case for many; you may not have recognized that you were a Prophet until you started attending the ministry that you are a part of today. It could be that for years you knew that there was a call on your life, but no one had pinpointed it down to that specific role in the body. Being under the tutelage of your leader will help groom and point you toward your purpose. From here things will make much more sense. Through these more mature ones overseeing you, you will gain more clarity on how your gifts fit with your call.

Mismanaged Gifts

People who mismanage their gifts know what their gift is but have trouble discerning exactly how or when to use it. They often feel insecure and uneasy about how to operate in it. They lack confidence and often get anxious when asked to use their gift.

Many people feel as though insecurity is normal but here lies the issue when you are insecure you will often find yourself one step behind on an assignment because you have a constant need for affirmation or confirmation. What insecurity does is take the attention away from God and put it back on man's ability. This brings God no glory as He has no room to move through us as He desires.

We see in the story of Gideon that he was very insecure (Judges 6). The Lord though, was very merciful toward Gideon because he did not have history with God. Up until the point that the Lord met Gideon by the winepress, he had only heard stories about his ancestor's experiences with God. However, there will come a point where you mature, as Gideon did, and have to be able to trust in the God that called you.

Neglected Gifts

Neglect means to leave something undone especially through carelessness. Neglected gifts are those who know what their gifts are but refuse to use them for reason of busyness, laziness or maybe even selfishness.

In the story of the stewards and the talents we see where each steward was entrusted with a certain number of talents. They were not all given the same, but they were all expecting to bring a return on what was given. God expects us to produce something from that which is given. When we neglect the gift that is given to us by God because we deemed it as insignificant, then we put ourselves in a bad place with the Almighty.

"Do not neglect the spiritual gift you received through the prophecy spoken over you when the elders of the church laid their hands on

you. Give your complete attention to these matters. Throw yourself into your tasks so that everyone will see your progress." 1 Timothy 4:14-15 NLT

Neglecting of the gifts or assignments God gave you will cause you to forfeit. When an assignment in ministry is given and you drop it God sees it as a neglect. Every assignment God gives you is important, and the gifts God gives you is always for the benefit of someone else. They are for the body and every part of the body is important. Even that gift you think is minute. Don't be like the man with the one talent who buried his gifts. That which he had was taken away because he neglected it.

Devalued gifts

We devalue our gifts by not readily using them or prostituting them out for personal gain. In this we hold our gifts hostage unless it benefits us. This is a misuse of that gift. We see where people in the Bible used their gifts to carry out their own personal agenda and it did not work out well for them. When you hold your gift hostage because you are offended or use it as a means to control others then you are abusing your gift. That is not what God gave us the gifts for. The gifts are for the body, and yes, He can use our gifts to make room for us, but their main purpose is to edify the body of Christ.

Jesus being moved with compassion, would look on the crowd of people and offer the gifts given by the Holy Spirit to heal and minister to the people. I am sure there were times when he was tired and sometimes healed people that never even came back to say thank you, but the accolades were not his driving force to operate what God gave him. He would often say "I come not to do my will, but the will of my father." This should be our attitude as well. Say this prayer

"Lord help me to use the gifts that you give me to serve your purpose and not my own."

Testing

"I the Lord search the heart, I try the reins, even to give every man according to his ways, and according to the fruit of his doings."
Jeremiah 17:10 KJV

As God raises you and brings you up in your prophetic call, He will first bring you through the place of testing. God always test his chosen vessels. Though He uses different ways and methods for each individual, the end result is still the same. He wants to reveal the inner working of our heart.

Do we love Him above all?

Matthew 22:37 KJV "Jesus said unto him, Thou shalt love the Lord thy God with all thy heart, and with all thy soul, and with all thy mind."

Will we put Him first?

Deuteronomy 4:24 NLT "The Lord your God is a devouring fire; he is a jealous God."

Are our intentions pure?

Proverbs 20:27 NLT "The Lord 's light penetrates the human spirit, exposing every hidden motive."

Will we obey Him no matter what persecution we may face?

Isaiah 50:6 NLT "I offered my back to those who beat me and my cheeks to those who pulled out my beard. I did not hide my face from mockery and spitting."

Testing of Patience

One of the hardest tests I believe any individual will encounter from God is the test of patience. Patience is one of the fruits of the Spirit. It is a character trait that every believer should endeavor to develop. As a Prophet in training, God will test you and allow you to go through great trials in order for you to birth patience. See, gifts alone cannot sustain us. They will only take us but so far. Character is what keeps us going strong for long. So, it is in the place of waiting that true character is developed. When one does not embrace this place of waiting, they are destined to self-sabotage. **Self-sabotage** *means* to intentionally prevent the success of a plan or action. I define it as to destroy one's own destiny or future due to lack of preparation, skip process and or ignored or undealt with character flaws.

Let it have its work

> *"But let patience have her perfect work, that ye may be perfect and entire, wanting nothing." James 1:44 KJV*

Patience is not easily moved, is not anxious for fame, spotlight, superiority, notoriety, or popularity. In this test God will allow situations and circumstances to come into our lives in order to produce the fruit of patience. So, what does patience look like? Patience is not about your ability to wait more than it is your attitude and disposition that you have while you wait. See, every part of the process is necessary. The journey is important. In the journey we build history with God, trust in God, faith, character and birth the fruit of the Spirit.

God desires a perfect vessel. One He can use fully, who is entire, complete, mature and is not tossed to and fro with every wind that comes to shift them. But maturity is produced over time and does not happen overnight. Those who desire to become and overnight success are inadvertently hindering their own success and potential. When you skip process, you must go back to do your first works over again, picking up the key and vital things that you missed along the way.

> *"An inheritance obtained too early in life is not a blessing in the end." Proverbs 20:21 NLT*

Opposites attract

People can see the development of a chosen vessel even before that individual realizes the anointing and influence that they carry. People are attracted to the next. Darkness is attracted to the light. Even when you cannot see the light that you are radiating in the spiritual realm, demonic forces are picking you up. Some will try to latch on, connect, use, manipulate, or even bribe the gift in the vessel before it's time. But remember patience is necessary for the birthing.

You must wait on the Lord for your advancement and revealing in the realm of the Spirit. Let's use Saul and David for example. Saul saw David's potential and his great enthusiasm when coming to fight Goliath. He wanted to use that to his advantage and told David to use his armor, which represented his influence as if it was his own. David knew he could not fight with something that did not fit him and respectfully rejected Saul's offer. Likewise, many times people who have great platforms or ministries will see the potential of a young Prophet and try to use it as their own. We must ask God to show us where the opposites and destroyers of our destiny are seeking ways to attach to us.

You must be aware of your blind spots and your weak areas. That is why character development and accountability is so important. If left unchecked, you can fall into the trap of premature birthing, causing spiritual death or even abortion due to unequal attractions. If you have undealt with character flaws, insecurities, and idolatries these can become bait traps of the enemy. The enemy is subtle and will use anything, if possible, to deceive and draw you away from your God given time of birthing into your purpose. Promises of wealth, notoriety fame, influence, popularity, and spotlight will all be used as a Delilah to draw you in.

Let's take another example from Saul. In the Book of 2 Samuel, Saul grew impatient. He had been waiting for Samuel to come so that he could offer sacrifices unto God. Unfortunately, Samuel took longer than Saul's patience capacity, so he went ahead of him and offered sacrifices himself. Likewise, many people do not want to wait on the next of God. The next elevation, open door or even assignment so we go ahead and do it on our own.

On the contrary, David who had been anointed to be next in line as king, waited patiently for his turn and served until the Lord brought him into the fullness of his ministry. Even after he was anointed by Samuel he went back and continue to be faithful over the work that he was given tending to his father's sheep. He didn't go around boasting that he was the next. He didn't throw his own party letting everyone know he had been anointed. He remained faithful, humble, and patient. We should take after David's example and do the same.

Now let's talk about some of the things that impatience will cause you to walk into so that you can avoid them.

1. Impatience will bring you into dishonor

When you "feel" as though you are ready and that your leader is holding you back or refusing to acknowledge your gift; if that mindset and thought pattern is not corrected it will bring you into a place of dishonor. David too was tested in this area. His companions almost cost him his Kingdom through dishonor by encouraging him to kill Saul in the Cave (1 Samuel 24:5). Thinking that you should be further than you are will cause you to miss out on the next promotion. There is weight in the wait. You gain spiritual muscles when you wait for God to elevate you to the next level and not look for the easy way up or try to cut your own way to elevation. God looks at the heart condition in the wait. David's heart remained pure and stood the test of time; even though on numerous occasions Saul tried to take his life.

2. Impatience will cause you to drop assignments

You may feel as though God is calling you into a different assignment. Whether that involves traveling, writing, producing content on social media or etc. Though he may very well be calling you to step out into this new arena, we must make sure that the first assignments that we have are not neglected. Most people go up but forget to pass the baton, thus leaving the people behind them to fend for themselves. Leaving sheep, churches, assignments unattended or neglected all in pursuit of vain glory and ambition. God does not honor such types of promotion.

God is concerned about his sheep and the care of the body. He will not cause any part of the body to be wanting. We must consider how we move an advance in the things of God. Our concern must always be for his sheep for that is the heart of God. Remember, our assignments are never about us but are always connected to those God gave us to serve. As God calls us to higher places in Him, we must make sure that the seat we last occupied is not left empty or being filled inadequately. Always remember your actions speak louder than your words, and the people that are behind you are watching what you do and the way you move as you go up.

The Test of Obedience: Idolatry

As stated before, the Lord's test come in many different forms. He comes to test us on many different levels and in several areas of our life. Some of the most difficult tests include the things and people we love the most. Let's look at one of the Patriarchs of our faith Abraham. In the Book of Genesis, we see where Abraham had been given a promise by God that he would bring forth a seed. Not only would he bring forth a seed from out of his own loins, but it would come forth out of the womb of his barren wife Sarah.

After years of waiting on the promise, and even trying to fulfill that promise on their own through Ishmael, they finally bore God's promise seed Isaac. But after all the waiting we see where God flips the script on Abraham and ask him to sacrifice the very thing that was promised to him.

"Some time later, God tested Abraham's faith. "Abraham!" God called. "Yes," he replied. "Here I am." "Take your son, your only son—yes, Isaac, whom you love so much—and go to the land of Moriah. Go and sacrifice him as a burnt offering on one of the mountains, which I will show you." Genesis 22:1-2 NLT

This could very well be one of the most difficult tests that we see any human walk through with God. This test is the test of idolatry where God tested Abraham to see if he would put anything before Him. What better thing to test us with than the thing that we love the most? God will often ask us for that very thing that is dear to our heart to reveal unto us the position of our heart in serving Him. Without question Abraham took his only son Isaac, gathered the things necessary for a burnt offering and headed to the place where God had showed him. In that moment God was not only testing Abraham but showing Abraham what was in his heart. We must remember that whether good or bad God knows what is in the inner crevices of our hearts.

"But I, the Lord, search all hearts and examine secret motives. I give all people their due rewards, according to what their actions deserve." Jeremiah 17:10 NLT

For Abraham this was a time of exposure. The Lord already knows what is in our heart, just as He knew what was in Abraham's heart, nothing is hidden from Him. But what the Lord wanted to do was use this experience to show Abraham that he was indeed a faithful servant and confirm his word to him that he had been chosen by God as a vessel in his Covenant promise.

Serving requires obedience

To **serve** means to perform duties or services for another person or an organization. When we serve, we are not doing what we desire, but the desire of the one we are under. In Abraham's case he was under God and through Abraham's willingness to sacrifice his only son he showed where his service lied. He put God's command above his own desires and fulfilled both parts of this Scripture.

"Obedience is better than sacrifice and submission is better than offering the fat of rams" 1 Samuel 15:22 NLT

Many times, being obedient to God's will cause us to do this. In reality being obedient to God is a sacrifice within itself. There will be times God will ask us to "sacrifice" our wants, desires, and ambitions in order to be in full submission and obedience to Him. I too have experienced the test of obedience by giving up something that was very dear to my heart. At first I didn't' understand but as I journeyed with God the importance of my obedience came to light. So, the question lies what is the "It" that God is requiring of you and are you willing to make the sacrifice for the call?

Act first

Sometimes it takes for you to obey the first command for God to give you the revelation and purpose behind it. There were many points in Abraham's life where we see God required him to obey without full understanding. Just as Abraham lifted his hand to slay Isaac, God's voice stopped him, and we see him reaffirm his Covenant to Abraham in a greater way. This took place because Abraham was willing to obey him in the greatest.

God always wanted to bless Abraham and make him the father of many nations, but it required his obedience for it to be fulfilled. See, God never requires us to make such a sacrifice if He didn't already have greater in store. What I realize is that God was not trying to take something from Abraham but was trying to get something to him. That is just the kind of God He is. If you have come to this place, know that God has your best interest at heart. Obey Him in the little and He will make you ruler over the more.

> *"This is what the Lord says: Because you have obeyed me and have not withheld even your son, your only son, I swear by my own name that I will certainly bless you. I will multiply your descendants beyond number, like the stars in the sky and the sand on the seashore. Your descendants will conquer the cities of their enemies. And through your descendants all the nations of the earth will be blessed—all because you have obeyed me."*
> Genesis 22:16-18 NLT

Test of Obedience: Respecter of Person

Let's explore another story in the Book of 1 Kings about a Prophet who was tested with obedience in the area of respecter of persons. In this story there was a king ruling in Judah named Jeroboam who caused the people to walk in error by setting up pagan places of worship. God was not pleased and sent a Prophet from Judah to pronounce judgment over them.

> *"At the Lord 's command, a man of God from Judah went to Bethel, arriving there just as Jeroboam was approaching the altar to burn incense. Then at the Lord 's command, he shouted, "O altar, altar! This is what the Lord says: A child named Josiah will be born into the dynasty of David. On you he will sacrifice the priests from the pagan shrines who come here to burn incense, and human bones will be burned on you." That same day the man of God gave a sign to prove his message. He said, "The Lord has promised to give this sign: This altar will split apart, and its ashes will be poured out on the ground." 1 Kings 13:1 NLT*

When Jeroboam heard the proclamation, he became angry and tried to capture the Prophet, but God caused sickness to come upon him, and immediately his hand shriveled-up. Jeroboam, seeing that this was the work of the Lord, asked the Prophet to intercede that God would heal his hand. The Lord headed the Prophets request, and his hand was restored that same hour. Now let's pay close attention to the actions of the Prophet in this next verse.

"Then the king said to the man of God, "Come to the palace with me and have something to eat, and I will give you a gift." But the man of God said to the king, "Even if you gave me half of everything you own, I would not go with you. I would not eat or drink anything in this place. For the Lord gave me this command: 'You must not eat or drink anything while you are there, and do not return to Judah by the same way you came."' 1 Kings 13:7-9 NLT

We see here where the Prophet quickly and sternly refused the wicked rulers offer. Why? Because the Lord had given him a command and he intended to follow it. Now let's venture to the second part of the story. As the Prophet begin to travel home, he was intercepted by an older Prophet who had heard about the pronouncement he had made against Jeroboam. The older Prophet then invited the younger Prophet in to eat with him, but again the younger Prophet explained the commands he was given by the Lord. This is the second time we see the Prophet explain the command he had gotten. It showed that he understood clearly what the Lord wanted and required of him. But the older Prophet continued to press him and even went as far as to lie to get him to eat with him.

"But the old prophet answered, "I am a prophet, too, just as you are. And an angel gave me this command from the Lord: 'Bring him home with you so he can have something to eat and drink.' But the old man was lying to him. So they went back together, and the man of God ate and drank at the prophet's home." 1 Kings 13:18-19 NLT

He used his influence of being an elder to him and the fact that he was a Prophet as well to deceive him into disobeying God, but the younger Prophet did not respond to him the same way he did Jeroboam by rejecting his invitation. He held the older Prophet in a higher regard. Due to this he compromised and accepted his offer. We see here that he was a respecter of persons. In this God was testing his heart as well as his capacity to obey Him above man. Unfortunately, the younger Prophet did not pass this test. He allowed the older Prophet to cause him to disobey the word of the Lord.

Likewise, it is easy for us, at times, to look at the world and the things that they do and reject it but override and compromise with those who look, and sound like us. Especially when they are someone in the body who we look up to or even maybe our leader. It is true that God will use those leaders and more mature ones to give us instruction but this was not the case here. He knew the instructions that God gave him, but the bias he had caused him to fall.

No one is higher than God

It is okay to have a healthy reverence, respect, and honor for leaders and other people in your life. What is not okay it's when we allow it to interfere with our obedience or allow it to supersede the word that God has revealed about them. When the Lord begins to show us things about people in our lives that we are close to or hold in high regard we must accept it as truth. If you don't, you will allow this to disrupt your ability to receive information from the Lord. My leader often tells me this "There is no one higher than God, not even me. If God said it, that is it!." No voice or opinion is above God. It does not matter if it is your mother, father, spiritual leader, mentor, protégé, another Prophet or close friend.

As humans it is often easy to ignore flaws and faults in the people that we love the most and are close to, but if you continue to ignore what the Holy Spirit is showing you, eventually you will become insensitive to what He has to say. It could be that He wants you to give that person a word of warning, pray or intercede for them, but because it is hard for you to accept the truth that that person has the capacity to struggle with that you ignore it. This shows there is an unhealthy attachment to that individual. We cannot be biased in our eyes, opinion, or discernment. This will hinder you and cause you to become *partial in judgment.*

This may be a struggle for you, especially when God begins to show you things about leaders and people you are close to. As Prophets, we must know God's Word is above his name, and no one is excluded. If you don't, you will find yourself compromising with His Word, not releasing words of correction, and not obeying instructions He gave you in order to please those who you hold in high regard. The younger Prophet made this mistake and it cost him his life. On his way home he was killed by a lion just as God said.

"Then while they were sitting at the table, a command from the Lord came to the old prophet. He cried out to the man of God from Judah, "This is what the Lord says: You have defied the word of the Lord and have disobeyed the command the Lord your God gave you. You came back to this place and ate and drank where he told you not to eat or drink. Because

of this, your body will not be buried in the grave of your ancestors." 1 Kings 13:20-22 NLT

If this is something you feel you struggle with ask the Holy Spirit to break every unhealthy attachment and relationship that could possibly be a hindrance in your life. Then ask Him to wash your eyes through the truth of His Word until no partiality is found. Ask Him to bring back to your memory anything that he might have told you about an individual that you ignored because of the relationship that they held in your life. Ask Him to show you how to work pass this place without losing your respect for that individual. Ask Him to give you the heart to love past faults and receive the instruction that he wants to give you concerning that situation. Ask Him for a heart of obedience to heed to His Word above that of man.

Testing through Assignments

The last test we will talk about in this section is testing through assignments. Now let's Venture into the parable about the servants and the talents to better expound on this concept. We see in the Book of Matthew where Jesus began to compare the kingdom of God to a man who went away on a long journey and left his servants in charge of some of his estate.

"For the kingdom of heaven is as a man travelling into a far country, who called his own servants, and delivered unto them his goods. And unto one he gave five talents, to another two, and to another one; to every man according to his several ability; and straightway took his journey." Matthew 25:14-15 KJV

The Scripture says he gave them the talents according to their abilities. He knew what they were capable of handling. At the time they did not know what the outcome would be, they were just given the talents and asked to govern them well. He used the first measure as a test to see how they would handle it. Just as the ruler did in this parable, God will often use the very assignments that He gives us to test if we will be faithful and consistent. The talents given to the servants did not belong to them. They belonged to their Master, but he gave them what we call stewardship over them. **Stewardship** is a job of supervising or taking care of something, such as an organization or property.

These men were set to steward a part of the master's estate, we as Prophets are a form of stewards that have been given a portion of God's *purpose* to help usher into the Earth. What I have come to find is God will use those very assignments that He gives you to test the position of our heart. Will you be faithful and consistent even when no one is looking? Can you be trusted with tasks that may not seem grand or get you attention from others. After the ruler returned, he found that two of the servants made a return on his investment while the third servant buried his talent. The ruler in turn rewarded the first two with more talents. He then cursed the last servant and took away the one talent that he had and gave it to another.

Can you handle the one talent?

His master called him *evil* and wicked because he did not take that which was given to him seriously. He saw the one talent as insignificant, as we also might see some of our assignments as insignificant. God may start you off with one assignment. It could be he wants you to intercede for a certain country or even an individual and continue in intercession until you see breakthrough. It could even be covering a certain ministry in your local church. He then instructs you that he wants you to do these things in private. Charging you not to share this with others, but still expect you to be faithful in them. *Can you be faithful when no one is watching?* Maybe you start off well and then become inconsistent. To you it may be no big deal but to God it is a different story. See, God is looking at the posture of your heart and how you carry out every assignment He gives you. We must remember that the assignment originated from God, and He holds you accountable to it. He only had one talent, in part because that is what he knew he could handle, but that one talent meant something to his master.

God expects growth

"But the master replied, 'You wicked and lazy servant! If you knew I harvested crops I didn't plant and gathered crops I didn't cultivate, why didn't you deposit my money in the bank? At least I could have gotten some interest on it." Matthew 25:26-27 NLT

When the master came back and found that which he had he gave his servant in the same condition, with no growth it angered him. What the master was looking for was effort not necessarily perfection. Just as it is with our father. He expects us to multiply that which He gives to us, to work the ground diligently to produce increase. Every intercessory assignment, word of encouragement, and prophetic word God gives you is important to Him. This is stewardship. We should govern the things of God just as if they were ours if not better. He told him he could have at least placed his money in the bank for it to build interest, but he was not even willing to put in that little effort to make some gain for his master.

<u>Testing for Promotion</u>

"Blessed is the man who endures temptation; for when he has been approved, he will receive the crown of life which the Lord has promised to those who love Him." James 1:12 NKJV

So, what is the purpose for God testing us in this capacity. As stated, before it is to reveal the inner working of our heart but also to increase us. Those who God proves; He rewards with what I call *promotions*. Testing always precedes promotion. What the man with the one talent did not know was that he was up for a promotion and was being evaluated by his master. But before that promotion could be granted, he needed to be proven.

See, God does not test us for us to fail, nor does He give us test He knows we are unable to pass. He is not that kind of God. He would never put more on us than we can bear. The servant in the previous story had the capacity to do more with what he had but he chose not to.

These promotions come in different forms, and you experience different levels of them as you grow in your journey with Christ. They can come in forms of prophetic graduations, (advancing you into greater levels of the prophetic), greater access, deeper revelation in the spirit, spiritual authority, favor, influence and so forth. When God has proven you through testing, showing that you have matured and are able to handle a greater capacity, then and only then will He promote you to the next level. Again, promotions may look different for everyone in different seasons of your prophetic journey, but as always, He will grant to you what He desires for you to have and only gives you that which He knows you can handle.

Another thing that the master was looking for was faithfulness. It was one of the things the master commended the other two servants that he did not with the third. God promotes and blesses the faithful (**Matthew 25:21**).

Faithfulness is the concept of unfailingly remaining loyal to someone or something and putting that loyalty into consistent practice regardless of excruciating circumstances. I must tell you that this will not always be an easy task, but it is one that comes with great rewards. You will see much opposition, resistance, and demonic warfare. You will encounter distractions and discouragement when striving to be faithful over that which God has given you. Especially when others around you seem to be less than faithful. Nevertheless, remain consistent and diligent, watching the strategies of the enemy to try and throw you off. He will try and use whatever tactics he thinks will work, but we must remain like Jesus said putting our hands to the plow and not looking back.

"You therefore must endure hardship as a good soldier of Jesus Christ. No one engaged in warfare entangles himself with the affairs of this life, that he may please him who enlisted him as a soldier." 2 Timothy 2:3-4 NKJV

Rewards of faithfulness

So, what does being rewarded because of faithfulness look like? To many it could mean a bigger platform, more exposure, adoration of men or popularity but that could not be more far from the truth. Though the assignments God gives us might warrant those things, in actuality the more faithful you are the more responsibilities God gives you.

Greater Responsibility

"The servant to whom he had entrusted the five bags of silver came forward with five more and said, 'Master, you gave me five bags of silver to invest, and I have earned five more.' The master was full of praise. 'Well done, my good and faithful servant. You have been faithful in handling this small amount, so now I will give you many more responsibilities. Let's celebrate together!" Matthew 25:20-21 NLT

Through the testing of assignments God sees that you are responsible. I like to say that means we are able and willing to *respond* to that which God gives us. Yes, promotion equals more responsibility! Who would have thought? Just like the two servants in the end of the story were blessed with more talents to steward or govern, so God will bless us with a heavier and more abundant workload.

Let's take a minute to pause and think about this concept. They were given not more influence but more to manage. See, because the harvest and souls of His people on earth are so important to him, he looks for faithful vessels to give His more precious assignments. Beloved do not be fooled; God knows the heart of man. If He sees you would not be faithful and consistent in the little, then He knows He could not trust you with greater levels of influence and assignments.

"He that is faithful in that which is least is faithful also in much: and he that is unjust in the least is unjust also in much." Luke 16:10 KJV

Now, let's take a moment and begin to ask the Holy Spirit if there are any inconsistencies in our life or dropped assignments that we have failed to carry out. When He has revealed to you those weak areas that need to be repaired, repent, and ask Him to give you a renewed and refreshed zeal to carry that assignment to its completion. Admit your fault and ask him to grant you with another chance at stewarding the next assignment.

How to combat inconsistency

One way the Lord has given me to keep up with the words and assignment that He gives me is to journal in a notebook. Because the Lord speaks to Prophets so often throughout the day, it is easy to forget those little words that He drops in your spirit. For you it might be your phone or another device. Sometimes at the end of the day it is good to sit quietly and allow the Holy Spirit to bring back to your remembrance those things that He talked to you about and write them down. You may even want to take these things into your prayer time.

Make it a habit to look through it every once in a while, to keep your memory fresh. This also works with remembering dreams and visions. By having the notebook or your phone close and available when you wake, you can quickly jot it down while it's still fresh in your mind.

Character

Character can be described as a person's moral, values or traits that define that individual. It is not something you try to have but the essence of who you are. What comes naturally for you to do, say, or think. It is the real you without show or pretense. This is why you can have either good or bad character. The Bible talks about how to distinguish an individual's character by their actions.

"Yes, just as you can identify a tree by its fruit, so you can identify people by their actions." Matthew 7:20 NLT

Thus, your true nature is hard to hide. We can only fake it to make it for so long. After a while, the persons true selves (fruit) will show. What's in you will most certainly come out one way or another. This is why character development is so important.

Have you ever seen people who were called and gifted? God allowed them to be raised up and opened doors of opportunity for them. They flourished for a season then what seemed like all of a sudden you saw them no more. This could very well be because of lack of character. Their character did not match their calling. Paul tells the Ephesians that they should live a life; or have character that is equal to their calling.

"Therefore I, a prisoner for serving the Lord, beg you to lead a life worthy of your calling." Ephesians 4:1-2 NLT

Go strong for long

Remember, gifts come without repentance (Romans 11:29). Gifts can get you through the door, but character is what keeps you there. Let's look at the animal kingdom. Cheetahs are very strong and are one of the fastest animals on the planet, but they can only maintain those fast speeds at short distances. This concept mirrors those who want to go up quick, they will fall even faster. So, then the desire is not to come up fast but to have character necessary for the level that we are on. Character gives you the ability to go strong for long.

"Wait on the LORD, and keep his way, and he shall exalt thee to inherit the land: when the wicked are cut off, thou shalt see it. I have seen the wicked in great power, and spreading himself like a green bay tree. Yet he passed away, and, lo, he was not: yea, I sought him, but he could not be found. Mark the perfect man, and behold the upright: for the end of that man is peace." Psalm 37:34 KJV

It is our choice how we walk out or calling and govern our gifts. This is why God will allow His chosen vessels to go through rigorous tests in order for character, which is the fruit of the Spirit, to be birth.

Characteristics of the old man

Paul lists some character flaws that we should endeavor to be delivered from, not only as Prophets but also as believers. He talks about the old man which includes lasciviousness, uncleanness, greed, corruption, deceitfulness, lust, lying, stealing, corrupt communication and admonishes us to put them away (**Ephesians 4:19**). At the same time, he also admonishes us to put on the new man that displays a righteous character of love, patience, and humility.

"Choose a good reputation over great riches; being held in high esteem is better than silver or gold." Proverbs 22:1 NLT

Our reputation speaks to the consistency of who we are. One who has integrity consistently practices what they preach thus proving that the fruit that they bear is true. While a lack of integrity ruins your reputation taking away your credibility. So how can one check if they are integral? By whom you are consistently. Are you a gossiper? Can you be trusted with confidential information? Do you always speak the truth? Are you honest? Do you have greed in your heart? Are you quick tempered, arrogant, or prideful? Do you treat others with dignity and respect? All of these are important aspects as we evaluate how we are stewarding our calling. Remember, our private life, character and prophetic ministry are not separate but all intertwined. We will dive deeper into the topic of character development in the next chapters.

Prophetic Integrity

In this new era, God is requiring the next generation of Prophets to walk into a greater level of prophetic integrity. **Integrity** is the quality of being honest and having strong moral principles, uprightness, firm adherence to a code of especially moral or artistic values. Due to the false representation that has been given to the church and world through *some* of the previous generations of Prophets, God is now coming to re-establish new foundations in the prophetic office. The Lord is now demanding that His chosen vessels to walk in higher levels of "uprightness of character and actions."

In this chapter we will talk about the different character flaws that a Prophet can operate out of and how to avoid them. We will use the term *demonic identities* to describe these character flaws. It is important to remember that anyone can find themselves operating in these identities. The purpose is not to condemn, but to bring awareness and to help you regain God's true identity for you as a Prophet.

As we journey through this chapter feel free to take notes as you identify areas in your own prophetic practice that need to be adjusted. Let's come through this space with open eyes and ears to hear what the Holy Spirit has to say about us individually. It is our desire to see His will in the earth and to operate our prophetic gift in the manner that He originally intended for us.

<u>False Prophet</u>

First let's talk about one of the most poisonous identities that any Prophet can have and that is one of the **False Prophet**. The Bible talks frequently in both the Old and New Testament about False Prophets.

> *"A wonderful and horrible thing is committed in the land;*
> *The prophets prophesy falsely, and the priests bear rule by their*
> *means; and my people love to have it so: and what will ye do in the*
> *end thereof?" Jeremiah 5:30-31 KJV*

We must remember that the gifts and callings of God come without repentance (**Roman's 11:29**). Likewise, the call of God is given to that Prophet without repentance. It is a gift given by God that He does not take back; whether we decide to embrace the call or choose to live an unrighteous life. None of these choices negate the fact that a person is a Prophet. With that understanding, let's dive deeper into what God considers to be a False Prophet.

The difference between what the Bible calls a *False Prophet* and a *true Prophet* comes down to intent. The False Prophet's intent is to deceive. That is why a Prophet can prophesy presumptuously and not necessarily be a False Prophet, because their intent is not to deceive. We will talk more about the presumptuous Prophet later in this chapter.

Anytime you prophesy with the knowledge that the information, prediction, revelation, or instruction you are getting is incorrect or did not come from God you become a False Prophet. Likewise, a born Prophet could come under the identity of the False Prophet if they chose to use their gift to deceive.

The Bible talks about False Prophets in both the Old and New Testament. Throughout these we find two distinct characteristics of a False Prophet.

1. The False Prophet teaches false doctrine that leads people away from God and into sin
2. The False Prophet follows and is influenced by filthy lucre (money).

If you would like to get a more in-depth knowledge about the False Prophet before we venture into this chapter, feel free to read 2 Peter 2, Ezekiel 13, Numbers 22, and Jeremiah 23.

The first distinction about a False Prophet is that they teach false doctrine and *lead people away from God.*

"Therefore," says the Lord, "I am against these prophets who steal messages from each other and claim they are from me. I am against these smooth-tongued prophets who say, 'This prophecy is from the Lord!' I am against these false prophets. Their imaginary dreams are flagrant lies that lead my people into sin. I did not send or appoint them, and they have no message at all for my people. I, the Lord, have spoken!" Jeremiah 23:30-32 NLT

These ones are not men and women of integrity and teach doctrine that is contrary to holiness and righteousness. Though it may not always be out right heresy, the underlying tone of their message is infiltrated with compromise, greed, luke-warmness and dumbs down the righteous standards written in God's Word. This leaves the person believing that it is okay to walk the thin line or to live in the gray area. They will often tell stories about their hypocritical lifestyle and use God's grace as being the okay for them living this way.

"Their destruction is their reward for the harm they have done. They love to indulge in evil pleasures in broad daylight. They are a disgrace and a stain among you. They delight in deception even as they eat with you in your fellowship meals. They commit adultery with their eyes, and their desire for sin is never satisfied. They lure unstable people into sin, and they are well trained in greed. They live under God's curse." 2 Peter 2:13-14 NLT

False Prophets weaken the heart of the Believer by making them believe a lie

They weaken the hearts of the believer by giving them false hope, security, and making them to believe things that will never come to pass (Ezekiel 13:10).

"This is what the Lord of Heaven's Armies says to his people: "Do not listen to these prophets when they prophesy to you, filling you with futile hopes. They are making up everything they say. They do not speak for the Lord!" Jeremiah 23:16 NLT

This part deeply saddens me as I have seen this all too often throughout the body of Christ. Where Prophets come to houses and prophesy falsely with the intent to deceive. The people then leave with a false expectation though not aware of it at first. Then the ultimate teller of truth comes (time) and exposes all the False Prophets lies. When their word does not come to pass, that person's heart becomes discouraged and begins to lose faith in God's Word and the prophetic voice. Thus, making it harder for them to receive from the true Prophets because of the damage that was done by those that went before them.

Am I saying that every prophetic word that you received that you have not seen come to pass was one given by a False Prophet? No, there are many other details that fall into play when interpreting a prophetic word. There may have been conditions to that prophecy that needed to be fulfilled in order for it to come to past. Or it could be that it is not the due season for that promise to manifest. With that said it is important for us to be able to discern the difference between those conditions and a flat-out false word.

False Prophets speak false words

"I have not sent these prophets, yet they ran. I have not spoken to them, yet they prophesied." Jeremiah 23:21 NKJV

"The Lord has not sent them." We see this phrase repeated numerous times throughout Scripture to distinguish born Prophets who go and speak without being sent by the Lord. The word is not in their mouth. False Prophets speak false words, and this is why it is important for a true Prophet to know how to judge a prophetic word correctly.

Let's venture into the Book of Nehemiah and see how he was able to discern between a false and a true prophetic word. In this passage Nehemiah is on a mission from the Lord. He is going back to Israel to rebuild the wall that was torn down during the siege of the Babylonians. While building the wall Nehemiah was faced with those who attempted to inhibit the work that he was doing. This opposition did not only come from outsiders but also from Nehemiah's own kinsman.

"Later I went to visit Shemaiah son of Delaiah and grandson of Mehetabel, who was confined to his home. He said, "Let us meet together inside the Temple of God and bolt the doors shut. Your enemies are coming to kill you tonight." But I replied, "Should someone in my position run from danger? Should someone in my position enter the Temple to save his life? No, I won't do it!" I realized that God had not spoken to him, but that he had uttered this prophecy against me because Tobiah and Sanballat had

hired him. They were hoping to intimidate me and make me sin. Then they would be able to accuse and discredit me. Remember, O my God, all the evil things that Tobiah and Sanballat have done. And remember Noadiah the prophet and all the prophets like her who have tried to intimidate me."
Nehemiah 6:10-14 NLT

We see here that even the true Prophet Noadiah began to turn and prophesy falsely against the work of Nehemiah. Nehemiah had to sift through many deceiving voices that were sent to put him in fear and throw him off course. Thankfully, Nehemiah had great discernment and perceived that the words that were being sent to him, even from the Prophets, were not of the Lord. For those with a pure heart it is hard to believe that a born Prophet would intentionally lie using God's name, but this happens all too often. That is why God is coming to purge and purify the prophetic voices.

Judging Prophetic Words

"Beloved, believe not every spirit, but try the spirits whether they are of God: because many false prophets are gone out into the world." 1 John 4:1 KJV

When receiving or giving a prophetic word one must ask

1. Does this condone my wrong behavior?
2. Does this reward my disobedience?
3. Does it inhibit my rebellion or wrong thinking?
4. Does this make me feel comfortable in my sin?
5. Does this go against instructions that have already been given by God or my leader?
6. Does this go against my conscience?
7. Does this cause division between me and another believer?

If you know you are in sin, and the prophetic word you receive makes you feel more at ease about your sinful condition, rather than piercing your heart to repentance, you need to reconsider that word. If you know that you have not been faithful in giving, and you receive a prophetic word that the Lord is going to bless you without first correcting you about your lack of obedience, you need to reconsider that as well.

If a Prophet comes with a word that goes totally against your leader or makes you feel as though it is okay to rebel against them, this word is not from the Lord. Remember, the Lord is not an author of confusion and will never cause you to dishonor authority (**Romans 13**). Even if the Lord is calling you to shift to another ministry it will be confirmed by him in a way that does not cause chaos or strife between you and the house that you are leaving. If a prophetic word calls you to question words that have already been confirmed to you by the Lord, this too is something that I would take back to God before fully receiving the word.

"But now I see that the prophets of Jerusalem are even worse! They commit adultery and love dishonesty. They encourage those who are doing evil so that no one turns away from their sins. These prophets are as wicked as the people of Sodom and Gomorrah once were." Jeremiah 23:14 NLT

I have received prophecies that I felt were not from the Lord because it "sowed discord among the brethren." If a Prophet comes and causes you to be suspicious about your brothers or sisters in Christ be very wary about receiving this word. If they come to big up your ego and cause you to think that everyone is against you or jealous of you again be wary to receive this word. Am I saying that you will never receive a word a warning concerning those around you who are not for you? No, but even those types of words should be delivered with grace and should prompt forgiveness, striving toward mercy for those individuals, especially if they are in the body of Christ.

Remember that the kingdom of God does not work like the world. The Lord says we should love our enemies as we love ourselves and pray for those who despitefully use us (**Matthew 5:44**). So, one must ask themselves did this word cause me to become bitter or hold unforgiveness in my heart? If so, it could be that that word did not originate from the heart of God or was not delivered properly.

Now let's look at the second characteristics of a False Prophet which is **filthy lucre.**

"They commit adultery with their eyes, and their desire for sin is never satisfied. They lure unstable people into sin, and they are well trained in greed. They live under God's curse. ¹⁵ They have wandered off the right road and followed the footsteps of Balaam son of Beor,ⁱ who loved to earn money by doing wrong. ¹⁶ But Balaam was stopped from his mad course when his donkey rebuked him with a human voice." 2 Peter 2-16 NLT

One of the things that sticks out about this type of Prophet is that they are driven by popularity, wealth, and a love of money but not the truth of God's Word. False Prophets are frequently associated with greed and covetousness. **Covetousness** is an evil, eager or excessive desire especially for wealth or possession. These Prophets will use their gift in order to get money or possessions. They love honor and the praises of men and equate it to success. They can most definitely be bought. They have a lack of prophetic integrity and allow their gifts to be prostituted which brings them into filthy lucre.

These Prophets...

1. Are not led by the Spirit of God but money and whoever sends for them
2. Are ambitious

Not everyone who endeavors to go into ministry comes into it with pure motives. Some see the call to ministry as a way to get money or to pay their bills. Let us look into a very familiar Prophet in the Bible whose name was Balaam. We start the story in the Book of Numbers around the time after the exodus of the children of Israel from Egypt. They are still journeying in the wilderness and have not made it to the promised land yet. But Balak the king of Moab has heard about the victory they obtained over the Amalekites (**Exodus 17:8-16**) and is terrified. Knowing that he could potentially be next, he devised a plan to hire Balaam the Prophet, to prophesy against the Israelites. From the passage, it seems as though Balaam was a Prophet known for two things; one who practiced divination and his ability to be bought.

> *"The king of Moab said to the elders of Midian, "This mob will devour everything in sight, like an ox devours grass in the field!" So Balak, king of Moab, ⁵ sent messengers to call Balaam son of Beor, who was living in his native land of Pethor[a] near the Euphrates River.[b] His message said:" Look, a vast horde of people has arrived from Egypt. They cover the face of the earth and are threatening me. ⁶ Please come and curse these people for me because they are too powerful for me. Then perhaps I will be able to conquer them and drive them from the land. I know that blessings fall on any people you bless, and curses fall on people you curse." Numbers 22:4-6*

At first it seemed as though Balaam was not going to consent to Balak, but in the end his love of money caused him to compromise. He sent them away the first time, but Balak was persistent and sent his messengers to Balaam again. Balaam agreed to go back to God to see if He had any more to say. This was not because he thought that God would change His mind, but because his desire for riches and prestige trumped his integrity. This was His response after Balak's second attempt.

> *"That night God came to Balaam and told him, "Since these men have come for you, get up and go with them. But do only what I tell you to do." Numbers 22:20 NLT*

On his journey he encountered an Angel of the Lord that stood in his way. Balaam, at first could not see the angel, who was standing there with his sword drawn about to kill him, but his donkey could. His donkey tried to turn away from the angel not once but three times. Balaam was angered because he did not understand what the donkey was doing and struck it. Then the Lord open Balaam's eyes and he was able to see the angel standing there with its sword drawn.

> *"And the angel of the Lord said unto him, Wherefore hast thou smitten thine ass these three times? behold, I went out to withstand thee, because thy way is perverse before me" Numbers 22:32 KJV*

Even though it may seem as though the Lord tempted Balaam in telling him to go and then later threatening to kill him, the Lord already knew what was in Balaam's heart.

> *"Let no one say when he is tempted, "I am tempted by God;" for God cannot be tempted by evil, nor does He Himself tempt anyone. [14] But each one is tempted when he is drawn away by his own desires and enticed. Then, when desire has conceived, it gives birth to sin; and sin, when it is full-grown, brings forth death." James 1:13-15 NKJV*

Balaam's heart was full of deceit and greed. This is what drew Balak to him. The Love of money and what the Bible calls *gifts of divination* that Balak was offering (**Numbers 22:7**). Balak offered Balaam money and prestige in exchange for speaking a false word. Balaam continued on to meet Balak in his attempts to override the Word of the Lord. By the end of the story Balak and Balaam tried three times to manipulate God into cursing the children of Israel, but God would not allow Balaam to use divination to speak against His chosen people. Balaam eventually gave up when he saw his attempt would not prevail against God, but this is not where his story ends. We see in a different book where Balaam eventually died along with the King of Moab in an attack from the Israelites (**Joshua 13:22**).

Filthy Lucre vs. Honor

Those who operate under the identity of the False Prophet will often pervert their gift by prostituting it.

Signs of spiritual prostitution

1. **Put a price on the Gospel**

   "You rulers make decisions based on bribes; you priests teach God's laws only for a price; you prophets won't prophesy unless you are paid. Yet all of you claim to depend on the Lord. "No harm can come to us," you say, "for the Lord is here among us." Micah 3:11 NLT

   The minute you put a price on your ministry by saying you will only go if they pay you a certain honorarium and meet certain conditions, you have entered into *divination* and are now pimping out your gift.

2. **Have their own agenda and will only go to those in your circle or are a part of your group**

   We see this all too often in many prophetic circles where Prophets tend to only prophesy in houses and groups they are affiliated with. This is not at all the heart of God as God is not a respecter of person or limited to a certain group, denomination, affiliation, or circle. We must go back to our original call and that is to go wherever God sends us. He may send us to people that may not look like us or even have our same beliefs. Even in discomfort we must remember that we are fulfilling the will of God and that is our priority.

3. **Show partiality with their words**

   "This is what the Lord says: "You false prophets are leading my people astray! You promise peace for those who give you food, but you declare war on those who refuse to feed you." Micah 3:5 NLT

   There have been times where Prophets have been hired out by ministries under the guise that they are to speak what God says, but some Prophets had been given an agenda before they even reached the pulpit. Through backdoor conversations, the leader of that ministry has already influenced their word. This purpose is to manipulate, correct, rebuke, condemn or even excite the people for that leaders own personal gain. Just like in the story of Balaam, God may have desired to pronounce a blessing on the people or house, but because that leader may have been going through some difficulties with their members, they infiltrate the need of correction and rebuke into the Prophet's word.

Or on the contrary where alignment and correction was needed for a house it did not happen because of the relationship they have with that leader or congregation. They ignore the promptings of the Holy Spirit and pronounce blessings, abundance, and wealth in a place where they knew the ground was not conducive for it. This is not the way to do prophetic ministry. Whether blessing or cursing, correction or encouragement, the root of the word needs to derive from the heart of God. No outside influences should sway our words. We must not allow friendships, partnerships, money, prestige, honor, or any other thing to coerce the word that God has put in our mouths for the people or house.

4.   **Allow themselves to be prostituted by only going to those who send for them like they Balaam, even if God tells them not to go**

"They went to Balaam and delivered this message to him: "This is what Balak son of Zippor says: Please don't let anything stop you from coming to help me. I will pay you very well and do whatever you tell me. Just come and curse these people for me!" Numbers 22:16-17. NLT

False Prophets are driven by the cares of this world popularity and wealth. Their prophecies are always biased in favor of those who can buy them. These ones allow the word in their mouth to be perverted by bribes and usury.

The Right to Profit from Ministry

Though Balaam was a Prophet driven by greed, it was not uncommon for Prophets to be given gifts for the word they gave (**1 Samuel 9:7;2 Kings 8:8**). It was a form of showing honor and not doing so was looked down upon. The difference here is that those Prophets did not allow the gifts they received to sway the word they gave.

In the Book of 1 Corinthians 9, Paul addressed the church of Corinth about the right of those who preach the Gospel to be supported by the ministry.

> *"Don't you realize that those who work in the temple get their meals from the offerings brought to the temple? And those who serve at the altar get a share of the sacrificial offerings. In the same way, the Lord ordered that those who preach the Good News should be supported by those who benefit from it." 1 Corinthians 9:13-14 NLT.*

Even Jesus, when sending out the 70, commissioned them not to take anything with them but allow themselves to be supported by those who welcomed them into their homes. Commanding them to eat whatever was put before then (**Luke 10**). As Prophets we too are ministers of God's Word and, have every right to be fed physically by what we put out to others spiritually.

> *"For the Scripture says, "You must not muzzle an ox to keep it from eating as it treads out the grain." And in another place, "Those who work deserve their pay!" 1 Timothy 5:18 NLT*

This is biblical, this is right, but what is not right is when we allow monetary contributions to dictate the who, what, when where and why of our ministry. The Apostle Paul understood this and would not allow this to happen in his ministry.

> *"If I were doing this on my own initiative, I would deserve payment. But I have no choice, for God has given me this sacred trust. What then is my pay? It is the opportunity to preach the Good News without charging anyone. That's why I never demand my rights when I preach the Good News." 1 Corinthians 9:17 NLT*

Paul's *why* was never moved by those who chose to or chose not to support him physically. He understood the dangerous position he would be in if he did not preach this Gospel. He was compelled by God to do so. He recognized that it was God who commissioned him to do this work and not of his own volition.

As Prophets, we are commission by God to prophesy and declare His works. This should not be something we take lightly. Nor is it something that should be influenced by money. The Old Testament Prophet went where God sent them, said what God told them to say, and God took care of them. Am I saying that you will never need the support of others to carry out the call? No, but it is to say that our first obedience should be to God not to men. Whether they are able to fulfill a minimum honorarium or not. If God sends us, we must go and know that God will supply all of our needs. He finances that which He commissions.

The Gospel is a free gift

> *"Is anyone thirsty? Come and drink— even if you have no money! Come, take your choice of wine or milk— it's all free!" Isaiah 55:1 NLT*

Paul boasted in his without charge ministry. Why? Because salvation is a free gift and so should the Gospel. After all Christ paid the ultimate price for us to be utilized in the first place. If it were not for His sacrifice, we would have nothing to preach about. It is God who freely gives us not only are calls and gifting's, but even the very prophetic word He downloads into us.

Remember the call

Remember, the call of the Five-Fold Ministry Office of the Prophet is not so we can make gain, but it is to fulfill the purposes listed in Ephesians 4. *Why?* To equip the saints, build up the church until we grow into the full stature of Christ (**Ephesians 4:11-12**).

We are his messengers sent to deliver His Word

In this season the Lord is calling His Prophets to rise to another level of obedience and becoming strategic in their movements. We are entering into a new era and the Lord is saying the season for *engagements* is over. This next season is a season of *assignments*. There will be times when we will be called on by people and houses to minister and God does not permit us to go. That is not to say that particular conference or program is bad, it might just not be a part of your assignment for that particular season.

We must be sensitive to His voice in these matters. As I stated before we are His messengers, and we carry the word that He sends us to deliver. Though an event or opportunity may seem good that does not mean that it is God ordained. We must submit our agendas to the will of God and not be driven by anything other than to please Him. No matter how appealing the offer may seem, at the end of the day our attitude must be this" *If God is not pleased then it profited me nothing*." This is how we keep ourselves unspotted from perversion and being led by filthy lucre. Remember, God will supply all of your needs according to his riches in glory. Keep the faith an only go where God sends you.

God's warning to false messengers

What does God say about those Prophets that choose to pervert their way? First if you have found yourself operating from this demonic identity you need to repent and ask for God's forgiveness. If you do so with a true heart, He is just to forgive you.

"Let the wicked change their ways and banish the very thought of doing wrong. Let them turn to the Lord that he may have mercy on them. Yes, turn to our God, for he will forgive generously." Isaiah 55:7 NLT

For those who decide not to repent, and continue in error, the Lord's hand is against them. In the Book of Matthew, the Lord talks about the end of those Prophets and people who worked miracles in His name that operated through the gift but never sought to do the will of the Lord.

"Not everyone that saith unto me, Lord, Lord, shall enter into the kingdom of heaven; but he that doeth the will of my Father which is in heaven. Many will say to me in that day, Lord, Lord, have we not prophesied in thy name? and in thy name have cast out devils? and in thy name done many wonderful works? And then will I profess unto them, I never knew you: depart from me, ye that work iniquity." Matthew 7:21-23 KJV

Yes, there will be many people who will find themselves being rejected by God because they used the gift without seeking the *Gift Giver*. All these that are stated here operated from a gift but were never connected to the heart of God. Those Prophets who practice such behavior will receive a spiritual demotion.

If you want to keep your oil pure and avoid operating from this demonic identity, then you must submit yourself under the authority of the Lord and the vessel He has chosen to place over you. Allow yourself to be spot-check frequently by the Holy Spirit and those close to you. Hold yourself accountable to His work to avoid becoming a hypocrite and endeavor, at all times to please the one who called you in the first place. Do everything with a pure heart unto him and not unto man.

"And whatsoever ye do, do it heartily, as to the Lord, and not unto men; Knowing that of the Lord ye shall receive the reward of the inheritance: for ye serve the Lord Christ." Colossians 3:23-24 KJV

The Popular Prophet

"What sorrow awaits you who are praised by the crowds, for their ancestors also praised false prophets." Luke 6:26 NLT

The Popular Prophet is one who's words are bent to the will of men. These ones care more about popularity, being "relevant" and accepted by men than carrying the true Word of God. So, they will often come under the deception of what I call trend prophesying. It is easy to fall into the temptation of **trend prophesying** where a Prophets words are formed based off what is "popular" or "trending" at the time. This can also be described as proph-e-lie-ing (to prophesy lies).

There are many prophetic trends that arise in the prophetic community depending on the season and what people are seeking to hear. These Prophets conform their words in order to be accepted by men. Often it is because of a lack of confidence and /or intimidation that they bend toward the "will" of the people. Often those who operate from this place will prophesy cars, houses, marriages and what many may seemingly call "blessings" from the Lord, but the truth is that may not be what God is really speaking.

God could be speaking and calling a house into correction and alignment, but because they have fallen into the place of trend prophesying, they just go along with what they know will make the people feel good. These Prophets intent is not to deceive but their fear of man causes them to compromise God's pure word.

Things that get us to **proph-e-lie.**

Fear of persecution

Fear of man

Presumptuousness

Self-promotion

Wanting to be accepted

Now let's take a lesson from Saul. In this passage the Lord gave Saul instructions to completely destroy the Amalekite Nation. When He said destroy, He meant everything.

> *"Now go and completely destroy the entire Amalekite nation— men, women, children, babies, cattle, sheep, goats, camels, and donkeys."* *1 Samuel 15:3 NLT*

Saul however did not comply fully to God's instructions only carrying out certain parts. Instead of wiping out the entire nation he spared King Agag's life and kept some of the animals as plunder (**1 Samuel 15:20**). God in turn ripped the kingdom from Saul because of his disobedience and sent Samuel to tell him the bad news. When confronted by Samuel, Saul insisted that he obeyed the Lord, but as Samuel pressed him, he finally admitted his guilt.

> *"Then Saul admitted to Samuel, "Yes, I have sinned. I have disobeyed your instructions and the Lord's command, for I was afraid of the people and did what they demanded. But now, please forgive my sin and come back with me so that I may worship the Lord." 1 Samuel 15:24-25 NLT*

By Saul refusing to obey the Lord's command, showed that his loyalty did not lie with God but with man. We must remember God never holds others accountable to the choices that we make. We all are held responsible for our own obedience to God.

> *"Fearing people is a dangerous trap, but trusting the Lord means safety." Proverbs 29:25 NLT*

Some may question Saul's true heart concerning this Scripture. Whether he truly was afraid of the people or not is left to be determined. What we do know is that Saul had a mind of his own and it was his choice to disobey God. What also is clear from this passage is Saul's motive. Even after the kingdom was ripped from him and being reprimanded by Samuel, he begged him to come back and worship. This was not from a place of true repentance, but so that his image could be upheld by the people. In wanting to be accepted by men, he rejected God's Word and in turn God rejected him.

Popular Prophets teach an imbalanced Word

The Lord spoke frequently about those Prophets who promised the people peace when there was no peace ahead. Thus, leaving them in a place of vulnerability. Where they should have been admonishing them to repent, so that God's judgement could pass over them, they instead put their heart at ease leaving them open to sudden destruction (**Ezekiel 13:5**).

When we omit parts of God's word in order to make it more tolerable, we come under the same deception. In order to not go over into the identity of this Prophet we must be able to receive God in His fullness. That means receiving God's rod of correction (**Lamentations 3:11**) and staff of comfort (**Psalms 23:4**). His blessings and His cursing (**Deuteronomy 30:19**). Mercy and judgement (**Jeremiah 33**).

All aspects make him who He is. God is loving, full of mercy but also hates sin and repays those who practice it with its wages which is death and will by no means pardon the wicked (**Exodus 34:6**). If we refuse to receive this truth about God, and only desire to see the loving blessing part of him, we will not be able to receive His revelation and bring correction to the body like it needs. We will never prophesy truthfully.

> *"Let these false prophets tell their dreams, but let my true messengers faithfully proclaim my every word. There is a difference between straw and grain! Does not my word burn like fire? says the Lord. "Is it not like a mighty hammer that smashes a rock to pieces?" Jeremiah 23:28-29 NLT*

Because the Popular Prophet is becoming more prevalent, even in this time it is more important for those who have sat in the counsel of God and sought His face to speak what he is saying. We should do so faithfully without fear of backlash knowing only God's words will stand. Obedience to God is not always an easy task. One must die to their image, how they look and appear to men in order to fully obey God. There will be some words that may seem unconventional or maybe even taboo, but obedience is something that we must master. If our loyalty lies in anything else whether it is our reputation, status, popularity, or followers we are headed for compromise.

Seek to please God

"Obviously, I'm not trying to win the approval of people, but of God. If pleasing people were my goal, I would not be Christ's servant." Galatians 1:10 NLT

In order to walk in this office, we must have a made-up mind to follow God at all costs. There is no way that you can fully please God and men. This is a part of the call. The very nature of the office mandates rejection and ridicule.

Now, am I saying that true Prophets will never be accepted or admired by man? Certainly not! There will most definitely be a group that God has called you to that will eat the word that comes from your mouth. But the reality is carrying the true word of God will not always align with the desires of the people they are meant for. We must be content with this harsh realization in order to carry out our call without compromise. We take comfort in knowing that we are pleasing God no matter what it may cost us in the natural.

Lying Prophet

Next let's talk about another kind of Prophet in that is one of a Lying Prophet. We spoke previously in this chapter about the False Prophet which is a spirit that I do not believe anyone wants to intentionally come under. Though it might sound similar, the Lying Prophet is different. A **Lying Prophet** is one who is not intentionally deceiving others but inadvertently doing so because they themselves are being deceived by their own desires. Let's look at this example from the Book of Ezekiel. In this passage, the Lord told Ezekiel to prophesy against the Prophets who left the true word of God and began to prophesy out of their own hearts.

"Son of man, prophesy against the prophets of Israel that prophesy, and say thou unto them that prophesy out of their own hearts, Hear ye the word of the Lord; Thus saith the Lord God; Woe unto the foolish prophets, that follow their own spirit, and have seen nothing!" Ezekiel 13:2-3

From here we see that it is possible for you to prophesy from your own heart and what you want to happen. In the Book of Jeremiah, the Lord confronted this same type of Prophets again (**Jeremiah 23**). At this time, the children of Israel were suffering judgement because of the many years of sin that they had committed against the Lord. The Prophet Jeremiah knew that they would suffer for a specific length of time (70 yrs.) before God would deliver them out of exile.

The other Prophets however could not believe that God would punish them so harshly so they began to oppose the words of Jeremiah, attempting to shorten the "set time" that they would be in exile (**Jeremiah 28**). They did not seek to hear the "Word of the Lord" in this case. So, because their own desires trumped what God said they began to prophesy what the Bible calls "out of their own heart ". How true this statement is in that we too can and go off when our desires are not checked. We must be careful to always say what God says even if it seems that it will not be beneficial for ourselves.

Characteristics of a Lying Prophet

They operate from a spirit of divination

Divination is the practice of seeking knowledge of the future or the unknown by supernatural means. Prayer is our confirmation that the word that we are hearing is from God. Prayer is our safeguard from operating under this spirit. It is a deterrent against demonic voices. Many Prophets prophesy and do not even realize they have entered into divination. This is because when there is not a consistent prayer life, you begin to operate merely through your gifts.

I must warn you that if you have not spoken to the Lord, humbled yourself and waited at the door to hear His voice, when you go to prophesy you open yourself up to other spirits to speak through you. Being a Prophet and having a gift is not enough. Our dependence must be on God in order to prophesy accurately. When a Prophet has not humbly sought the face of God and hastily attempts to go speak His Word, they are prone to error.

Remember that a Prophet's position is not just to prophesy, but we must first be wholly committed to a lifestyle of prayer. In this we can almost always ensure that the words that we are receiving are from God. If one is not fervent in prayer or consistent in their personal time with God, they can become manipulated into prophesying out of their own heart and desires, deceiving not only themselves but those around them. A Prophet who does not pray or receive counsel from God is considered illegal in the spirit realm.

They see false dreams and take them as a sign from God

We saw from both the Book of Ezekiel and Jeremiah examples that it is possible for you to be deceived and prophesy out of your desires. You can also desire something so strongly that you begin to dream about it. Yes, it is possible for you to dream a false dream and see a false vision. These are what the Bible calls *lying divination*.

> *"I have heard what the prophets said that prophesy lies in my name, saying, I have dreamed, I have dreamed. How long shall this be in the heart of the prophets that prophesy lies? yea, they are prophets of the deceit of their own heart;" Jeremiah 23:25-26 KJV*

Dreams that derive not from the Spirit of God but from your own soul. King Solomon also spoke about this in the Book of Ecclesiastes where the mere busyness of life or over-thinking can cause you to have these false dreams (**Ecclesiastes 5:3**). In the Book of Ezekiel, their rejection of God's Word caused them to enter into vain visions and lying divinations. So how does one avoid prophesying from this place. One way is to always take our opinion, desires, ideologies, thoughts and present them to God. In this honest place of prayer is where we allow the Holy Spirit to draw the dividing line between that which is of us and that which is of God.

Another distinction of a Lying Prophet is that *the Word of God is not in them.*

> *"And the prophets shall become wind, and the word is not in them: thus shall it be done unto them." Jeremiah 5:13 KJV*

These Prophets do not carry the true Word of God. That is why that which they speak does not come to pass. God is not responsible to bring forth a word that He did not conceive. God will never fulfill false prophecies. This is where we see a lot of *hit* and *miss* in the prophetic, meaning their prophetic track record is not consistent. This is not to say that they are not a true Prophet but rather the lack of consistency in prayer causes them to fluctuate in and out of their soulish realm. This often times is what causes people to see the prophetic as not credible. Which is not the case at all. The prophetic is very much real and credible it is just that God is not responsible to birth a word that did not originate from him. We must recognize this difference so that we can maintain the integrity of our prophetic ministry.

They operate under a Lying spirit

Along with the Spirit of divination, there is also something called a Lying Spirit that one must be careful of. This spirit deceives the Prophet and in turn causes them to deceive others. Let's Venture into the Book of Chronicles to further understand how this spirit operates and why God allows it to hinder His Prophets.

"Then Micaiah continued, "Listen to what the Lord says! I saw the Lord sitting on his throne with all the armies of heaven around him, on his right and on his left. And the Lord said, 'Who can entice King Ahab of Israel to go into battle against Ramoth-gilead so he can be killed?' "There were many suggestions, and finally a spirit approached the Lord and said, 'I can do it!' "'How will you do this?' the Lord asked. "And the spirit replied, 'I will go out and inspire all of Ahab's prophets to speak lies. You will succeed, said the Lord. Go ahead and do it.' "So you see, the Lord has put a lying spirit in the mouths of your prophets. For the Lord has pronounced your doom." 2 Chronicles 18:18-22 NLT

In this passage King Ahab was requesting guidance as to whether he should go to war with a certain nation. Though he knew there was a true Prophet (Micaiah) who was credible, he still chose 400 False Prophets to prophesy before him. Why might you ask? King Ahab chose these 400 Prophets because he knew that they would prophesy in His favor. They had already set in their heart to prophesy good things concerning the king no matter what God said. God knew this so he allowed a lying spirit to come and influence the Prophet's words.

This can be a very difficult subject to understand but we must remember that God is righteous in all that he does and does not tempt man (**James 1:13**). However, the Bible does say that when you choose to reject His Word, he will give you over to your own desires to cause you to believe a lie (**2 Thessalonians 2:11**).

Ahab rejected The Prophet Micaiah because he knew he would tell him the truth. When first approached by the king, Micaiah spoke from a place of sarcasm urging the king to go to war (**2 Chronicles 18:14**). Ahab knew Micaiah was not being honest and did not buy into the Prophets sarcastic jokes. Yet he still chose to believe the lies of the 400 False Prophets. This is how we allow a Lying Spirit to influence our messages. When our intent is to please man, or our own desires and not God..

Consequences of speaking falsely in God's name

Whether you come under the category of the False Prophet, Lying Prophet or Popular Prophet there are consequences for speaking falsely in God's name. In the Book of Jeremiah, we see where one of many occasions where the Lord anger kindled against the Prophets and priests who had turned and begin to prophesy falsely in His name. In this particular passage, the Lord gave a stark warning for Jeremiah to give to them.

> *"If any prophet, priest, or anyone else says, 'I have a prophecy from the Lord,' I will punish that person along with his entire family. You should keep asking each other, 'What is the Lord's answer?' or 'What is the Lord saying?' But stop using this phrase, 'prophecy from the Lord.' For people are using it to give authority to their own ideas, turning upside down the words of our God, the living God, the Lord of Heaven's Armies. "This is what you should say to the prophets: 'What is the Lord's answer?' or 'What is the Lord saying?' But suppose they respond, 'This is a prophecy from the Lord!' Then you should say, 'This is what the Lord says: Because you have used this phrase, "prophecy from the Lord," even though I warned you not to use it, I will forget you completely. I will expel you from my presence, along with this city that I gave to you and your ancestors. And I will make you an object of ridicule, and your name will be infamous throughout the ages." Jeremiah 23:34-40 NLT*

God had gotten so fed up with His Prophets prophesying falsely to where he basically told them to stop using His name. God was and is still serious about His namesake. In the Old Testament Prophets suffered severe consequences for speaking false words. He would not allow even His born Prophets to tarnish His name. I believe we don't see such extreme measures taking place now because of Jesus Christ's sacrifice on the cross. Now the mercy of God is expounding greatly upon all mankind. Though this is true we should not dismiss the fact that God's prophetic word should not be treated lightly.

Is this to say that you would never prophesy inaccurately or make mistakes? No, it is not. On the contrary, In the beginning of your journey you will make many mistakes and will continue to make mistakes even in the process of God training you. He knows this and makes allowances for it through those who cover you and other Prophets. However, this is where motive and knowledge come into play. There is a real difference between one who is in the process of learning God's voice and one who speaks falsely with full knowledge that the Lord hath not said.

> *"Listen to me, you who know right from wrong, you who cherish my law in your hearts. Do not be afraid of people's scorn, nor fear their insults." Isaiah 51:7 NLT*

So, what can we take away from this? As Prophets we must speak what God tells us to speak. Our words are not our own. We cannot allow ourselves to be influenced by any other voice but the voice of the Lord. That includes man as well as our own desires.

The Presumptuous Prophet

Now let's talk about the Presumptuous Prophet. There is a distinct difference between what the Bible calls a False Prophet and a true Prophet that speaks presumptuously. To **Presume** means to supposed something to be true without proof; failing to observe the limits of what is permitted or appropriate. Remember, the False Prophets' intent is to *deceive*. A Presumptuous Prophet intent is not to deceive nor are they being influenced by the fear of man like the popular or lying Prophet. However, any true Prophet can prophesy presumptuously if they assume something based on God's previous actions or words.

The Old Testament talks about Prophets who were presumptuous. Let us go to the Book of 2 Samuel to learn more about the difference between a False Prophet and a presumptuous Prophet. We will begin by examining the Prophet Nathan. If you are not familiar with this Prophet, he is one of the Prophets who served under King David's rule. This was the same Nathan that brought a word of correction to David about his sin of sleeping with Bathsheba and killing her husband Uriah.

The Bible speaks of him as one who could be trusted, who heard from the Lord and upheld his Integrity. He was by no means a False Prophet, but the Bible records an instance in which this true Prophet gave a word based off what he thought, without consulting God first. In this passage it starts where

King David had just brought back the Ark of God from the place where it had been resting temporarily, to his place of residence in the city of David. After looking at the beautiful house he lived in, it prompted David's desired to build God a house.

> *"The king summoned Nathan the prophet. "Look," David said, "I am living in a beautiful cedar palace, but the Ark of God is out there in a tent!" Nathan replied to the king, "Go ahead and do whatever you have in mind, for the Lord is with you." 2 Samuel 7:1-3 NLT*

We see here that Nathan gave a word to David without first consulting the Lord. In the next verse, we see where God visited Nathan and gave him the word that He wanted him to give David.

> *"Go and tell my servant David, 'This is what the Lord has declared: Are you the one to build a house for me to live in? I have never lived in a house, from the day I brought the Israelites out of Egypt until this very day. I have always moved from one place to another with a tent and a Tabernacle as my dwelling. Yet no matter where I have gone with the Israelites, I have never once complained to Israel's tribal leaders, the shepherds of my people Israel. I have never asked them, "Why haven't you built me a beautiful cedar house?" 2 Samuel 7:5-7 NLT*

What Nathan said was true. God was with David and had been with him but building him a house was not in God's will. It does not appear that Nathan had any malicious intent to deceive David, but his mistake was that he did not consult God first. As Prophets we must always consult God first. It may have seemed to Nathan that David building God a house was "no big thing" as I have encountered things in my life that I felt like were "no big thing." I am sure we have all made moves and decisions that looked good and thought God would be okay with, only to find out after the fact that was never His will.

Again, we must never get familiar with God that we get to the point where we think we know how He moves. We must always ask for His direction and instruction. Can you imagine a leader coming to you for advice and because that leader has a good reputation, or you may have seen God move in a certain way in their ministry before, assume that it must be the same for now? You give an answer based off of these observations but never consult God. Then, after hearing from the Lord, have to go back and correct yourself.

This would be a difficult position for anyone to be in. But Nathan held his integrity and did the right thing. He went back to David and corrected his mistake. There is a lesson for all of us to learn from Nathans' error. We must always surrender our mind, thoughts, opinions, ideologies, and beliefs to God. Even in the smallest of instances we must consult God. If not, we will form our prophetic words around these assumptions and come out in error.

Jesus while in the wilderness was tempted by the devil. One of the things the enemy tried to get him to do was to tempt God. The enemy used the very Word to try and cause Jesus to go into error. One of which involved the Scripture that states, "He will give His angels charge over you to uphold you that not even your foot would dash against a stone." (**Matthew 4:6**). He wanted Jesus to jump off the top of a high building to prove this. Jesus however being God in flesh discerned that though this was true he was not to test out his power just to prove a point. That was not the will of God.

As Prophet's God honors the words that comes from our mouth. Even in this we don't want to speak carelessly assuming that God will make happen everything that we say. For example, you may encounter a situation where someone is seeking God for healing for a terminal illness. Well based off of certain scriptures we could definitely declare that we are healed in Him. But the reality is there are many illnesses that have led to death. This is seen in believers and unbelievers alike. So how we handle this type of situation is very crucial. What is the Holy Spirit revealing concerning this issue? Does He desire to work a miracle on their behalf or is He showing you that this person will soon die? Speaking presumptuously in these matters could cause devastating results to those involved. Causing unnecessary heartache and disappointment. So, when in doubt always ask.

Prophesying off partial knowledge

> *"Now our knowledge is partial and incomplete, and even the gift of prophecy reveals only part of the whole picture! But when the time of perfection comes, these partial things will become useless." 1 Corinthians 13:9 NLT*

From this Scripture we learn that we prophesy in parts. When God reveals to us information through whatever form, it is always a piece of the picture and not the whole part. Many different denominations and ideologies have been birthed from a piece of revelation and not necessarily the whole picture. This is dangerous and should not be taken lightly as not all things can be understood with just one piece. Revelation must be revealed and increases over time. Subsequently all prophecy is limited to pieces and will continue to be until all is revealed at the return of Christ. That is why we must prophesy *carefully* the piece that we have, being aware that it is limited and be open to further revelation.

Many of the Old Testament Prophets had to prophesy things that they did not fully understand. God gave them a word and it was their job to release what He said. Even the visions that many of the Prophets saw were beyond their time and left them in a state of awe and wonder. Though they did not fully understand everything, and only had a piece of it, it was not their job to try an interpret the fullness of it. It was, however, their responsibility to portray the message and revelation of the part they did receive.

Let's look at the Prophet Daniel for example. In a span of time Daniel had received three major visions from the Lord about times to come. The last one he received left him perplexed to the point where he went into mourning. He refused to eat anything pleasant for three whole weeks as he prayed to God for clarity (**Daniel 10:1-3**).

The things that Daniel saw could not be understood with his natural mind. They were mysteries and had to be revealed. The Lord released the answer to Daniel's prayer the first day he prayed, but the angel that carried Daniel's answer was delayed by the prince of Persia (**Daniel 10:12-14**). Though Daniel received the vision he still had to wait on the *revealing* of that word. This is where many of us fall short. In the waiting process. It is in this time where God produces patience in us and temperance. It is in the place of waiting where we must position ourselves in humility. Daniel positioned himself in this posture, and because of that he received his answer.

Impatience will lead you into presumptuousness

Another characteristic of this type of Prophet is that they are very anxious to release the words that they hear. This is what leads them into presumptuousness.

"Then he added, "Son of man, let all my words sink deep into your own heart first. Listen to them carefully for yourself. Then go to your people in exile and say to them, 'This is what the Sovereign Lord says!' Do this whether they listen to you or not." Ezekiel 3:10-11 NLT

Just like God told Ezekiel, we too must let the word sink deep into our heart so that God can reveal to us the mystery of the thing and bring us into clarity. In all things you want to make sure you get an understanding. Remember, everything that we hear or see is not meant to be released, that is why it is important to receive the word and then wait on the revelation and the application. We will talk more about this subject in the chapter entitled *Receiving Prophetic Revelation*.

Never forget we are receivers of information. We can never assume to know it all. That is God's job. We are not omniscient, He is. It is perfectly fine to not know. Matter of fact it is better to admit you do not know so God can teach you than to pretend to know and be presumptuous. That should take a weight off your shoulders. Though people may come to you expecting you to always have a word, you do not have to succumb to that pressure. Stay in a place of humility and seek God for His revelation and trust that what He desires you to know He will tell you and what He does not He won't.

You may not have the interpretation of every dream, or answer to every mystery and that is ok. There are some things that God is not going to release or reveal to you and that is ok as well. Never go ahead of Him without getting the clarity. Ask God and wait patiently for the answer. When He does release it, then you can move in confidence of the revelation that He does give to you.

The Lazy Prophet

"Never be lazy but work hard and serve the Lord enthusiastically." Romans 12:11 NLT

Now let's look at another demonic identity and that is one of the Lazy Prophet. As my leader began speaking to me about this character flaw the Lord brought me deeper into how we operate under it and its characteristics. What defines this Prophet is the unwillingness to push beyond comfort zones into the deeper things and revelation of God.

Some key characteristics of this type of Prophet are

1. They Lack consistency- only operate from their office part-time
2. Operate from their gifts and not the mantle
3. Impatient – Do not like to wait on the *revealing* of a prophetic word which leads them into presumptuousness
4. Lack maturity and growth

Now let's take a look at a very familiar parable, the five foolish virgins.

In this story there are 10 virgins that are waiting for a wedding party to arrive. They all have their lamps with their oil trimmed but only five of them brought extra oil. Unfortunately, the bridegroom took longer than expected to arrive. By the time they arrived, the five foolish virgins had run out of oil. They asked the other five if they could borrow some of theirs. The wise virgins refuse to share their oil and told them to go to the market and buy more of their own. By the time the foolish virgins came back with the extra oil the bridegroom had already entered the chamber and the door was locked. From this story we can gain the understanding about the importance of preparation. The five foolish virgins fail to prepare properly. They did not expect the bridegroom to tarry. Not only that, they were not willing to go the extra mile but rather expected to receive from those who did.

God is a God of motion

> *"Take a lesson from the ants, you lazybones. Learn from their ways and become wise! Though they have no prince or governor or ruler to make them work, they labor hard all summer, gathering food for the winter. But you, lazybones, how long will you sleep? When will you wake up?" Proverbs 6:6-9 NLT*

We see here that God hates laziness. Why? Because it is not in His nature. God is a God of motion, so much so that God did not even take a rest until He completed all of His work (**Genesis 1-6**). In order for you to complete your work it will require great dedication. Dedication is the quality of being dedicated or committed to a task or purpose. Not only for a Prophet but all five-fold ministry offices. Dedication= time and energy. Paul in his letter to Timothy admonished him not to be lazy but to fully engage in the tasks that were given to him.

Janell Edmondson

"Until I get there, focus on reading the Scriptures to the church, encouraging the believers, and teaching them. Do not neglect the spiritual gift you received through the prophecy spoken over you when the elders of the church laid their hands on you. Give your complete attention to these matters. Throw yourself into your tasks so that everyone will see your progress." 1 Timothy 4:13-15 NLT

Paul was encouraging Timothy to remain faithful and diligent even though he was not there to oversee him. **Diligence** is careful and persistent work or effort, steady, earnest, and energetic effort. The Lord too requires us to take initiative and to be self-starters. This is our responsibility to be self-determined and not wait on others for us to be faithful in that which the Lord has given us. Remember, like the five wise virgins, diligence pays off. What you do behind the scenes matters. Your season of preparation matters. The five foolish virgins had to find that out the hard way.

Not just when we are called

Diligent Prophets are always prepared. God is always speaking, moving and doing something in the earth and He wants to engage us and what He is doing. We should be always sitting, seeking to hear what God has to say. The question is have we proven ourselves to be dependable? Some people believe that the main call of a Prophet is to go around prophesying at different churches, conferences, or events, as I too once had this same perspective, but that is just not the case. In fact, this pandemic has shaken the foundation of many prophetic ministries. As Prophets, we must remember that our purpose is not just to prophesy. There is a lot that is required to carry out our call in its fullness. If we only focus on that aspect, then we missed the point and the purpose of the Prophet.

The Lazy Prophet only prepares if they are called to minister in a service. They are not diligent or prudent. They are not ready in *all seasons*. Whether we have an opportunity to minister in a church setting or not it is important for the Prophet to always be *instant*. We should always be prepared. Sharpening our tools doing self-study, self-development, pruning, learning, and perfecting our craft should be a part of our daily regimen. We must prepare our self to be fit for the master's use. It is what God expects of us and it should be our desire if we desire to become masters of our trade.

"Study to shew thyself approved unto God, a workman that needeth not to be ashamed, rightly dividing the word of truth." 2 Timothy 2:15 KJV

The mantle requires great dedication

Remember, gifts come without repentance. It is not difficult to operate in gifts and charisma, but in order for you to operate from your mantle it will require *great dedication*. Unlike the mantle, the familiar place does not require for you to be consistent in order to operate out of it. It is a place of the old. Where we operate from old word, anointing's, and moves. It is a place where you offer no real sacrifice. The Lord always desired for us to seek Him consistently. God designed us to have a relationship with Him that includes daily communion. In this place of laziness, we do not come to God daily to receive a fresh word. We see this mirrored in the Book of Exodus when the Lord rained down Manna from Heaven in order to feed the children of Israel in the wilderness. (**Exodus 16:4**).

He gave them fresh new bread every day. It was their job every day, except on the Sabbath, to go out and gather the manna. If anything were left over until the next day worms would develop in it. The children of Israel did not understand the revelation of this concept. The Lord was trying to teach them that just like the manna, He was their daily bread and they needed to pursue Him every day in order to receive the new life.

This is the beauty of our relationship with God. That He gives us a fresh new breath every day. When we operate from the familiar place, we become complacent and comfortable with the old revelation and word that we have received. We do not set our ears to hear what He has to say in this new day. We do not come to receive the update because we become content with the former things that He has given us. Eventually just like the manna, our word will become stale and will no longer be acceptable to eat. This is a dangerous place to operate from as God is always moving. Though He himself does not change, there is always new insights, revelations and mysteries waiting to be revealed.

Laziness leads you into presumptuousness

We also must remember that we prophesy in part, but just because you have a part does not mean you have the full understanding. God does not always give us everything at once. As a matter of fact, most of the time He does not reveal everything at once. We can see here and perceive without necessarily putting in effort. When you operate from this Spirit you do not push to receive revelation. You then are tempted to move on the one word or part the Lord has given without getting full *clarity* and *how to apply it*. Those two things are necessary to accurately convey a prophetic word.

Just like we stated previously, when you run without receiving this piece it leads you into *presumptuousness*. Where you assume you understand what God is saying or has showed you, but in reality, you really do not know. Wise Prophets are prudent and always *pray into prophecy* before releasing it. We must seek God and wait at wisdom's door to gain clarity, revelation, and application.

> *"Keep on asking, and you will receive what you ask for. Keep on seeking, and you will find. Keep on knocking, and the door will be opened to you. For everyone who asks, receives. Everyone who seeks, finds. And to everyone who knocks, the door will be opened." Matthew 7:7-8 NLT*

Laziness Leads to demotion

We can learn much about the importance of being diligent in what God gives us from the parable of the three servants (Matthew 25:14). Like the ruler, God gives to us according to our abilities. He knows what we can handle. The first two servants were self-starters, while the third was lazy. He hid his one talent just as the lazy Prophet buries their gifts, not cultivating what they have. In the end he was demoted and the very talent he had was taken away.

> *"But the master replied, 'You wicked and lazy servant! If you knew I harvested crops I didn't plant and gathered crops I didn't cultivate, why didn't you deposit my money in the bank? At least I could have gotten some interest on it.' "Then he ordered, 'Take the money from this servant, and give it to the one with the ten bags of silver." Matthew 25:26-28 NLT*

If you can remember from the previous chapter *Honoring the gifts*, though you are born a Prophet and have different gifts does not mean they flow freely. They need to be cultivated. You must put time and energy into perfecting, maturing, and mastering your gifts. *Mastery* entails comprehensive knowledge or skill in a subject or accomplishment. To be an expert takes effort and consistency. People start off well but then delay themselves because they do not remain consistent. Consistency is what brings growth. Lazy Prophets are inconsistent. They lack consistency in prayer, reading of the Word, and assignments. When one operates under this identity it only hinders their own growth.

Must remain consistent

Let's imagine you have a new plant. You spend time getting the right soil, digging the hole deep enough, making sure it is placed in an area that has enough sunlight, and water it frequently. After much time and care, it finally begins to grow up and bear fruit. You get so excited that you can now enjoy the fruit of your labor. You start extracting the fruit off the tree and eating from it. In your excitement you stop watering it. After a while there will be no more fruit and the plant will wither away. Same with the gift, just because you see it blossoming does not mean you can stop pouring into and developing it. The same dedication and energy that it took for you to get to the level you are at now is the same dedication you will need in order to maintain it. Eventually you will have to add on to it in order for it to increase and expand. If not, after a while you are going to be running on fumes like the foolish virgins and run out of oil.

We never arrive

Some reach a certain point and believe they have "arrived" and do not put in as much effort as they did in the beginning. But what I have found is we never really arrive. Though we grow and mature, we never reach a point where we have no more capacity. This is a vain perception as even in our Christian walk there is always room for growth. There is always higher heights and greater revelation that the father desires to reveal to us if we are willing to seek Him and put in the effort.

The Parking lot Prophet

The next type of Prophet we will discuss is the **Parking lot Prophet**. You may have heard of this term use frequently when describing people who like to give words and counsel outside of the overseeing of their leadership. These words are often given in a private settings through phone calls, or after a church service in the parking lot thus coining the name "Parking lot Prophet." The parking lot Prophet is one who has no accountability. They often release words without getting them checked first.

This demonic identity takes many forms and must be identified early on before it grows into a ferocious fire. It's often in times where a person feels unseen and as if their gifts are being overlooked that they will yield to this identity. Though they may seem very confident in their ability to prophesy, they have no real track record to verify that their words are accurate. These are what my leader calls "Lone Ranger" Prophets. They prefer to work independently. We see this often in prophetic ministries where a Prophet will travel from place to place, town to town, city to city, church to church without any headship or covering, many times leaving a trail of destruction behind them.

Some key indicators that one is operating under this identity is that

1. **They have no Home Base or leadership that they serve under.**

As stated before one of the roles of a Prophet is to bring edification, comfort, and exhortation to the body of Christ (**Ephesians 4:12**). It is important that each five-fold ministry gift is connected to a local body where they are able to serve in this capacity.

"And let us not neglect our meeting together, as some people do, but encourage one another, especially now that the day of his return is drawing near." Hebrews 10:25 NLT

2. **The majority of their prophetic words are released in private without a witness.**

Paul stated in the Book of Corinthians that prophetic words must be *judged*. That is not to say that all prophetic words will be released in a public setting, but it is to say that they need to be checked for accuracy and to ensure that they line up with the Word of God. This is especially true when releasing words concerning personal relationships such as marriages, transitions in ministry including those who are considering leaving one ministry and moving to another, and also releasing words that confirm an individual's calling or gifts.

3. **They feel threatened by the concept of accountability and see it as a place of control.**

The Bible frequently makes distinctions between those who are foolish and those who are wise. A wise person embraces correction and accountability. While a foolish person does not (**Proverbs 9:7-9**). King Solomon was said to be the wisest man that ever lived, but even he had people around him to help guide his decisions (**1 Kings 4:5**). We must not need to be fearful or threatened by accountability because it is a safeguard to help us not go off the right path. When we reject this concept, it shows that there is a place in us that does not like to submit to authority.

"So don't bother correcting mockers; they will only hate you. But correct the wise, and they will love you. Instruct the wise, and they will be even wiser. Teach the righteous, and they will learn even more." Proverbs 9:8-9 NLT

4. **They lack stability and roam wherever they *feel* led.**

When God gives us an assignment, He expects us to produce fruit and see it to its completion. With the parking lot Prophet this is not so because they are trying to find their way on their own. When they come up to difficulties or resistance, they will often switch plans or assume the Lord is *leading* them in a different direction. This is a key indicator that they are not submitting to the authority and voice of God.

Accountability keeps us consistent even in our ministry endeavors. You will often see those who lack accountability be very inconsistent in their building. Producing new plans or ideas sometimes suddenly. This is because God will often use that overseer to help align the Prophet's vision. Though it is true that sometimes God will cause you to change direction or give you new instructions, in the midst of it, his voice is consistent, and you should be able to see at least a pattern of that which He is trying to accomplish in your life for any given season. We must remember that our heart is deceitfully wicked and can deceive us without us being aware of it. All the more reason why having someone watching our blind side is important.

5. **They don't birth into new levels and dimensions**

In the Book of Timothy Paul admonished Timothy not to neglect the gift that was given to him by the laying on of Hands by the Presbytery.

"Do not neglect the spiritual gift you received through the prophecy spoken over you when the elders of the church laid their hands on you." 1 Timothy 4:14 NLT

We see here that God will use those senior leaders to stir up the things that are hidden deep inside of us. With the Parking Lot Prophet, we will often see them come to a place of a spiritual plateau. We must remember that even after one has been *called* and *ordained* to be a Prophet, they will still need that place of development. It is that overseer or senior leader that can help push them into the next dimension of their ministry.

You will often gain the anointing and receive the oil that flows from the head. It is important to serve in order to get the release of this oil. Timothy served and was submitted to Paul. Joshua submitted himself to Moses. Elisha submitted himself to Elijah. The 12 disciples submitted themselves unto Jesus and even Jesus submitted himself unto the father. They all were able to gain and be elevated from the position of service. If one desires to go up, he must first go down and become a servant. It is in the lack of leadership that we see these types of spiritual stagnation.

If you have discovered that you are one that has been operating under this identity, I would have for you to seek the face of God on how you should move forward. Ask Him to give you direction, bring you into his counsel and lead you to your God ordained covering. There is refreshing and restoration waiting for you when we submit to God's authority and do ministry his way.

The Cussing Prophet

The Lord began to speak to me on this next type of Prophet. He said to me "Stay away from the "**Cussing Prophet**." As I begin to inquire of God on this topic, what I found was quite surprising. So, what is the cussing Prophet? The Cussing Prophet is an overly critical and judgmental Prophet. This may very well be one of the easiest identities to operate under. When one is said to be *judgmental* it means they display or have an excessively critical point of view. This type of Prophet does exactly that, especially to those who don't look like them or may have fallen into sin.

Correction in the body

Have you ever seen where someone in Christ, either well known or in a high position had fallen or was caught in some type of scandal? It seems like almost immediately after we see a slew of critical blogs, post or videos concerning the matter. Most of which are casting judgment on the situation often without having all the details or facts. This type of behavior puts the church in a negative light as a body divided against itself surely cannot stand. The Bible talks extensively about correction within the body of Christ, so when and how to we do this?

> *"Dear brothers and sisters, if another believer is overcome by some sin, you who are godly should gently and humbly help that person back onto the right path. And be careful not to fall into the same temptation yourself." Galatians 6:1 NLT*

First, one must be qualified, mature, and do it from a place of humility. There is a place for correction amongst believers, and sometimes open rebukes are necessary (**Proverbs 27:5**), but the heart in which you do it is very important. We see where Paul corrected Peter and called him out on his hypocrisy because he would act one way around the Jews and then another way around the Gentiles (**Galatians 2:11**). This open rebuke was done in a way to reconcile and to set Peter back on the right track. Not to embarrass him.

Unfortunately, the Cussing Prophet's purpose is not to do so. In fact, their motive is to point out the faults and flaws of others in order to make themselves look more righteous. Thus, putting the one who has fallen into an open shame and hindering them from receiving restoration. This is not the heart of Christ. This is not the example the Lord told us to live by.

> *"Your love for one another will prove to the world that you are my disciples." John 13:35 NLT*

When we feel as though it is our job to go around and point out the failures of others, we become just as hypocritical as the Pharisees and Sadducees. They were waiting and watching Jesus but for all the wrong reasons. They were going around looking for anything to cast Jesus in a negative light (**Mark 3:2**). Looking for him to fall or say something so they could bring an accusation against him. Jesus continually rebuked them for their hypocritical ways.

As Prophets we should be an example to the body of Christ to show the love of God and correction in a manner that he would do it in. Yes, there will be times when correction will be needed but it will always fulfill the purpose of Christ which is to reconcile and restore. It will be done in a way that does not bring shame to the body of Christ nor hurt that individual past the point of restoration. It is also important to note that if you are not in a position to help that person into reconciliation or restoration then more than likely your words of criticism are doing more harm than good.

Remember, no one is perfect and under the right circumstances we could find ourselves falling in the same situation of the very person we are trying to judge. The scriptures say for God so loved the world that he gave his only begotten son. This was before the world acknowledge him, knew him, or even loved him. If that love was so great that he was willing to die on the cross for sinners, how much more is his love for one of his children that have backslidden and fallen away.

"Turn, O backsliding children, saith the Lord; for I am married unto you: and I will take you one of a city, and two of a family, and I will bring you to Zion." Jeremiah 3:14 KJV

Jesus loves his children even when they have done wrong. He says he is willing to go as far as leaving the ninety-nine who have not left him, to go after the one who has gone astray (**Matthew 18:12**). This should be the heart of every believer toward their fellow brothers and sisters in Christ. This is the light that the Lord desires his church to shine and not the light of criticism, hypocrisies, or judgment, but rather the light of love, long-suffering and patience (**Jeremiah 31:3**).

Differences of opinion

Another distinction of this type of Prophet is that they have a very critical point of view toward those who may not look or believe like them. In the body of Christ there is an array of different opinions concerning biblical concepts. Depending on what kind of church you grew up in, your background, or even your culture will determine your outlook on certain biblical beliefs. As he began to speak to me about this type of Prophet, he brought to my attention this word *"bigotry."* **Bigotry** is an intolerance toward those who hold a different opinion from oneself. There are many things within the body of Christ that we may call "differences of opinion" that can cause a great separation, and we even see where because of the many differences of opinion, denominations have been birth.

Denominationalism is the division of one religion into separate groups, sects, schools of thought or denominations: the act of categorizing or making a category. Denominations highlight certain truths in the Bible, putting more emphasis on some more than others. Some of what we call denominationalism is actually rooted in man-made tradition rather than biblical truths. Due to these "differences of opinion" certain people become very intolerant of those who do not carry the same beliefs as they do. Some will go as far as even refusing to fellowship with those of different denominational backgrounds.

This is not to say all denominations are wrong or erroneous. The error lies when we allow these differences of opinions to become "walls" that keep us apart. Though this has become very common in the church, it is not at all the heart of God. Even with these different teachings and beliefs the common foundation should be Jesus Christ and that is what binds us together.

"For there is one body and one Spirit, just as you have been called to one glorious hope for the future. There is one Lord, one faith, one baptism, one God and Father of all, who is over all, in all, and living through all." Ephesians 4:4-6 NLT

Intolerance in the Early Church

The place of intolerance and bigotry is not new to the church. As a matter of fact, even the early churches found themselves coming up to these places of disputes. Let's venture into the Book of Romans chapter 14 where Paul talks about these "differences of opinion ".

"Accept other believers who are weak in faith, and don't argue with them about what they think is right or wrong." Romans 14:1 NLT

He talks about those who have strong convictions concerning worshiping on certain days and even eating certain meats. Paul instructed them not to pass judgment on fellow believers who honor God differently than them. I believe here Paul made a distinction between those who are operating under a spirit a religion and those who just simply chose to honor God from a pure conviction.

Paul reminds us that these convictions are not wrong as long as we do it unto God and do not condemn (make a determination that others are not righteous) others if they do not practice under those same convictions. He makes it clear that these types of disputes and intolerances do not display the love of Christ. How we honor God whether it be through the things that we eat or the day we choose to worship him should be recognized as a sacrifice to God. God is the one who sees the heart and will receive that sacrifice.

Zeal can turn into intolerance

Sometimes we can be very zealous, and this zeal can quickly turn into intolerance. We see this pictured in the story of Paul. He thought he was doing God a favor by persecuting The Christians. He was set in his ways and views. It took a divine encounter with Jesus, Paul falling off of his high horse which represents religious pride and zeal, to show Paul God's true nature, purpose and love for humanity. Jesus then sent Paul back to the same ones he persecuted to be a minister unto them.

They are not of us

The disciples also experienced this when they saw a different group from theirs using Jesus' name to cast out demons. They tried to convince Jesus to stop them. However, Jesus would not give in to their ignorance. He said this "If they are not against us than they are for us (**Luke 9:50**). We must remember the mind of God. If it is building His body, then they are for us. But if they go against God's Word, then that should be rejected (**1 John 4:1**).

We must recognize if we are not building the body, bringing believers together, restoring those who may have backslid, or drawing unbelievers to Christ, then we are being a hindrance to the work and move of God. We must always filter our passions through the lens of Jesus and the love of God. This will prevent prejudices and offences from occurring.

"There is neither Jew nor Greek, there is neither slave nor free, there is neither male nor female; for you are all one in Christ Jesus."
Galatians 3:28 KJV

Unity in the body

The Lord is raising up a new breed of Prophets that will not be afraid to cross denominational lines and breakdown barriers to do his Kingdom will and agenda. They will have eyes that are renewed, and the religious scales removed just as Paul did (**Acts 9**). It brings God no glory when his church is divided based on different convictions.

As Prophets we must not give in to the strategy of the enemy to become intolerant to those who may have a different view than us. I am sure all of us have been guilty of this identity. We must ask God to open our eyes and show us our own intolerances, then repent and allow the truth of His Word to reshape our mind.

Prophetic Bully

The way you treat people with your gifts speaks about your character and is very important. As the Lord began to speak to me more intently on character, he revealed to me this next identity which he calls the **Prophetic Bully**. So, what is a *Prophetic Bully*? A Prophetic Bully is any individual who uses their gift to control others by instilling fear and intimidation through the revelation and information they receive from the Spirit.

So how does one become a Prophetic Bully? The Lord began to show me that many people ignorantly come up under this system because they have not been taught how to *govern their gift with grace*. Oftentimes people are afraid of the prophetic because God allows Prophets to see and hear sensitive information, but many have mishandled and abuse this ability. You may have heard one of your favorite preachers use this quote while ministering "Don't make me come down your row." These mishandling's can cause people to be afraid of the prophetic because they do not know what could potentially be revealed about their life.

The purpose of the prophetic should never be used to *instill fear*. We also should not try to *coerce* any one into receiving our prophetic word as well. **Coerce** means to persuade (an unwilling person) to do something by using force or threats. You might say, "That would never be me." But never say never. Many people have used their gifts in the wrong way and were not aware.

The Holy Spirit is Gentle

The Lord will use a Prophet to release sensitive information in their prophecies for multiple reasons. It could be to instruct, correct, or even rebuke. One thing that we must remember that even in this the Holy Spirit is gentle. There are times when he will only allow you to tell information in a private setting, as Jesus did with the woman at the well (John 4). He could not invite the twelve into that space because they were not mature enough yet. They were not ready to handle the word he was about to release to her. This was evident in their reaction when they finally did see Jesus talking with her. See, Jesus's purpose in that encounter was not to expose or to put her to shame, but to deliver her. So, being full of wisdom and compassion, he sent them away so that he could confront her issues in secret and through her deliverance many other people from her hometown came to know and believe on Christ.

To say or not to say

"A talebearer revealeth secrets: but he that is of a faithful spirit concealeth the matter." Proverbs 11:13 KJV

Then there are some things that God will show you and will require you not to say anything because that person is either not mature enough to receive the correction or is not at that point in their deliverance process. For example, the Lord may give you a word for someone about a specific struggle that they are struggling with i.e., lust, but he also revealed to you that they also have pride and unforgiveness. This is where wisdom and grace are needed. Just because the Lord shows you something about an individual does not necessarily means he wants it to be released.

So, then we must consider, what is the Holy Spirit's immediate concern? We can crush someone in their deliverance process by pointing out all their flaws and shortcomings all at once. At that moment God may choose to only be concerned about their immediate struggle with lust. We do not want to be a bully and further crush them by revealing too much too soon. This is not the way of our Lord and savior Jesus Christ. Just as Jesus with the woman at well, He chose to deal with her adulteress lifestyle. That was his immediate concern. I am sure there was more Jesus could have told her about her history, but he knew what was needed to bring her through this first deliverance process. We must also learn to discern the same.

Crossing Boundaries

Then there are times when we can allow our own hearts to move us into bullying someone. What do I mean by this? As God speaks to us about individuals, we can often feel the burden of God's heart for them and the urgent need for them to repent. This was seen through the Old Testament prophetic writings where they pleaded with Israel to turn in order to escape God's judgement. God allows us to carry this burden, but it is sometimes easy to misplace it in that we become overly aggressive with the prophetic word

God gives us. For example, God gives you a word to release to an individual(s), you are obedient and do so, but the person(s) does not receive the word or make the necessary changes. Then out of our own self-will we continue to make attempts to coheres that person to change or receive the word. Often reminding them of the word. The first time was God ordained but the other times were not prompted by the Holy Spirit, but by our own desire.

This is Prophetic Bullying. These repeated attempts are equal to us using our prophetic gift as a stick to beat that individual with to *make them change*. This is not the way of grace. This is actually the way of condemnation because even God himself allows us time to come to our deliverance and does not continuously overload us about how sinful and off we are. Most important to remember he gives us all free will. We must have the heart of Christ to operate our gifts in the way that he would.

Is this to say God will never send you to reiterate a word? No, it is not. Repeated words of warning from God are not uncommon. We see in the Bible where God in his love and mercy would send words of warning to people or peoples who were about to receive God's judgement. He would send a Prophet to warn them and if they would not receive them or made corrections to their behavior then he would send another (**Jeremiah 7:25**). This is because God never wants to destroy anyone. But because he is just, he must bring justice to sin, so then we must discern between the Holy Spirit's *prompting* and our *emotions.*

> *"Therefore, I will judge you, O house of Israel, every one according to his ways, saith the Lord God. Repent, and turn yourselves from all your transgressions; so, iniquity shall not be your ruin. For I have no pleasure in the death of him that dieth, saith the Lord God: wherefore turn yourselves, and live ye." Ezekiel 18:30, 32 KJV*

Then there comes a point where God will stop sending warnings. Yes, there is a cut off point for prophetic warnings. This may not be necessarily a bad thing because he is patient and still gives all of us time to repent, but at the end of the day it is that person's choice to change and God's choice as to what happens if they don't. This is not to say God's grace has run out just because the warnings have stopped. Remember, the Holy Spirit plays a huge part in the conviction process and sometimes God is actually working on the heart of a man even though we don't see the outward manifestation of it yet.

It is to say that you have done your part in the *delivery* process, and in that God is pleased. Though our intentions may seem right, and our heart honestly wants to see the person change, we cannot make the decision for them. If we continue to pursue an individual in this manner, then we have overstepped our boundaries.

We don't have to show or prove that we hear from God

Oftentimes our insecurities will push us into to becoming a Prophetic Bully. When we are unsure of our gift it causes us to overexert it in order to feel validated by others. We must remember that the gifts were not made to make us feel or look good. They were given to the body by God to edify his bride (**Ephesians 4:11**).

Do no harm

As stated before, some words can do more harm than good. It may be that God wants us to pray and intercede for that specific area, cover their sins, or stand as an encourager with them in their deliverance process. We must remember that we are all on a journey to sanctification. This is a process, and we must give those around us the same grace that God gives us. *Word of Wisdom*: Just because we see does not mean we always have to say.

The Tongue of the Learned

We must ask the Lord to give us the tongue of the learned.

"The Lord GOD hath given me the tongue of the learned, that I should know how to speak a word in season to him that is weary: he wakeneth morning by morning, he wakeneth mine ear to hear as the learned." Isaiah 50:4 KJV

The tongue of the learn comes with being sensitive to the Holy Spirit and through experience. The tongue of the learned is the ability to know when to release a word so that it brings a benefit to those that hear it. In the beginning of the training process, we will make many mistakes in this area. But God is patient. He will guide you through if you are willing to yield and be obedient.

The Disobedient Prophet

"But Samuel replied, "What is more pleasing to the Lord: your burnt offerings and sacrifices or your obedience to his voice? Listen! Obedience is better than sacrifice, and submission is better than offering the fat of rams." 1 Samuel 15:22 NLT

Disobedience is failure or refusal to obey rules or someone in authority. A Disobedient Prophet is one who refuses to obey a command that God has given them. We find in Scripture a few Prophets, who at one point in their prophetic ministry operated from this identity.

Jonah – instead of going to warn the people of Nineveh, went in the opposite direction to Tarshish, running away from his assignment.

Elijah – ran from Jezebel and his assignment was given to another.

Jeremiah – refuse to prophesy what the Lord said until it consumed him like fire shut up in his bones.

So, you might ask this question. Why would a Prophet choose to not obey the voice of the Lord? There are a few reasons why one would follow down this road. What I have come to find is generally a Prophet is disobedient in order to preserve him or herself. Sometimes the assignments of the Lord can put us into dangerous situations where we will be persecuted. Many of the Old Testament Prophets faced severe persecution and some even death, but God never promised a persecution free ministry. So then we see that Prophet become disobedient in order to protect themselves. **Protection** is any measure taken to guard a thing against damage caused by outside forces; the state of being kept from loss. **Self-protection** are mechanisms we put in place to ensure our security and well-being.

Humans have a natural desire to feel secure. It is the second level on Maslow's hierarchy of needs. It is natural to try to defend ourselves and the ones that we love, but as believers Jesus teaches us the opposite. He says we should not try to save our own lives. Let's look into the story of Elijah to see the place of self-preservation in action.

> *"When Ahab got home, he told Jezebel everything Elijah had done, including the way he had killed all the prophets of Baal. So Jezebel sent this message to Elijah: "May the gods strike me and even kill me if by this time tomorrow I have not killed you just as you killed them." 1 Kings 19:1-2 NLT*

Jezebel threatened Elijah's life because of what he did to the False Prophets in the previous chapter. Instead of facing a threat head-on and allowing God to fight his battle, Elijah ran from his assignment, leaving his servant behind in order to save his own life. He found a tree to take refuge under and then requested of the Lord to take his life.(**1 Kings 19:3-4**).).

Elijah went straight into self-protection mode. It was not that he wanted to die, as he tried to make it seem, but it was that he did not want to face the battle. He wanted God to have pity on him and take the battle away. He had abandoned his servant and his assignment and went on the run. The Lord showing patience and mercy toward Elijah, sent an angel to feed him. From there Elijah journeyed to Mt. Horeb. There the Lord confronted Elijah.

> *"Elijah replied, "I have zealously served the Lord God Almighty. But the people of Israel have broken their covenant with you, torn down your altars, and killed every one of your prophets. I am the only one left, and now they are trying to kill me, too." 1 Kings 19:10 NLT*

The Lord asked Elijah the same question twice. What are you doing here? Twice Elijah gave him the same reply. Here we see plainly what Elijah's fear was. The fear of persecution. He did not want to end up like the other Prophets who became martyrs while doing the work of the Lord. Unfortunately, God was not looking for Elijah to reply. God already knew why Elijah was there. He also understood the persecution his Prophets were facing for being obedient to their assignments. What the Lord was looking for was Elijah to move into action and finish what he gave him.

The Sacrifice of Obedience

Everything God gives us has a purpose behind it, beyond what are natural eyes can see. That is why we must move beyond our flesh, how our obedience will affect us or how our obedience may seem to others. See, Jezebel was Elijah's assignment, and he had the ability and the authority to take down that demonic stronghold, but obedience is not always easy and often takes sacrifice. This was something that Elijah was not willing to do. His insecurities and fear for his life caused him to abandon the assignment that God gave him.

When faced with difficult assignments from God, we like Elijah try our best to find a way out. The Lord will even test us in these areas to see if we are willing to pay the price to carry his glory. There will be assignments that the Lord gives us that are not clean cut, which do not include words of encouragement and blessings. There are times when we will have to stand against opposition and go against the grain. This will cause us to be ostracized, ridiculed, and rejected. This could come from those close to us or from those in the body of Christ. This is why it is important for a Prophet to first count the cost before choosing to commit to this ministry. It did not turn out well for Elijah in the end because he never fulfilled his assignment. God passed over him and gave it to another, commissioning Elijah to go and anoint Elisha, the very one who would take his place.

Undesired assignments

Another reason why a Prophet would become disobedient is because they do not like the assignment that God gave them. We do not get to choose what type of word we get to release. We also do not get to choose where the Lord sends us to fulfill our assignments. Let us look at Jonah for an example. Jonah was sent to Nineveh and was given the assignment to tell them to repent or God was going to bring judgment. Now to give Jonah some credit, he was being sent into a very hostile territory. The people of Nineveh were Assyrians, known for their barbaric acts. They treated their prisoners more like animals instead of humans. Many would believe this played a part in the reason why he rebelled, but then something unexpected happened and Jonah gives us another reason for his disobedience. In chapter 3, the people of Nineveh repented after hearing Jonah's prophetic word . God then forgave them and turned away his judgement (**Jonah 3:10**).

This was Jonah's response to God's forgiveness.

> *"But Jonah was not pleased at all, and he became angry. He prayed to the Lord and said, "O Lord, is this not what I said You would do while still in my own country? That is why I ran away to Tarshish. For I knew that You are a kind and loving God Who shows pity. I knew that You are slow to anger and are filled with loving-kindness, always ready to*

change Your mind and not punish. So now, O Lord, take my life from me. For death is better to me than life." Jonah 4:4-3 NLT

Jonah had an issue. Unforgiveness. The Assyrians were enemies of the Jews and Jonah knew that if they repented God would forgive them. This was not his desire. He could have wished nothing more than to see God's judgement upon his enemies, but that is not how God saw it.

God saw the people of Nineveh as his creation and not merely an enemy to his chosen people Israel (**Jonah 4-11**). See, Jonah had his own agenda, and this assignment did not fit into it. Seeing the people of Nineveh get off scott free was not a part of Jonas plan, but it was in God's will. Just like Jonah there will be times when God will give us assignments that do not fit into our desires. Having to pray for our enemies or those who persecute us. This is where the real testing takes place. Do we allow our hearts to lead us into rebellion like Jonah or into full submission and obedience to God's will?

There are no small assignments

There are times that God will give us assignments that may seem small in our eyes. This world views success much different than God does. Many times, success to us equates to having a big platform, speaking to large numbers of people, or being connected to people who are well known. But what if God calls you to do something totally different? What if he calls and sends you to a place that is not "popular" or to a people that may seem to you as "insignificant" by their size. What if the assignment God sends you on will not get you fame or recognition from men? Will you still do it? These are the questions that many Prophets and servants of God alike must face every day. This too is an area of testing by God to see where our true motive lies. Are we truly in this for God and what pleases him? Or are we in it for fame, money, or notoriety.

"The sacrifice of an evil person is detestable, especially when it is offered with wrong motives." Proverbs 21:27 NLT

When our heart is not conditioned, re-molded and shaped into the purity of God we will often succumb to the pressure and standards of this world. This will lead us to only go after assignments that we feel will bring us glory, fame, and adoration. This is not at all the heart of God, as he sees every individual life as significant. Whether or not we will receive accolades from that assignment we must remember that God sees our obedience as a sacrificial offering unto him. It is him that we should aspire to please in all things. After all, when we leave this earthly realm and enter heaven it is God who rewards us.

"His lord said to him, 'Well done, good and faithful servant; you were faithful over a few things, I will make you ruler over many things. Enter into the joy of your lord." Mathew 25:24 NKJV

The Prophetic Junkie

The last type of Prophet we will be dealing with in this section is the "Prophetic Junkie." So, what is a Prophetic Junkie and how does one avoid from becoming one. A Prophetic Junkie is someone who hoards prophetic messages. This is what the Bible calls having itchy ears.

"For a time is coming when people will no longer listen to sound and wholesome teaching. They will follow their own desires and will look for teachers who will tell them whatever their itching ears want to hear." 2 Timothy 4:3 NLT

They will go to and fro listening to any and every prophetic declaration or message that comes their way. Most times people succumb to this prophetic hoarding because they are in a desperate search for a "word from the Lord". As Believers we never have to go on a treasure hunt to hear what God has to say. For he has given us a surer Word of prophecy (**2 Peter 1:19**) which is the Word of God. God is always speaking to his people, but many have become lazy and don't seek him for themselves through His Word.

We can apply any biblical prophecy and declare it over our lives. Whether if we are in a time of confusion, we can speak peace according to Isaiah 26. Whether we are facing times of uncertainty Proverbs 3:6 says that if we acknowledge Him in all of our ways, he will direct our path. Even in time a fear he promises to be with us (**Psalm 23**). God has given us a word for every situation that we will face as humans sojourning through this earth. We should endeavor to seek him for the answers to the problems we encounter in our lives.

Using Discernment with prophetic messages

Though we all like to hear an encouraging word once in a while, and God will use his Prophets to speak to the body as a whole, it is very important that we use discernment in what we allow our spirit man to take in. One must remember that there are False Prophets masquerading as true men and women of God (**Matthew 7:15**). Wolves in sheep's clothing whose desire is to do nothing more than to deceive, manipulate and instill fear. They come with false doctrines and teachings that causes us to go away from the truth of God's Word and also gives us a sense of false hope. With this in mind we must not "eat from everyone's table." Doing so will only cause us to become spiritually sick.

God of order

Remember, God is a God of order will often use those around us such as our spiritual leaders or Prophets that reside in our local assembly to speak to us first. We must learn how to eat from the table that God has set for us. Every table that is set is not fit to feed us and like I mentioned before, eating from the wrong table can make you spiritually sick. God is not an author of confusion.

If you begin to receive instruction for your life from your local assembly and then begin to hear messages on social media or online that are contrary it can cause confusion and hinder the progression of what God desires for you. Many times, it is not that the prophetic word is inaccurate or not from God, but it could be that it is just not what God is speaking to you for this season in your life. This is where we must use our spiritual weapons of discernment and accountability in order for God to confirm what is for us and what is not.

A child of God needs not to become desperate for a word from God as God is always willing and available to speak to his children. Whether it be through prayer, His Word, your leader, your local assembly, or a word that he will bring to you himself. I do not want to confuse you to think that God will not use outside sources to give you instructions or direction but always know that it will be in alignment with what God has already spoken to you.

No mixed messages

This is also true for a Prophet. Not all Prophets are mature enough to discern what is good or what is bad. What is being prophesied from one's soulish realm and what is being prophesied from the Spirit of God. There are even some true prophetic words that God will not want his Prophet to hear. Why is this? It could be that the Lord desires for the Prophet to gain the revelation straight from his mouth. This helps the Prophets ear to become in tune with him and to discern when it is him speaking.

There are also times when the Lord could be revealing information to a Prophet and if they begin to listen to similar prophecies, it can cause confusion and that Prophet will come out with a *mixed message*. What does that look like? A prophetic word that has a portion of what God was trying to relate to them and also the things that they heard from other sources. Though the word is "accurate" it still may not be the direction that God was trying to take them or the revelation that he was trying to release to them, but because they heard it before getting clarity, they assume that was the finishing piece that God was trying to release.

Again, this is not the case in all times as we prophesy in part and God will use other prophetic voices to confirm his word and piece together the whole picture. This is why discernment is imperative. There'll be times when God will have you in a season where he calls you in a place of seclusion. Causing you to shut everything down, for you to put your ear to his heart to hear what he has to say. If our wombs are filled with too many other prophetic words, it could cause an interruption in the receiving of the revelation that he wants to give us.

Many times, especially in the development process, God will designate certain voices in your life for you to listen to. These voices are those that can be trusted and will nurture you in your immature state. This could include those you are familiar with as well as some from outside your local community. These are the ones that God has designated to speak to you in this season of your life so *embrace this select group of individuals.* Tune in to the words that he will speak through them and do not allow the itching of the ear or anxiousness to cause you to heap up prophetic words. If you do, you will then have to go through a place of spiritual detox in order to flush out what was of God and what was not. If you have been struggling with this identity pray and ask the Lord to reveal to you the designated people that he has placed in your life. Ask Him to teach you the true role that the prophetic voices were meant to have in your life. Pray for the desire to seek Him in a greater way so that you can hear His voice clearly through His Word for yourself.

Receiving Prophetic Revelation

The Lord uses many different ways to speak to his Prophets. Therefore, the way we all receive prophetic revelation will be different. Some may come through hearing, other visions and dreams, the reading of Scripture, experiences and so on. Oftentimes these words are like pieces of puzzles that you receive bit by bit. Until it all finally comes together, and you received the *revelation* or *insight* of what God is trying to relay to you. This happened many times in the Bible where God used imagery, metaphors, hyperboles, and analogies all to explain to the Prophet his message (**Ezekiel 12:3**). Let's look at one example from the Book of Jeremiah chapter 13.

In this passage the Lord instructed Jeremiah to go buy a loincloth (underwear) and wear them but to not wash them.

"So I bought the loincloth as the Lord directed me, and I put it on." Jeremiah 13:2 NLT

Then he instructed him to take the loincloth and hide it in a hole in the rocks by the Euphrates River. From the outside this could look very strange because the Lord had not given Jeremiah any revelation behind the instructions that he gave him. This is the same with many prophetic words that God will give us. At first, they may seem uncorrelated to one another and not make much sense. But Jeremiah was obedient and continued to do what God instructed him. After some time had passed, in verse 6, the Lord told Jeremiah to go and remove the loincloth from the rocks where he had hidden it. By this time, it was rotting and no longer usable. Then finally in verse 8 Jeremiah received the insight behind the instructions God gave him.

"Then I received this message from the Lord: This is what the Lord says: This shows how I will rot away the pride of Judah and Jerusalem." Jeremiah 13:8-9 NLT

God went on to explain that just like the loincloth he made Israel to cling to him, but they refused to listen. Instead, they chose to follow their own desires serving other gods and stubbornly refusing to serve the Lord. This was the insight that the Lord was trying to relay through the use of the rotted loincloth. Though Jeremiah received this *Revelation* it was still not the *message* that the Lord wanted Jeremiah to give to the children of Israel. He doesn't give him the message to release until verse 12.

"So tell them, 'This is what the Lord, the God of Israel, says: May all your jars be filled with wine.' And they will reply, 'Of course! Jars are made to be filled with wine!' "Then tell them, 'No, this is what the Lord means: I will fill everyone in this land with drunkenness—from the king sitting on David's throne to the priests and the prophets, right down to the common people of Jerusalem. I will smash them against each other, even parents against children, says the Lord. I will not let my pity or mercy, or compassion keep me from destroying them." Jeremiah 13:12-14 NLT

The *Revelation* was for Jeremiah, but the *message* was for the people. We must have understanding of what part of our prophetic words are meant to be shared and what is just for us. There are many things that the Lord would share with the Prophet, but from that not everything was meant to be *published* to the people (**Jeremiah 46:14, Amos 3:9**).The Lord may give you a word of warning through a dream but it may be that he only wants you to release the *message* or interpretation and to not share the details of the vision.

Made to carry Revelation

See, a Prophet's womb has been created to be able to receive words but then we must wait for the interpretation, insight, and revelation. Prophets' wombs were made to receive prophetic information and then digest it so that it is broken down to a form that is understandable for the people. We must allow that word to breakdown and mature in our wombs so that we can fully understand what God is saying. Once we received the revelation, we must ask God what part of this information if any needs to be released. Not everyone can understand the way in which God speaks to us and if we release too much information it can cause confusion. You don't want to go around like a loose cannon sharing every dream, vision, or Revelation the Lord shows you.

> *"Then he added, "Son of man, let all my words sink deep into your own heart first. Listen to them carefully for yourself. Then go to your people in exile and say to them, 'This is what the Sovereign Lord says!' Do this whether they listen to you or not." Ezekiel 3:10-11 NLT*

The part of the word behind the revelation that God desires for his people to know is called the *main message.* Once we receive this, we must ask him what the best way is to *release* it so that the hearers can properly *apply* what it is God is saying or requesting of them. We must "make it plain" so that those who hear can run with the message. Words saturated in revelation can cause more harm than good because it does not give them the opportunity to fully comprehend and then act on the word .If the word is alignment, then what exactly is God saying is out of alignment. If he is calling for repentance, what areas have we missed the mark. If it is blessings, what forms of blessings should they expect (tangible, spiritual) and so forth.

Also remember we prophesy in part, so there will be times when you only have partial information that you have to work with. Even in this we must make it as clear as possible so that it will benefit and edify the receiver. These four steps are important for every prophetic word; receiving the **information**, obtaining the **revelation** (insight), understanding the **main message** and how to *deliver it.* Once we master this process, we will be on our way to releasing the right word, in the right form, that is easily understood by the hearers.

Prophetic Accuracy

"So a prophet who predicts peace must show he is right. Only when his predictions come true can we know that he is really from the Lord."
Jeremiah 28:9 NLT

Whether you are an ordained, activated, one who has been told that you are a Prophet, or just coming into the realization that you have a call on your life, the topic of prophetic accuracy is one that you must hone in on. Walking in the prophetic office means we hear from God, speak for God, give warnings, instructions, and counsel as the Spirit leads us. With that being said if it is the Spirit of God leading us to speak then that prophetic word should come to pass right? Right! In fact, one of the marks of the Prophet is that their word comes to pass. This is where the topic of prophetic accuracy comes into play. Let's dig in.

"I will raise up a prophet like you from among their fellow Israelites. I will put my words in his mouth, and he will tell the people everything I command him. I will personally deal with anyone who will not listen to the messages the prophet proclaims on my behalf. But any prophet who falsely claims to speak in my name or who speaks in the name of another god must die. But you may wonder, 'How will we know whether or not a prophecy is from the Lord?' If the prophet speaks in the Lord's name but his prediction does not happen or come true, you will know that the Lord did not give that message. That prophet has spoken without my authority and need not be feared." Deuteronomy 18:18-22 NLT

In the Old Testament we see there was harsh punishment for those Prophets who prophesied falsely in God's name. Here we see God not only warns the people about failing to heed to the Prophets words, but also warned those Prophets about the consequences of prophesying without God's authority and taught the people how to discern the difference.

For further Clarity let's read that last verse in the King James version.

"When a prophet speaketh in the name of the Lord, if the thing follow not, nor come to pass, that is the thing which the Lord hath not spoken, but the prophet hath spoken it presumptuously: thou shalt not be afraid of him." Deuteronomy 18:22 KJV

Note the word used here is "presumptuously ". This word in its original form does not have the same meaning as we spoke of before in the chapter "The Presumptuous Prophet". Here the word presumptuous means **Pride** which is Insolence; arrogance (rude and disrespectful behavior). This word literally means to boil or to seethe up. In this case the Prophet is not acting in ignorance but rather speaking boastfully in pride. Those Prophets who acted in this manner were abusing their authority and were to be put to death.

This may seem extreme to many, but this punishment was not meant to detour the Prophets from prophesying but rather for them to have a reverent fear for the Word of God. With God everything is about the heart. He looks at the heart and intent of a man when he is doing anything. It is easy for one to become boastful and arrogant getting carried away and speaking things that are contrary to God's will. Or neglect to consult God before we speak. When we become overconfident, proud or arrogant in our position or call then we run the risk of boiling and seething up. This is a place where God is displeased. So, we see in both the Old and New Testament that in these cases the people had a right to hold the Prophets accountable for their words.

Developing a good track record

There is a common misconception that if you miss or give an inaccurate word that you are not a Prophet. This is not the case at all, in fact your accuracy matures overtime as you grow with God, learning his voice and the way that he speaks to you. This however does not happen overnight.

"As Samuel grew up, the Lord was with him, and everything Samuel said proved to be reliable. And all Israel, from Dan in the north to Beersheba in the south, knew that Samuel was confirmed as a prophet of the Lord." 1 Samuel 3:19-20 NLT

As the Prophet Samuel grew up and his words came to pass, he built what I like to call a **prophetic track record**. This is a consistent record of accurate prophetic words. This is what the people will look at to prove that your words are reliable. Though it helps you gain credibility it is not a required means for man to *affirm* (validate) you as a Prophet, but rather it is more like a tree bearing fruit. Your accuracy *confirms* that you are a Prophet. This is the fruit that you bear. It speaks to what is already true.

Staying at his feet

So how do you become an accurate Prophet? It is a process, and that process takes time, patience, practice, training and making mistakes along the way. However, one of the first and most important steps in developing accuracy is the fear of God. In order for you to prophesy accurately you will have to have a level of humility and a healthy reverential fear of God. Remember, the fear of God is the beginning of all wisdom. Those who fear God have a life that is submitted to his will. This includes having a right perception of God, his holiness, righteousness and who he is. Secondly, we must be in constant communication with him in order to receive the revelation and learn how to discern his voice. This will cause you to more easily interpret *when* he is speaking to you and *what* he is speaking to you.

This essential place of constant communication for prophetic accuracy is prayer. This is your oil. Remember, in order to hear the words we must receive his counsel (**Jeremiah 28**). This is not something that we can just pull down out of the air at will. If you don't want to pervert your gifts and speak out of the soulish realm you must live in the presence of God. The fear of the Lord, prayer, worship and staying in the Word keeps us fresh and accurate.

Learning how God speaks to you

"Samuel did not yet know the Lord because he had never had a message from the Lord before." 1 Samuel 3:7 NLT

As we see in the case of the Prophet Samuel when God first spoke to him, he did not recognize his voice as being the Lord's. We see through Scripture as time went on Samuel learned God's voice. Depending on how God relays his information to you will determine the length of time for you to mature in accuracy. Those who hear God's audible voice like Samuel, may come more quickly into understanding while those who receive visions or deal more heavily in revelation may take a bit longer.

<u>Why we can miss</u>

We are receivers of information and sometimes that information can be misunderstood. You may understand God to be speaking of something very specific when he may be speaking something more broadly. In these learning areas are where a Prophet can easily misinterpret what God is saying. It is the place between *receiving* and *perceiving* revelation. It's not that you don't see or hear but rather you have not matured in your perception. Remember, it is in the perception that we process, interpret and understand a thing. God is not in the business of rushing our process so neither should we. Give it time, God will mature you. Stay at his feet. Keep your ears to his heart and as you learn his voice you will grow in accuracy just as Samuel did.

False information

One can easily give a false prophetic word if they try to interpret something that did not originate from God. For example, dreams, visions, or information that does not come from God. Remember, we have a soul, and the mere busyness of life can cause soulish dreams. These can also originate from demonic spaces, us trying to operate from our gifts, divination, suspicion or even superstition.

When one tries to interpret and then speak on this false information this leads to soothsaying. If one mistakes a soulish dream as a spirit given one and seeks to interpret it the results can be devastating. As we mature, we began to filter what God is saying more easily. Deciphering from that which comes from our soulish realm, desires, ideologies, beliefs and that of what God is speaking to us. This is where prayer and prophetic accountability will be your safeguard.

We must also understand the enemy disguises himself as an Angel of light and will oftentimes seek to mimic God's voice or the way you receive revelation. Again, if we perceive these false voices to be true then they will cause us to prophesy inaccurately. Suspicion is one of the major pitfalls of a Prophet and arises from a place of impatience and will cause us to miss. Our flesh, wrong motives and desires can also trick us into believing something that is not true. God will often use this area to train us in our discernment.

This is why you must give yourself room for mistakes. You will make mistakes. It is in our mistakes that we learn the most, it also keeps us humble and provides us with an opportunity for growth. What I have also learned is that in the pursuit of perfection is where we miss the most. When we overanalyze what God is speaking, or delay releasing words for fear of failure. This is pride and can hinder our ability to hear from God accurately.

Am I saying we should go around carelessly releasing words in hopes to get one right? Certainly not. There are times that we will miss. We are human and prone to error, but that, should not stop us from striving to have an accurate track record. Not for our own image or in our own strength, but with the help of the Holy Spirit and for his namesake. Having a good prophetic track record not only makes us credible but it is also a part of our prophetic integrity. We should strive to be Prophets of great character that speak only things we know to be true.

Factors to Prophetic Manifestation

"People scoff at me and say, "What is this 'message from the Lord you talk about? Why don't your predictions come true?"
Jeremiah 17:15 NLT

It is important to note that there are contingencies to prophecy as well. Just because a Prophet prophesies something and it does not come to pass does not mean that Prophet missed. We must remember there are many variables that play a part in the word coming to pass. Some prophecies require human cooperation for them to come to pass. When they don't it may seem as if a Prophet prophesied inaccurately, but this is not the case.

Some contingencies in prophesy include

Prayer

Obedience

Repentance

Time

Like we learned in a previous chapter, every prophetic word is not set in stone. Though God does not repent in a sense, we can touch God's heart and remove judgment through a repentant heart. There are many instances noted in Scripture where a prophetic word was reversed due to that individual(s) repenting. Hezekiah was given a word by the Prophet Isaiah to get his house in order because he was about to die. He was able to obtain the mercy of God by bringing God into remembrance of all the sacrifice he had made for him. After delivering the word the Prophet Isaiah was sent back by God to Hezekiah.

> *"But before Isaiah had left the middle courtyard, this message came to him from the Lord: Go back to Hezekiah, the leader of my people. Tell him, 'This is what the Lord, the God of your ancestor David, says: I have heard your prayer and seen your tears. I will heal you, and three days from now you will get out of bed and go to the Temple of the Lord. I will add fifteen years to your life, and I will rescue you and this city from the king of Assyria. I will defend this city for my own honor and for the sake of my servant David."* 2 Kings 20:4-6 NLT

The word of the Lord for Hezekiah was "set your affairs in order," then his prayer changed the outcome. This was not an isolated incident. After king Ahab killed Naboth while acting under the influence of his wife Jezebel, the Lord sent the Prophet Elijah with the word for them both (**1 Kings 21**). The prophecy declared that God would send disaster on his family and all his male descendants, but after hearing the prophecy Ahab response was unlike those he had displayed before. This time he humbled himself before God. Though God did not totally undo his Word, he showed him grace in that the destruction would not come in his lifetime (**1 Kings 21:28**). Just like Hezekiah, he received another Word from the Lord.

Our change of heart can change God's heart, our posture of humility can take away judgment. This works both ways as we have seen God promise David that if his descendants served and obeyed him that he would establish his dynasty and that someone from his line would always serve as king. (**1 Kings 9:5**). However, David's son Solomon did not heed God's warning. When he became king, he allowed his many wives to sway his heart into serving other Gods. God kept his promise, and the kingdom was rented from Solomon.

> *"The Lord was very angry with Solomon, for his heart had turned away from the Lord, the God of Israel, who had appeared to him twice. He had warned Solomon specifically about worshiping other gods, but Solomon did not listen to the Lord's command. So now the Lord said to him, "Since you have not kept my covenant and have disobeyed my decrees, I will surely tear the kingdom away from you and give it to one of your servants." 1 Kings 11:9-11 NLT*

Time tells

> *"This vision is for a future time. It describes the end, and it will be fulfilled. If it seems slow in coming, wait patiently, for it will surely take place. It will not be delayed." Habakkuk 2:3 NLT*

Many times, prophecies are not for the present, sometimes not even for our lifetime. Many of the Prophet Isaiah's prophecies dealt with the coming Messiah, and some even spoke to the end times. I am sure as Isaiah prophesied, he did not realize how much of what he said was for now, the future or which prophetically spoke to both. Much of what he spoke he never actually got to see "come to past." In these instances, it may seem like your prophecy is off. It is not the case at all, that prophecy is just not for now. So what God was speaking in the Book of Habakkuk was "Just because it hasn't happened *yet* does not mean it is not going to happen at all. One must have faith to believe God even if we don't see it and prophesy anyhow. These are just a few examples of the many conditional aspects to prophecy.

Practice makes perfect

Another key aspect of accuracy is actually practicing. With anything you do if you want to master it, it will take practice. God himself will provide opportunities for you to practice your craft. Most times it will start in your local body or maybe with those closest to you like your family and friends. Training is a necessary component of developing accuracy and it takes time. Remember, God is a trainer, and he will train your senses to know his voice like he did with Jeremiah before he sends you out. You will not be commissioned as a novice so don't attempt to rush this process. The Lord will only send you out when he knows that you are capable and ready to fulfill the task.

Give yourself space

Oftentimes it is those who have never given a prophetic word let alone an accurate one who will be most critical of the prophetic. Skeptics love to criticize what they don't fully understand. I have rarely heard of a true Prophet call out or criticize another Prophet when they miss or incorrectly interpret revelation. Why is this? This is because a true Prophet knows the process. God brings us into his classroom for us to learn and grow and just as it is in the natural, so it is in the Spirit. As you learn you will make mistakes, get some not so good grades, have to repeat some tests, or maybe even have to relearn some information. God gives us the grace to do all of this as he trains us.

A mature Prophet understands this place and will help facilitate that less mature Prophet into better understanding, helping to right the wrong instead of finding fault. We are humans prone to error. Do not allow the criticism of man to discourage you from prophesying or stunt your growth. Your voice is important. Keep moving, growing, and learning and as you do you will be skilled and grow in accuracy.

Delivering a Hard Word

Not all words that the Lord will give you to release will seem favorable for the receiver. There are times when you will have to release words of judgement, correction, alignment, warning, and calls to repentance. These are what I call **hard words**. Though they may not be the easiest words to release, it is necessary for a Prophet to become comfortable with delivering these types of words in wisdom and in love. If not, we will cause people to walk in ignorance, receiving God's wrath and the blame will be put on our shoulders.

> *"If I warn the wicked, saying, You are under the penalty of death, but you fail to deliver the warning, they will die in their sins. And I will hold you responsible for their deaths." Ezekiel 3:18 NLT*

God's will, as seen throughout biblical history is to draw the hearts of men back to him. In God's Love and mercy he sends warning and words of correction in order for us to escape his judgements. His judgments are a byproduct of his righteousness. God would not be righteous if he did not judge sin.

Delivering a balanced word

Prophets of the Old Testament were very familiar with having to deliver these types of words. If you spend any length of time in prophetic ministry, you will as well. Even when delivering hard words, the Lord will always leave room for a place of reconciliation and repentance. We see this concept in the Book of Revelation where the Apostle John wrote letters to the seven churches of Asia minor. Many of these churches received strict words of rebuke, but along with the rebuke Jesus gave them room to right their wrong.

There will be times where the word is just an announcement of judgement that is inevitable, but you should always leave room for hope. Who knows maybe their repentance and humbling of themselves can change God's mind?

"Perhaps they will listen and turn from their evil ways. Then I will change my mind about the disaster I am ready to pour out on them because of their sins." Jeremiah 26:3 NLT

When delivering a hard word, one must carefully consider different factors. First, what is God's heart concerning this matter. Why is God sending you to release the judgments or correction? What is his desired outcome? Are there adjustments that can be made in order to correct the wrong? Can repentance change the outcome? What is God desiring or requiring from this person(s), or place. All of these factor into the message you will release.

Don't Sugar Coat

Never add to God's word. Adding to God's word in order to provide a cushion or relief to a wound is dangerous. Omitting parts of a word is also considered compromising. We must remember partial obedience is still disobedience. Should we speak the truth in Love? Quite certainly we should, but there is a difference between speaking the truth in love and sugar-coating God's word in order to make it more tolerable to the hearer.

Clear communication is also key when giving prophetic words. We must make plain what God is communicating to the hearer without adding to it. The Bible says that we should let our yes be yes and our no be no. Anything other than that comes from the evil one (**Matthew 5:27**). When God speaks to us there is no need to assume or try to interpret beyond what he has given. We say what he gives us and leave the rest up to God to reveal when he sees fit.

Then one must carefully consider how and when to release this word. You want the delivery to be concise. As with all prophetic words how it is released is important. Is this an open rebuke or something that should be done in a private setting? Do you need a witness to the word? Does this require face to face delivery or can it be done by other means such as a phone call or text message. Leave no room for error or misinterpretation. You want to be firm but not come off as arrogant, judgmental, or apathetic.

Speak God's Truth no matter the cost

> *"That these people are stubborn rebels who refuse to pay attention to the Lord's instructions. They tell the seers, "Stop seeing visions!" They tell the prophets, "Don't tell us what is right. Tell us nice things. Tell us lies. Forget all this gloom. Get off your narrow path. Stop telling us about your 'Holy One of Israel." Isaiah 30:9-11 NLT*

We must remember that we will face opposition. Especially when releasing words of correction or alignment. Let's just be honest, flesh does not like to be corrected. We see even in the Old Testament where the people did not want to hear the true word of God from the Prophet but instead wanted to hear "nice things." They'd rather hear a lie that would give them momentary relief than to hear the truth that would help them in the long run.

So it is also in this time. Many people would rather hear good things. Words of blessings and prosperity than to hear the judgment and correction of God. This is not to say that all encouraging words are considered *trend prophesying* as all of God's blessings and promises in Scripture apply to his bride and can be received as such (**2 Timothy 3:16**). However, as Prophets we should be carriers of God's message in whatever capacity that may be. We must tell the people the truth whether they want to hear it or not. Whether they accept it as truth or not, it is our duty.

<u>Governing the Prophetic</u>

The Apostle Paul spoke about the releasing of prophetic words in a public setting.

> *"Remember that people who prophesy are in control of their spirit and can take turns. For God is not a God of disorder but of peace, as in all the meetings of God's holy people." 1 Corinthians 14:32-33 NLT*

Many times, we see the Holy Spirit as a force that does not allow us to control ourselves, but this is not true. Yes, an unction can feel overwhelming, but we still have self-control. As Prophets and prophetic people, we must do things in decency and in order. Every house will function differently so one must learn what is considered out of order and what is not. When another minister is speaking, if we hear a word and are confident that it is something God wants us to release, then one must *wait their turn*. The prophetic can seem very vibrant at times to say the least, but Paul shows us that even in the unction to prophesy we have the ability to govern our own spirits.

This holds true not only for a church setting but for the outside as well. You may be prompted in the grocery store to give a word of comfort. You don't have to start speaking in tongues shouting "Thus sayeth the Lord!" This would be very unseemly and probably make the person receiving the word uncomfortable. You can release a word without drawing a scene or bringing attention to yourself. Jesus was a perfect example of this. He was very gentle in his approach, sensitive where needed. He sat and prophesied to the woman at the well so effortlessly it was like he was having a casual conversation with her (**John 4**). So, if Jesus could do it so can we.

Sometimes a Prophets' spirit can be stirred up by another Prophet while they are prophesying. In that we begin to receive all sorts of prophetic downloads and revelation. That does not necessarily mean that word needs to be released. It is just the prophetic bubbling inside of you. I have experienced this on many occasions. What I have found is that if I am patient the person who is ministering will end up saying the same word I received. If not, I can either pray and ask God for an opportunity to speak or wait on wisdom for the proper timing to interject. Again, it may not need to be said publicly. We must learn to discern the difference.

You have the right to remain silent

"The secret of the LORD is with them that fear him; and he will shew them his covenant." Psalms 25:14 KJV

Silence is not usually a word you hear associated with a prophetic gift or calling. As Prophets and prophetic people, it is our calling to speak, declare and to proclaim the word of the Lord and what God desires to do in the earth. But I want to show you something that the Lord taught me on the gift of silence. There are times when God will bring you into his secret space and show you things about individuals; things that will happen in the future and will require you not to tell a soul. These are called *God's secrets,* and this is something that I had to learn coming up as an undeveloped Prophet.

As the Lord begins to elevate you and show you things in the Spirit, at first it can be overwhelming. You may have a slew of emotions, excitement, fear, confusion, and nervousness. This was my experience as well. Not knowing what I should do with what I was seeing, I would immediately come out of my prayer closet or wake up from my vision and share. This was in my innocence and ignorance that I did such things.

At first some things he would show me were very heavy and I needed clarity so I would just write them down and wait. Then there were other times when I would experience visions in such an intense way that it would burden me to the point where I felt like I needed to release it. After doing this many times with my spiritual leader, she came back to me with instructions. She had been in prayer and the Lord told her that some things he was going to release to me I would have to hold them in my prophetic womb and not tell anyone. This is how I learned of God's *secrets*.

> *"Surely the Lord GOD will do nothing, but he revealeth his secret unto his servants the prophets." Amos 3:7 KJV*

Secrets

There are things you will see, hear and experience that are not to be shared. Let us look at one vision the Apostle John had when he was exiled on the island of Patmos.

> *"Then I saw another mighty angel coming down from heaven, surrounded by a cloud, with a rainbow over his head. His face shone like the sun, and his feet were like pillars of fire. And in his hand was a small scroll that had been opened. He stood with his right foot on the sea and his left foot on the land. And he gave a great shout like the roar of a lion. And when he shouted, the seven thunders answered. When the seven thunders spoke, I was about to write. But I heard a voice from heaven saying, "Keep secret what the seven thunders said, and do not write it down." Revelation 10:1-4 NLT*

God reveals his secrets to those he can trust. God allowed John to hear the mystery of what the seven thunders said but instructed him to keep it a secret. God is all wise and would not reveal this to John if he knew he could not handle the responsibility.

Secret prayers

Then there are times when the Spirit of the Lord will show you very sensitive things about people for the sole purpose of intercession. This is where your secret closet comes into play. These assignments may not even be intended to share in group intercession. Though corporate intercession is important, there are times when heaven will engage you in private missions where you must remain *silent in intercession*. He will have you intercede for a person, group of people, state, or country in order for his will to be accomplished and the plan of the enemy to be disannulled.

These are our *rights to remain silent*. These are the moments when the Spirit of God will *arrest you* for an assignment. Silent engagement with heaven to fulfill its agenda. This is where you *pray more and talk less*. What do I mean by this? There will be times on your assignment when it seems as though the total opposite of what you are praying for is occurring. Especially if you are praying for a particular person's deliverance.

This can be a difficult process, but you must remain diligent and intensify your prayer until you see the manifestation of what God said. A Prophet must be matured in this area to be able to hold and house the secrets of God without having to release everything that they see. These secrets must remain so, even after manifestation. There will be many prophetic things that the Lord will show you and when you see them come to past you must continue to hold your tongue. The enemy and our flesh will tempt us to release information in order for us to feel validated, but we must resist. This is maturity, this is humility, this is patience, this is a place of being trustworthy.

<u>Sensitive Information</u>

Everyone is not able to house nor are they spiritually mature to understand certain things that the Lord will show you. This is also true for intercession. In the instance that you need the power of agreement in prayer, you must use discernment with whom you choose to partner with. There are some prayer assignments that everyone may not need to be privy to. You can do more harm than good if you open weighty things to an immature believer. This could damage their faith or hinder them from coming into the deeper things of God. In this case maturity level is important and we must be careful not to be a stumbling block with our prophetic gift.

Time sensitive

"But you, Daniel, keep this prophecy a secret; seal up the book until the time of the end, when many will rush here and there, and knowledge will increase." Daniel 12:4 NLT

Then there will be some things that the Lord will show you that is for a future time and not meant to be released in the present moment (**Mark 9:9**). It is time sensitive and if you release it prematurely it can cause more damage than good. Some things the enemy does not know and is not aware of unless we speak it. He is privy to some information but not all.

"But he said, "Go now, Daniel, for what I have said is kept secret and sealed until the time of the end. Many will be purified, cleansed, and

refined by these trials. But the wicked will continue in their wickedness, and none of them will understand. Only those who are wise will know what it means." Daniel 12:9 NLT

Remember, God is omniscient, he knows all things about the past, present and future. The devil is not. This is a place where you must grow in wisdom and ask God for understanding to discern between what is a *secret*, what was *confidential*, what was *sensitive information*, what needed to be shared publicly for the purpose of *intercession*, and what was meant to be prophesied publicly before the people. Just like in the army, there are levels a confidentiality. Something's only high-ranking officials can be briefed on. Some things are top secret. And something's are just for those inside of the service and are not to be known by civilians.

<u>Confidential</u>

Some things are not secrets but are considered *confidential information* and they are not to be shared with everyone. There are some things that you will only reveal to your leader or prophetic mentor to get clarification, instructions, or directions. This happened a lot in the beginning when I would begin to receive mysteries from God. There will come a point in time when the Lord begins to deal with you in ways that you are not use to. This is the place where you go to your leader for guidance.

There are some things that God will show you that may seem very strange to you but may not be strange to a more seasoned Prophet. Again, this is why accountability is important. I remember when I experienced this as well. A new revelation of God that I had not known or experienced before. Quite frankly it frightened me. I did not want to totally dismiss it so after a while I took it to my leader, and she began to confirm to me that yes, this was of the Lord. Even after receiving this new revelation from my leader, I knew that this was not something that needed to be shared with others. This takes some time to develop your discernment to know what is and is not ok to share, but take heart, God makes allowances for our growth process. As long as we are not purposely testing him to see what we can get away with. Again, always be accountable and try your best to use discretion in these matters.

Governing His Influence

In this chapter we will discuss the power of God's influence and how we should govern it. **Influence** is the capacity or power of persons or things to be a compelling force on or produce effects on the actions, behavior, opinions, etc., of others. As Prophets we will all have a certain sphere of influence that we operate under. It is that which the Lord gives us to fulfill our assignments. There are some Prophets whose ministries maybe on a larger scale compared to others. This has nothing to do with them being better but has everything to do with the grace God has given them, the influence that they carry, and the people God has called them to reach. This influence has the ability to either affect someone negatively or positively. Due to this fact we must be careful how we govern it.

"For we speak as messengers approved by God to be entrusted with the Good News. Our purpose is to please God, not people. He alone examines the motives of our hearts. Never once did we try to win you with flattery, as you well know. And God is our witness that we were not pretending to be your friends just to get your money! As for human praise, we have never sought it from you or anyone else." 1 Thessalonians 2:4-6 NLT

An ambassador is an accredited diplomat sent buy a country as its official representative to a foreign country. These ambassadors must carry themselves in a way that brings honor and dignity to the country that they represent. Anything that they do while in the foreign country could affect their native country either in a positive or negative way. When we choose to take on the assignment of carrying God's Word, we become God's representative in the Earth. To many people, our lives will be the only Bible they will ever read. Thus, it is imperative that we pay careful consideration to the way we live and conduct our lives in and out of the public view.

Our private lives become intertwined with the call upon our lives. Now everything that we do has a direct impact on his kingdom whether good or bad. Many people have failed to come to terms with this truth. The influence that God gives us is not ours but his. It is an attractiveness that he clothes us with in order for the people connected to our assignment to be drawn to us and the message that we carry. The purpose of this influence is to bring glory to God. Whether it be by bringing unbelievers to Christ, building up his church, restoring back a backslider, or any other capacity that he uses; the end result should always point back to Christ. If used properly it can be of much benefit to the kingdom of God, but if mishandled it can turn many potential believers away from the Gospel. That is why we must be careful with the platform that he gives us.

Social Media Presence

Have you ever considered how influential singing artist and athletes are in our generation? Throughout history, models and actresses have created hair and fashion trends that influence an entire generation. They have the ability to influence culture, start movements and so much more. All it takes is one photo or Instagram post and all of their followers gravitate to whatever thing they are promoting. This is the power of influence, and we must remember that it is a gift. Even on our public social media platforms we have to consider these things. We have the power to create change in our generation so we must use it to promote Gods will and not that of our own.

"For I have come down from heaven to do the will of God who sent me, not to do my own will." John 6:38 NLT

Our ministry should be Christ-centered. The things that we promote, the words that we speak and that which we do in public should all originate from the will of God. After all, just like the three servants in the parable of Matthew, we are just stewards over that which God gives us. The ministry that he gives us was first his idea and not our own, so anything that stems from it should by default flow from that same place. This is how we stay in line with what God desires and not go off into the self-places.

Our brands, books, channels, podcast etc. must be God inspired and not self or man inspired. Every good idea is not a God idea. I love how Stephanie Ike states it in one of her teachings, "We must not get caught up in the latest "moves" or "trends". If not, that which we build will last for a moment but eventually fade away." God maintains what he births. He is not required to take care of something that was not his idea. By retaining this type of attitude, we guarantee Gods' stamp of approval and longevity in our prophetic ministry.

Be careful what you say

Once you cross over from called to being commissioned and the world knows your name as being God's Prophet everything you do will be put under a microscope for all to see. The smallest thing you say could be taken out of context if it is not carefully presented.

This goes especially for our social media. We must be careful not to use our social media as a place for ranting, or a substitute for our diaries. Though we all process things differently and may have an opinion on many different subjects (as that is our right), unfortunately our opinions do not always line up with God's will. Many times, within the body of Christ and also in the prophetic community is a sense where we feel as though we must address every social issue, or newspaper headline. We have become more reactive than responsive. This has created a lot of division and confusion within the body of Christ. This is because often people cannot discern between the Word of the Lord that you are releasing and your own opinion.

Am I insinuating that God does not allow us to be human and express our feelings? No, but we must remember that for those who are looking up to us, even the minor words that we speak in innocence become law, especially for the babes in Christ. Paul encountered this when he wrote to the Church of Corinthians. He addressed many issues some of which concerned marriage and singles. He made sure to make a distinction between that which was given to him by God and is own convictions.

"But I speak this by permission, and not of commandment. For I would that all men were even as I myself. But every man hath his proper gift of God, one after this manner, and another after that." 1 Corinthians 7:6-7 KJV

This is why it is best to keep these types of conversations in a private setting with those close to you, who know you well enough to make these distinctions and with whom it will not affect in a bad way. So, then what are we to learn concerning these matters? We must consider how our words will affect others more than our own desire to speak on any given topic. In this we create a safeguard for not only the body of Christ but our prophetic voice.

Humility

"When pride comes, then comes shame; But with the humble is wisdom." Proverbs 11:2 NKJV

People are drawn to the prophetic and especially Prophets because of their unique ability to *behold* or see into the future. This can easily stroke anyone's ego and temp you to fall into pride, but God is very serious about his glory and absolutely refuses to share it with anyone.

Praises of men

Have you ever preached a dynamic word and afterwards people began to flock to you and shout your praises? This recognition can in many cases tempt us into taking God's glory as our own. Let's take an example from King Herod about the dangers of vain glory.

"So on a set day Herod, arrayed in royal apparel, sat on his throne and gave an oration to them. And the people kept shouting, "The voice of a god and not of a man!" Then immediately an angel of the Lord struck him, because he did not give glory to God. And he was eaten by worms and died." Acts 12:21-23 NKJV

Whew! That seemed harsh didn't it but let's look deeper to see where Herod went wrong. See, the issue with Herod is not necessarily the fact that men gave him praises rather than the fact that he did not give the glory back to God. The Bible says that we should let others praise us and not ourselves (**Proverbs 27:2**) . When we praise our own accomplishments and set our hearts to be lifted up and seen by men this is called vain glory.

The praises of men cost Herod to take God's glory which intern cost him his life. We must learn from this example and not make the same mistakes. Let's look at an example from the Apostle Paul when he was faced with a similar temptation. In this story Paul and Barnabas were ministering in a certain town called Lystra. There was a man there who had been crippled in his feet from birth. When Paul saw that he had faith to be healed he called out to him to stand up, and immediately the man was healed.

After seeing this the people in the city decided that surely, they were Greek gods that had come down in human form. They immediately gathered bullocks and sheaths of flowers to offer sacrifices unto Paul and Barnabas. How similarly when God uses us to do great and mighty exploits that people do the same. They may not necessarily call us gods but the praises that they give us can oftentimes transcend to that of worship, and that should only be given to God. Unlike Herod this was their response.

> *"But when the apostles Barnabas and Paul heard this, they tore their clothes and ran in among the multitude, crying out and saying, "Men, why are you doing these things? We also are men with the same nature as you, and preach to you that you should turn from these useless things to the living God, who made the heaven, the earth, the sea, and all things that are in them." Acts 14:14-15 NKJV*

In the Scripture we see that their response to human accolades was not that of self-gratification but humility. They offered to take no glory but put the focus back on God and also called the people back to his supremacy, sovereignty, and saving power. Though it may feel good at first, the praises of men only cause one to be puffed up and swell the ego. This is a fertile ground for the seed of pride to grow that will eventually become a great tree that consumes and ultimately destroys that individual. So, in this day and age where vain glory and pride are at an all-time high, how does one govern this gift with humility? Here are a few keys to help ensure that we remain humble as we endeavor to carry out our prophetic ministries. These should be avoided at all costs.

1. **"I saw this coming"**

Often times when one of our prophetic words has come to pass, we will be tempted to publicly boast about it. Pride always desires to bring the attention back to "I." Saying things such as "The Lord told me this would happen." or "I saw this coming.." These phrases only speak to validate oneself and does not bring glory to God. First of all, we must remember that we are mere messengers. It is God's Spirit that is speaking and working through us that causes us to be able to see, here and perceive. Without him enabling us we would not have this ability. So, we have no room or need to boast. Let your prophetic track record speak for itself. People will see the consistency and in turn honor the gift. We need not to validate ourselves with the continual blasting of "My prophecy came to pass, did you see?" ministry. This is self-validation and far from humility. There is a way to do it that doesn't draw attention to oneself but gives glory to God. One must ask for wisdom on how not to become boastful and arrogant about such matters.

"When people commend themselves, it doesn't count for much. The important thing is for the Lord to commend them." 2 Corinthians 10:18 NLT

2. Avoid too much spotlight

When we begin to grow and become more accurate with our gift, we build our prophetic track record. People will recognize the authenticity of our gifts and begin to give us accolades. Jesus encountered a similar experience. When Jesus performed the miracle of the two fish and five loaves, the people began to shout, "Surely this is the Prophet we have been expecting." They went as far as attempting to make him their King (**John 6:14**). When Jesus saw this, he immediately retreated away by himself. This shows that even he knew the dangers of the praises of men. It is true that God will allow others to honor your gift and use men to confirm the gift of God inside of you, but as humans we can only take so much before it starts becoming displaced. This is why we must discern when to retreat like Jesus did, when the spotlight begins to get too bright. It is at this moment where we must deflect the attention off of ourselves and become the reflection of Christ. I like how John the Baptist said it in this Scripture.

"You yourselves know how plainly I told you, 'I am not the Messiah. I am only here to prepare the way for him.' He must become greater and greater, and I must become less and less." John 3:28, 30 NLT

3. **Self-promotion**

"For the world offers only a craving for physical pleasure, a craving for everything we see, and pride in our achievements and possessions. These are not from the Father, but are from this world." 1 John 2:16 NLT

Self-promotion is a dangerous spirit and can often be camouflaged. We live in an age of technology and because of this many of our words will be delivered in this manner. With that said the way in which we promote ourselves is very important. There is a very thin line between innocently advertising for the purpose of presenting information and self-promotion. When one heavily promotes themselves, accomplishments, success, they are what the Bible calls **vaunting(1 Corinthians 13:4)**. This is what we call boasting; excessively proud and self-satisfied talk about one's achievements, possessions, position, or abilities. This spirit is characterized by excessive pride or self-satisfaction. Even our attire can become a place where we can be tempted to vaunt. When one operates under this Spirit, they only seek to draw attention to themselves. The Apostle Paul warns us that love does not operate in this manner. So, let's ask ourselves this question. Does your Facebook, Twitter, YouTube, Instagram, or any other social media outlet that you use scream, God gets the glory! Or does it present pride and vainglory. These are very serious questions.

No matter how accurate we are, how busy our itineraries get, or how big our following is we must remain in a place of humility. In the Book of Luke, Jesus tells a parable about two men who prayed to God. The first man prayed out loud in the street so that everyone could hear, boasting about his righteousness. How much he gave to the poor and gave a tithe of everything that he had. The second man however who was a publican, humbled himself to the ground asking God for mercy, confessing that he was a sinner. The Lord had more respect for the second man than the first because of his humility.

"I tell you, this man went down to his house justified rather than the other: for every one that exalteth himself shall be abased; and he that humbleth himself shall be exalted." Luke 18:14 KJV

Humility is a Spirit that one must choose to wear. We must choose to take the lower seat in order to lift the name of Jesus higher. When you wear the Spirit of humility you seek to put the attention back on Christ and deflect it from yourself. C. S. Lewis says this, "Humility is not thinking less of yourself; it's thinking of yourself less." Yes, God will use you in great and mighty ways but remember that it is his power working through you and not of yourself. God can use any available vessel, even a donkey! That fact should be humbling in and of itself to know that the God of all the universe has chosen to use you as his voice in the earth. Let us let love become the conduit through which everything we do flows, including our prophecies. In this way we will walk perfect before God fulfilling the whole law.

> *"Now our knowledge is partial and incomplete, and even the gift of prophecy reveals only part of the whole picture! But when the time of perfection comes, these partial things will become useless. Three things will last forever—faith, hope, and love—and the greatest of these is love." 1 Corinthians 13:9-10, 13 NLT*

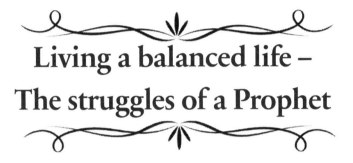

Living a balanced life – The struggles of a Prophet

Don't live in the future

As Prophet's, one of the most difficult areas is to maintain balance. Though common, if left unchecked this can become detrimental. The prophetic realm can weigh heavily on a Prophet's mind, the area where many Prophets battle. This is especially true for those who are seers or dreamer Prophets, with whom God deals heavily with the future. Many times, it feels as though we are constantly seeing, hearing, or receiving revelation. These glimpses of the future can feel like a dark cloud looming over your head. Our minds can sometimes *"stare"* at the thing God shows us to the point that we are now *living in the future*. So much so, it can be difficult to just live in the moment, but that is not what God has destined for our life. When we fail to enjoy our present moment, we leave and open door to fear and anxiety. The Prophet Daniel is a perfect example of this. He mourned for three whole weeks because of the Revelation he received about the feature of his people.

"I said to the one standing in front of me, "I am filled with anguish because of the vision I have seen, my Lord, and I am very weak." Daniel 10:16 NLT

He was filled with anguish concerning the future, but God heard his prayer and sent Gabriel to bring him understanding. Even after getting the insight his heart was still discontent and the word weighed very heavily on his mind. So it is with us. "So don't worry about tomorrow, for tomorrow will bring its own worries. Today's trouble is enough for today." Matthew 6:34 NLT

God shows us the future then tells us not to concern ourselves about it. Let's take Jesus for example. From the start of his ministry, he knew there would come a point where he would be crucified. We see it multiple times throughout Scripture where he would hint to his disciples and those around him of his imminent death (**Matthew 16:21; 17:22**). Every so often he would speak of it as a way to remind them what His purpose of being in the Earth was. That was the most pivotal point of his ministry. To die that we might be saved, but he did not allow it to overtake his mind or keep him from living in the moment. So, neither should we.

Again, there are many reasons God allows us to see things to come. First, the Lord does nothing unless he reveals it to his servants the Prophets (**Amos 3:7**). Also, as we discussed in previous chapters, it could be to warn, pray, intercede, or prevent. Then there are times when God will show you secrets because he considers you a friend. We must learn how to see and release back to God. Pray but don't allow the burden of the future to consume you. This is what God wanted Daniel to understand. His responsibility was not to gaze but to seal up the things he saw until the appointed time. The angel Gabriel brought him back to what he needed to be concerned about and amid his despair, gave him comfort and peace about his future.

"As for you, go your way until the end. You will rest, and then at the end of the days, you will rise again to receive the inheritance set aside for you." Daniel 12:13 NLT

Daniel was precious to God and so are you. He did not want him to live in that state of worry concerning the things he showed him. The mantles, gifts, callings, and revelations from God were never given to take over our life. Though difficult, we must learn how to carry the revelation from the future while still being present and active in our now. He had to remind Daniel that he is God, and he is still in control.

Spiritually Imbalanced

There is a saying that is popular in church, "You are so heavily minded that you are no earthly good." Though this is not scriptural, the concept behind it is biblical. We are spirits that live in a body that have a soul. This is true for every human being on the earth. Those who are Christians have been born again by way of the Spirit and are no longer restricted to this natural world but gain the Spirit of adoption and access to a heavenly seat in another location. So before, where we lived in the flesh to fulfill the lust thereof, now we can walk in the Spirit because our eyes have been opened. We are now aware that the invisible things are more real than what we can see with our natural eyes but *being spiritually aware does not denote the need for natural wisdom.*

If one desires to live in the Spirit and focus solely on that aspect, they will begin to neglect their natural body and responsibilities. For example, it would not be wise to go on an extended fast particularly one beyond 40 days because our physical bodies would eventually start to deteriorate. This would be considered foolish. Especially if you have underlying health conditions. Why is this? Because no matter how spiritual we are, God made our bodies to need proper nutrition. Likewise, it would not be wise to pray all day without ceasing in your prayer closet with your kids or spouse at home to fend for themselves. Why is this, because the Lord gave you that family to be a good steward over them.

This may seem extreme but for many balancing the spiritual and natural is a real struggle and can be due to many reasons. One is an overzealous desire to please the Lord with sacrifices, but this type is one God never asked for. Paul talked about this type of pious self-denial in Colossians.

"These rules may seem wise because they require strong devotion, pious self-denial, and severe bodily discipline. But they provide no help in conquering a person's evil desires." Colossians 2:23 NLT

Self-neglect in the name of ministry

The go hard or go home mentality has crept its way in the format of many ministries, prophetic and those alike. So, what is to be said to those who feel like they are not pleasing God if the majority of their time is not dedicated to ministry? This was never God's blueprint for ministry. Remember that we are three parts: body, mind(soul), as well as spirit. All these aspects of we need attention. We are not robots. Those who practice self-neglect will most certainly in time self-destruct. Unfortunately, this has become the norm for many. Having what appears to be a successful ministry while battling to stay afloat in our private lives. Again, this was never the way God wanted us to do ministry.

Let's take the Prophet Elijah for example. In this chapter, right after experiencing a great move of God on mount Carmel, Elijah found himself under a Juniper tree trying to escape a death threat from Jezebel (**1 Kings 19:5**). Elijah went into a state of depression refusing to eat or drink. The Lord sent and Angel to Elijah who brought him food and drink, why was this? See, although we see Elijah do great miracles and exploits, he was still human and had human needs. I would imagine Elijah had many self-destructive patterns in his life that led to this point. Like so many of us who try and run off the fuel of the anointing, but one must remember the anointing is not for us. It is for others. It most certainly makes teaching, preaching, laying hands, counseling, doing miracles easy, but then after it has accomplished its goal what is left of you? Unfortunately, it is not the Holy Spirit's job to take care of our natural man. As much as the Angel came down and brought Elijah supernatural food, he still had to make a choice whether he was going to eat it or not. We have that same choice whether we choose to make ourselves priority or not.

Let's do an evaluation. How is your personal life? Is it well-managed? How is your mind? Do you struggle to carry on from day-to-day but somehow seem to find the strength to minister when under the anointing? Do you battle with thoughts of suicide or bouts of depression but are still able to pour and speak into the lives of others? This is certainly not God's desire for you. Are your finances prospering, do you have self-control? Is your house in order or disarray. How is your health? How well do you take care of your body? Do you find yourself always eating out or do you have a well-balanced diet? This all speaks about how well balanced you are and guess what, it is perfectly ok to be balanced. Comb your hair, build both your spiritual and physical muscles.

When fasting Jesus told them to wash their face and anoint their head(**Matthew 6:17**). You don't have to look rough to be spiritual. Learn to keep your physical man up and mind as well as your spiritual man. Make time for rest. Pour back into yourself just as much as you give out to others. Seek the same counseling that others pull on you for. Think about it, how well can we really take care of others if we are emotionally, mentally, and physically depleted. I would think not well at all. So, let's stop hiding behind the mantle of self-neglect for the sake of ministry and eat for our journey is great.

Another reason for an unbalanced life could be an unbalanced approach to Scripture, where some teachings are taken literal with no consideration for what the Bible was really trying to speak. For example, Jesus says if our hand offends us, we should cut it off (**Mathew 18:7**). For it is better to enter the kingdom with one hand than to enter Hell with your whole body. Did he really want us to mutilate ourselves in order to ensure safe passage into heaven? Of course not! He was using it to teach to them how to resist temptation and have self-control. Those who give into every fleshly desire could not possibly live a life pleasing to God.

The Bible also teaches that we should not love the things of this world (**1 John 2:15**). It goes on to say what that includes such as sinful earthly pleasures, desiring everything we see and having pride in our achievements. This however does not mean we can't enjoy life. It's perfectly ok to enjoy friends, go to an amusement park or even watch a family friendly movie. Remember, Jesus did not die just for us to go to heaven. If that were the case, he would not have placed Adam and Eve in the garden of Eden here on earth, which by the way means "place of pleasure." One reason he died is to give us life more abundantly. That includes not only freedom from the weight of sin, but to enjoy all the beauty of this earth he created for us without being ensnared by it. Solomon said it best.

"So, I concluded there is nothing better than to be happy and enjoy ourselves as long as we can. And people should eat and drink and enjoy the fruits of their labor, for these are gifts from God." Ecclesiastes 3:12-13 NLT

Balance all

Jesus was the perfect example of a balanced life. He had friends, attended marriages, dinner parties, carried out his ministry, had those he mentored including the 12 disciples, stayed connected to God, but also spent time alone with himself. He was our example, the perfect example of a balanced life.

Not just ministry

The father affirmed Jesus actions telling those around him "This is my son in whom I am well pleased (**Matthew 3:16**). What is so amazing about this is that this was before we even see him start his ministry. Before ever doing a single miracle. From this we see that it is not just our serving in ministry that God is concerned about, but rather the whole aspect of how we live our lives. Jesus' life was relatable. He showed us that God desires us to live a full life. Meaning It's okay to take vacations, spend time with friends and family and just be present. This is all a part of living an abundant life. His life pleased God, yet he was not spiritually imbalance. So, what does this confirm about what really pleases the Father?

Burnout

Many Prophets and ministers alike have experienced burnout, mental breakdowns, failed marriages, failed relationships, and sickness all because of an unbalanced lifestyle. They put most of their energy into trying to build what ultimately belongs to God anyhow. Failing to fall into his grace and come to grips with their human frailty. We are human, he is not. We have limits, he does not. Yes, he has given us great responsibility, but also grace for every assignment. When we push ourselves beyond the limits of what God has asked of us then there is no grace there. This is where we break under the pressure of trying to be God. So, I say to you; don't break. Give God back his weight. We cannot carry everything, but we do our best and give God the rest.

<u>More than one ministry</u>

Minister means to attend to the needs of someone. There is more than one type of ministry God has given you to steward over and they are all equally important. Let's take a look at the Prophet Deborah.

> *"Deborah, the wife of Lappidoth, was a prophet who was judging Israel at that time. She would sit under the Palm of Deborah, between Ramah and Bethel in the hill country of Ephraim, and the Israelites would go to her for judgment." Judges 4:4-5 NLT*

Here we see the Prophet Deborah was a minister with many responsibilities. Many things she had to attend to. For one she was a judge over Israel, an overseer. This meant she was required to hear matters and render judgment, but she also was a Prophet like many of us who are reading this book. She stood in the office to hear from God and speak what he said. I am sure there was some counseling aspects in this role as well. My goodness! That's a lot to handle, but even before all of that the first part of this Scripture said she was a wife. That comes with a whole slew of responsibilities of its own. The Bible doesn't say if she had children but if she did that would be another piece she had to carry. What a big responsibility! God still expecting her to carry each piece with care. He knew she could handle it or else He would not have placed her in such a role.

I would go as far as to say that for Deborah to be successful she had to treat every aspect of her life as a ministry. Something that needed attention and care. Understand that your home is your first church, and your children are your first disciples. This is our first ministry. In order to have a successful marriage there are needs that must be met for both parties. You must be present, give emotional care and so forth. In order to raise respectful God-fearing children, you have to pour time and attention, nurturing them and training them in the ways of God.

If we cannot handle the natural things, then how could we expect God to trust us with the spiritual. The Apostle Paul gave Timothy the qualifications for a potential leader in the church. Most of the prerequisites had to do not only with their character but home life (**1 Timothy 3**). Imagine that, not even how gifted they were but how well their house was in order. God never changes. I would not doubt God required the same things from his Old Testament Prophets and us today.

So, what has God given you to attend the needs of? It could be your family, husband or wife, children or even those you mentor. You may not have a spouse or children, but this still holds true for you as well. Doing ministry requires you to be able to juggle. Meaning you give attention to whatever is in your hand but keeping in mind your other responsibilities so that nothing and I mean nothing falls. Not even you.

You could even think of it as you are cooking on the stove. You have a front burner and a back burner. That which is on the front burner is what gets most of your attention. That doesn't make the things on the back burner of any less importance. Surely you must keep in mind to check on them periodically or else they will burn. Sometimes it will be your family on the front burner and ministry will have to take a back seat and vice versa. That doesn't mean you totally neglect them; it just means the majority of your focus is on a different space. With this concept in mind everything gets its required time, care, and attention.

Let's take a moment to do a self-examination. Is there something burning in your life. If I were to ask those closest to you about your life what areas what they say are lacking? Does your spouse frequently ask for more attention? Do your kids feel valued and care for? Do your friends feel like they are an important part of your life? What about yourself? Are you well taken care of, or do you sacrifice your own well-being for the sake of ministry? We should not let our prophetic ministries concern us to the point where we neglect our home, family, children, spouse or even our own selves. Leave nothing neglected, not even yourself for this does not please God.

If you have found yourself struggling in the area of imbalance, ask God for his breath. Repent for every place you have displaced ministry or taken it on as an idol. Give God back his people, words and even your own purpose. Cast every fear and anxiety about your future on him and leave it there. Ask him how to manage every assignment that he has given you without neglecting anything. Then allow him to order your footsteps in this new way of doing ministry.

Seclusion not Isolation

Another struggle for many Prophets is the place of isolation. The walk of the Prophet is often associated with being a lonely one. What I have found is that this walk does not necessitate isolation but rather Prophets often feel more comfortable being isolated. This is indeed true for many reasons. For one, because of the realm we operate from we encounter many strange and uncommon things, which in turn causes us to have a hard time relating to others. This is especially true for those who have not come into the full understanding of who they are. They themselves feel out of sorts about their own experiences and have an even more difficult time relaying it to others. This leaves us much of the time feeling misunderstood. We in turn detach ourselves physically, emotionally, socially or all three. We retreat to this "safe place" for fear of being rejected or mislabeled.

However, justified we may feel this is just pride masking itself. God never wanted the Prophets walk to be this way. Why can I say this? Because he has made all humans for connection and community. God made us for relationship. This includes not only our spouses, but family and friends. Over the past few years due to the pandemic, we have seen the detrimental effects of prolonged isolation on the human psyche. I am sure this is only the tip of the iceberg concerning the mental health crisis because we were never made to be totally disconnected from others. Think about it. In the prison system one way they deal with an unruly inmate is to put them in isolation and we have observed the outcome. So whether it is by choice or not, the effects of isolation are still the same.

Another issue that arises is the fact that Prophets discern or "see." That means we see the good, bad, and the ugly in others. For some this reality can be intense and often cause mistrust issues. This too causes us to run from covenant relationships. We see spirits operating in others and often don't know how to handle it. Should I connect to this individual? Do they have the right motives? And so on. This again is pride masking itself as fear and also shows a lack of maturity. This Gift of Discerning of Spirits was never given to use as a weapon against others.

Jesus knew Judas's motive was off and the fact that Peter would deny him, but he never treated them any different. We all have issues, and it is often the hardest for us to see what is operating in our own selves. It is also easier for us to give grace in our own shortcomings but very difficult to give that same grace to others. We must allow the grace of God to be thoroughly worked in us to love and receive people through their flaws just as Christ does. We must have God's love formed in our hearts in order to be in covenant relationship without feeling the need to correct or be judgmental.

It is true God will often call his Prophets periodically into the place of seclusion. Drawing them away with him for them to recharge, refresh, download new insights and perspectives. Many times, what God releases to you in these moments will almost always directly impact how you interact with others. Just like he did with Paul, when he knocked him off of his high horse and drew him away for a time of redirection and training (**Acts 9**).

This is the difference. Isolation is self-driven while seclusion is God driven. These moments also include times of purging and deeper deliverance, but never should this be our everyday life. Does this mean you will be totally disconnected from people in seclusion? Not necessarily, it could mean the time you would usually spend doing things like traveling, or hanging out with friends or family may be more limited. Where you would pick up every phone call and chat for hours may decrease to only important matters, but never will God have you to cut off communication with those closest to you especially your spouse, children, Pastor, or prophetic community.

"Two people are better off than one, for they can help each other succeed. If one person falls, the other can reach out and help. But someone who falls alone is in real trouble." Ecclesiastes 4:9-10 NLT

We draw strength from the connection of others. As we talked about in a previous chapter, the company of Prophets helps you to sharpen your gifts and gain deeper revelation. Iron sharpens iron. Even in these times of seclusion God will use them as a means of support and encouragement.

If you have found yourself struggling in the place of isolation, ask God to help you deal with the root of pride and fear of being rejected. There will be many times in your walk where you will feel misunderstood, but remember God understands you even when others don't. He sees you and knows you better than anyone else could, even your own self! He knows the true intentions of your heart. Find comfort in this but don't allow it to become an excuse for you to withdraw yourself from others. Yes, there will be times when those you try to connect to will reject you.

Yes, there will be times where you will find yourself in circles that may not always look like you, causing you to feel a bit uncomfortable. Yes, there will be times where you covenant yourself with others and end up getting the bitter end of the stick. When opening yourself and putting trust in people there is always a risk of getting hurt. All of these are possibilities, but he still does not want us to run from them. God will even use that hurt in order to form his perfect love within us. Do not rob yourself from the new things God may want to do in your life. Allow yourself to be vulnerable, open yourself to whatever God wants you to gain from or pour into new covenant relationships.

Persecution and Rejection

"Then Amaziah sent orders to Amos: "Get out of here, you prophet! Go on back to the land of Judah and earn your living by prophesying there! Don't bother us with your prophecies here in Bethel. This is the king's sanctuary and the national place of worship!" Amos 7:12-13 NLT

We talked about the different aspects of the Prophet earlier in this book (mouth, eyes, ears, etc.). Yet there is another aspect that sets them apart and that is the *Mark of the Prophet*. Needless to say, anyone who carries a true Word of God will suffer. That includes his disciples, but prophetic ministry comes with a heavier level of persecution and rejection, more than that of any other five-fold ministry gift.

That is what marks them. That is what sets them apart. I might go even further to say that it is how God proves them. If you have been in prophetic ministry for any amount of time you are sure to have already faced some form of persecution or rejection. There is just no way around it. It has nothing to do with your demeanor, your accuracy, persona, how you treat people or anything else, but a part of the call and the suffering that we must endure as we carry our cross.

No greater

"Do you remember what I told you? 'A slave is not greater than the master.' Since they persecuted me, naturally they will persecute you. And if they had listened to me, they would listen to you." John 15:20 NLT

Jesus did no wrong, as a matter of fact he did everything right. He was the only perfect man to walk the earth, yet he still suffered persecution. Jesus's messages convicted the heart of men. The truth that he carried brought light into every hidden and deep place of their soul. It cut them to their depth and demanded that they make a decision. This is why many people hated and rejected him. At the end of it all, even the ones who were for him in the beginning persecuted him. We surely are no greater than he, so we must accept that same fate (**1 Peter 3:13**). Just look through the history of God's Chosen Prophets and you will see the pattern that echoed throughout their life. Rejection and Persecution.

"What blessings await you when people hate you and exclude you and mock you and curse you as evil because you follow the Son of Man. When that happens, be happy! Yes, leap for joy! For a great reward awaits you in heaven. And remember, their ancestors treated the ancient prophets that same way." Luke 6:22-23 NLT

He goes on to say if anyone desires to be his disciple, we must first count the cost (**Luke 14:26**). We must be willing to bear our cross as Jesus did. You must be willing to suffer for the sake of pleasing our Lord and savior. As you start on your prophetic journey you must consider this fact. You must ask God for his grace to carry his word and to be delivered from *the opinion of man*.

Remember, False Prophets are rarely persecuted by men. Why? Because they tell the people what they want to hear. Jesus warned us that if we are liked by men then there is a real chance that we are not carrying the light. Remember, the Prophet Micaiah from 2 Kings 19. He was persecuted and thrown into prison because of his refusal to conform to the words of men and the False Prophets.

The king knew what Micah was saying was true but because he did not want to agree, he rejected that word. You will be faced with this same type of situation as well. Rejected for doing the right thing. Hated without a cause. Accuracy does not always equal acceptance and sometimes you can do all the right things and still be mistreated. The question then is what is the most important thing, being accepted by men or accepted by God?

<u>Fear of persecution</u>

Let's look at Jeremiah for an example. Jeremiah was a Prophet of much persecution. Though persecution was not uncommon in those times for a Prophet, we don't see them respond or express it in the way that Jeremiah did. That is why he has been coined as "The Weeping Prophet."

Jeremiah's Complaint

> *"Then I said, "What sorrow is mine, my mother. Oh, that I had died at birth! I am hated everywhere I go. I am neither a lender who threatens to foreclose nor a borrower who refuses to pay— yet they all curse me." Then I said, "Lord, you know what's happening to me. Please step in and help me. Punish my persecutors! Please give me time; don't let me die young. It's for your sake that I am suffering." Jeremiah 15:10, 15 NLT*

See, this was Jeremiah's fear. He was afraid that he would die young and become a martyr like many of the other Prophets. Jeremiah had become a point of ridicule for his community. Even his friends turned on him and nicknamed him "The man who lives in terror." They threatened him, even wished harm on him yet he did nothing wrong (**Jeremiah 20:10**). Everywhere he turned he faced rejection and persecution all because he decided to speak the words that God gave him. Ouch! That must have hurt. I could only imagine having to live under these extreme conditions. Blow after blow, hit after hit, rejection after rejection. Not from outsiders but his own family, friends, and community. This was Jeremiah's coat. This was not something that he asked for, but rather what was given to him.

See, many times when we think of persecution, we believe that most of it will come from the outside. Especially in the time that we are in where technology is advancing at an alarming rate. Social media platforms are popping up everywhere and now everyone has an outlet to voice their opinion. Once you post something publicly you are at the mercy of the media. You are now open to both compliments and criticism. Accolades and arguments.

Though it is true you will be judged by people who don't know you personally and whom you may never meet, but what I have found is that most of your rejection will come from within and not without. Those closest to you. This kind is what causes the most damage to your heart as it did with Jeremiah.

The sting of bitterness took root in his heart and brought him to the place where he felt like he could not go on any longer. He even expressed where he felt like God had tricked him into taking on the office (**Jeremiah 20: 7**). He was not prepared for the suffering he would have to endure in order to carry God's word. At some point the persecution got so intense that Jeremiah decided to stop prophesying. This is where we see this very popular Scripture.

"But if I say I'll never mention the Lord or speak in his name, his word burns in my heart like a fire. It's like a fire in my bones! I am worn out trying to hold it in! I can't do it!" Jeremiah 20:9 NLT

The fire that Jeremiah was expressing was not a pleasant feeling. It was a burden and if you have ever carried a burden from the Lord, you know exactly what Jeremiah was experiencing. It is the war between your flesh and your spirit and ultimately through all his complaints and weeping, the spirit won. He yielded himself to die to himself and let God's will be done through his life.

There is purpose in it

Rejection and persecution have their place. Though it does not feel good, they have a purpose. Persecution is what aids in birthing a Prophet. God uses it to help build their character and keep them humble. It tests your motives to see where your *why* really lies. Are you in it for recognition or is your intent truly to serve and obey God? You don't know if you will really stand until you are faced with persecution. This is when the real test comes. Will you buckle? Will you compromise? Will you refuse to speak God's word as Jeremiah did? These are all tough questions that we will face as we walk out our prophetic ministry.

It is important to note that though the mark of the Prophet is persecution and rejection, we should not take it on as if it is *who we are*. It is not who you are. Though it is happening *to us*, we should not allow it to become *a part of us*. We are not rejected but have been accepted into the body of Christ whereby we call him Abba father (**Romans 8:15**). Our father accepts us as his own, and though some may reject you, know that there are many more that will be for you and are waiting for the word that is in your mouth. We must embrace this truth, if not then you will begin to embody the spirit of rejection. Remember, whatever you embrace is what you will attract. So, if you walk around always feeling defeated and rejected then rejection will always find you.

Defending God's Word

Then there will be times you feel so attacked that you will be tempted to retaliate or in many cases defend God's Word. These attacks can come from people who publicly mock you, leaving you feeling as though you must respond in the same manner. Going above and beyond in order to prove God's Word to be true. Let's see what the Bible says about correcting a mocker.

> *"Anyone who rebukes a mocker will get an insult in return. Anyone who corrects the wicked will get hurt. So don't bother correcting mockers; they will only hate you." Proverbs 9:7-8 NLT*

The world would say to defend yourself at all cost, but wisdom says hold your peace and let God fight your battles. Responding to the word of a mocker rarely ends in a peaceful resolution. Oftentimes it causes more confusion and chaos. This is true especially within the body of Christ where serious public disputes and dissensions only reflect negatively on the church. We must be honest and ask ourselves what is at the root of our motive to respond. Is it to bring clarity and understanding to the individual, or is it to defend our name? This is not to say that we will never respond. There will be times when God will unction you to respond but when He does it will be in a way to bring edification to the hearer and not out of a spirit of retaliation, defense or to prove a point. This is also a sign of maturity, when one can be ridiculed, but through the love of God hold their tongue in order to do no harm to that individual(s).

God defends his Prophets

The Prophet Isaiah faced persecution as well, but his disposition was different from Jeremiah's. It was one of hope and courage in that God would defend and take care of him. This was his proclamation in Isaiah 50:5.

> *"The Lord God hath opened mine ear, and I was not rebellious, neither turned away back. I gave my back to the smiters, and my cheeks to them that plucked off the hair: I hid not my face from shame and spitting. For the Lord God will help me; therefore shall I not be confounded:*

therefore have I set my face like a flint, and I know that I shall not be ashamed." Isaiah 50:5-7 KJV

Isaiah refused to back down from ridicule just to be accepted by men. He knew God would help him and defend him. *God defends His Word*, and He will not allow any of them to fall to the ground. Even when you have to deliver a *hard word*, remember that you are only a messenger and that word and outcome belongs to God. All He asks is for us to be obedient.

Dealing with Discouragement and Disappointment

Now let's talk about something that every Prophet at some point will face and that is a place of discouragement. Discouragement can be defined as a lack of confidence or enthusiasm, or dispiritedness. I really want to dive deep into this place because I believe this is something many Prophets and ministers alike are facing right now all around the world. There are many reasons why we could become discouraged. One of which is a place of rejection. This happens when our words are not received by the people we were called to give them to. Let's take Ezekiel for example. The Lord knew that the children of Israel were a stubborn and hard-hearted people but He still required Ezekiel to release the word even though they would reject it.

> *"But the people of Israel won't listen to you any more than they listen to me! For the whole lot of them are hard-hearted and stubborn. Then go to your people in exile and say to them, This is what the Sovereign Lord says!' Do this whether they listen to you or not." Ezekiel 3:7, 11 NLT*

Even though God sent Ezekiel to warn the people, it did not automatically mean that they were going to receive his word. God has given every man a free will and it is up to the individual to receive and act upon that word. These types of predicaments can weigh heavily on any individual, especially those who face repeated rejection. This is why it is imperative that we remember that we are God's messengers, and the message does not belong to us. Therefore, when one refuses to receive the message that we are releasing, they are not rejecting us but God.

> *"Whoever listens to you listens to me; whoever rejects you rejects me; but whoever rejects me rejects him who sent me." Luke 10:16 NIV*

It is when we take on God's Word as our own that the sting of rejection becomes a poison and can-do lethal damage. I do not believe the Lord faults us for feeling this way, but I also believe that we should not stay in a place of discouragement for an extended period of time. When we become overwhelmed by these feelings, they can spillover into our prophetic words, and prayers. We see this in the prayers of King David, in the Book of Psalms, where he frequently prayed for vengeance and judgment upon his enemies. It can become a dangerous place because if bitterness is set in our heart toward those we are meant to intercede for, then we fail to see correctly leaving them vulnerable to the enemy. As we discussed in other chapters the voice of the Prophet is very powerful. Elisha became angry when a group of young people began to tease him. In his anger he cursed them and caused a pack of bears to attack them (**2 Kings 2:23**). I do not believe this is what God gave the voice of the Prophet for. It should be our endeavor to do good and not evil. Therefore, our heart has to be rightly positioned when we speak. We must ask God to heal us from the place of discouragement in order for our words to be pure when they are released.

Recognition often comes later

This may seem like a harsh reality to many, but it is rare that the full extent of that Prophet's ministry is appreciated until after they are long gone. This is not only true for Prophets but for other ministers as well. Jesus showed his disciples how John the Baptist was the Prophet that the children of Israel had long been waiting for, but they failed to recognize him while he was living (**Matthew 17:11**). He came in a way they were not expecting so they rejected him. This was history repeating itself.

In the Old Testament we see where the children of Israel didn't want to hear the words of warning from the Prophets of their generation as well. Again, it wouldn't be until the next generations came up that they realized the words of that Prophet were true. If only their ancestors had heeded the warnings, they could have spared themselves from judgment. True Prophets in the Bible seemed to only truly be honored after their death. Jesus mocked the religious leaders for building extravagant burial tombs for the same Prophets that their ancestors persecuted and killed (**Matthew 23:29**).

There is nothing new under the sun. Today we see the same, where it is not till after the fact that people will pull back from the words that the Prophet or minister have spoken and recognize the importance of the gift they carried while here on earth. Don't allow this truth to discourage you. Find peace that a life lived to honor God by fulfilling your purpose is all that matters. It is our ultimate duty to obey God and in the end; He gets all the glory.

Then there is the place of disappointment.

Disappointment comes when our hopes, desires or expectation are failed to be fulfilled. There are many things that can cause a Prophet to become disappointed; one is a delay of the promise. As Prophets we are called to prophesy and proclaim the word of the Lord. There will be times when you won't see the fulfillment of prophetic words in the time that you thought they would manifest. There are even words and promises God will make over our lives that seem like they are in a delay. This is what the Bible calls hope deferred; it can damage your spirit and create a place of grief in the heart of a Prophet.

"Hope deferred makes the heart sick" Proverbs 13:12 KJV

I have experienced this place of discouragement in waiting. It can often leave you with questions and attempt to make you doubt if you heard God correctly. In this place I have found that the Lord will always come to bring encouragement to his Prophet through His Word. See, God's Word is precious and as we begin to declare and intercede over God's prophetic word it is important that we carry that prophetic promise in the right position. He watches over his word to perform it and He will never let any of his words fall to the ground. (**Jeremiah 1:12, Isaiah 55:11**).

It may seem as though the word He instructed you to release is in delay, but you must remember God's timing is not our timing. There is a set time, due time, and fullness of time. Prophets in the Old Testament sometimes waited years to see the fulfillment of their prophecies. Some even passed away before seeing it come to fruition and many of them still have yet to be realized. Due to this fact it is important to remember that it is God's word and through his omniscience and infinite wisdom, He creates the most opportune time of manifestation. It is good to look back at God's faithfulness in seasons of discouragement and disappointment to remind yourself that if He did it before He will surely do it again.

It is a Journey

First, I would like to congratulate you for making it to the end of this book. I am sure that there are Prophet's reading this book who are on different stages of their prophetic journey. Some of you may have been operating in ministry for some time, some of you may just be starting off. Some of you may just be realizing that you are even a Prophet. My prayer is that you feel more confident in your calling and how to operate in your gifts. Even with all the knowledge and insight that you have gained as you journeyed through these pages, I want to remind you that the making of a Prophet is still a process. One that did not start when you came into the acknowledgement of who you were called to be. God had his hand on your life and has been processing and navigating you this whole time. If you look hard enough, I am sure you will see it as well.

No matter where you happen to be on this pendulum; new, old, undeveloped, or seasoned, know that it is a journey. We never really arrived. Though we sometimes imagine it in our minds, there is no prophetic "High Point," or stage in this walk to where we can say, we have learned all that we can learn or know all that we can know. We will be forever learning, growing, and evolving in our prophetic call until the day that we go home to be with Jesus Christ. The only difference is the more we go with him the more knowledge and experience we gain.

As much as you are reading this book today, I am sure there are things written in it that God will bring me into deeper revelation of and my perception is sure to evolve on some level. So, release yourself from the rush of *being* and enjoy the journey of *becoming.* You are in the making. Though it may appear as though some are progressing faster than others, know that God has predestinated this process and tailor made it for you. As long as you continue to partner with him you will never skip process nor end up behind schedule.

Words of Encouragement

New Prophets

Now I want to encourage the New Prophets. Those of you who are just really coming into your prophetic call. It may be that you have known that you are a Prophet but are now really beginning to accept it and grow into greater levels of maturity. At this point in your journey, you may feel discouraged and disappointed because it seems as though your words are not being accepted in the same manner that other Prophets are. Firstly, we must remember that Prophets are not accepted in their own home. They were so use to Jesus being Joseph's son that when God propelled him into his ministry his own kinsman rejected him (**Luke 4:24**). I want to let you know that this is normal. You have been in the secret place with God, building history and gaining confidence in your abilities to hear from him and speak his words. Unfortunately, this is something that the rest of the world has not witnessed. Let us take Samuel as an example. He was trained from a young child under Eli, carrying out priestly duties. Then one day the Lord visited him and gave him a word. Though he was confident that the Lord was speaking to him, it was new to those around him. Due to this fact it took some time for Samuel to become established as a Prophet.

> *"As Samuel grew up, the Lord was with him, and everything Samuel said proved to be reliable. And all Israel, from Dan in the north to Beersheba in the south, knew that Samuel was confirmed as a prophet of the Lord." 1 Samuel 3:19-20 NLT*

It is God who affirms and validates you as a Prophet, so do not feel as if your words do not matter. Though it seems very difficult to face rejection, this is normal, continue to prophesy. It is your responsibility to be consistent in what He gives you and it is God's responsibility to bring the word to past. Just like Samuel, your words have to be proven. Your reputation must be built as one who is credible. These things take time. Do not take this place personal because it is a place of building trust through prophetic accuracy. As you learn and grow, God will establish who you are through your *prophetic track record.* Most importantly remember to stay humble, it is not about you but about God.

The Seasoned Prophet

"Don't be misled—you cannot mock the justice of God. You will always harvest what you plant. So let's not get tired of doing what is good. At just the right time we will reap a harvest of blessing if we don't give up."
Galatians 6:7,9 NLT

Now I want to encourage the seasoned ones. The Prophets who are not new to this journey. First, I want to say thank you for journeying through these pages with me. I hope something you read inspired you on your walk. You may be suffering from prophetic fatigue and discouragement. You may not have seen the responsiveness or growth that you may had hoped to see in your ministry. It may seem as if you have been toiling with little production. This may have caused you to pull back from sowing as much as you did in earlier seasons. We must remember time and season. Some seeds require a greater germination period than others. The sacrifice that you have made for God's kingdom did not go in vain. The pouring that you have done into the lives of others was not futile. Never forget God rewards faithfulness. He is not a man that He could lie, every seed you have sown is remembered in his eyes and you will reap if you do not give up. Remember what this ministry is all about. Though we are the ones that toil, in actuality, it is not really about us at all. These are God's people and though we may plant and water, it is him who brings the increase and him who gets the glory from it. It is God who purposes it and makes all things beautiful in his timing. Your wisdom is so important to the next generation of up-and-coming Prophets. You have jewels that are very valuable to the kingdom of God. Maintain momentum and continue to build like Caleb. God sustained his strength and stamina to endure even in his last seasons. Do not hang up your mantle, the hour of fathering and mothering has just begun.

Young Prophet

"The Lord replied, "Don't say, 'I'm too young,' for you must go wherever I send you and say whatever I tell you. And don't be afraid of the people, for I will be with you and will protect you. I, the Lord, have spoken!" Jeremiah 1:7-8 NLT

Do not despise your youth. No, you are not too young to prophesy. Just like God used Jeremiah, He is no respecter of person. He wants to use you as well. It is God's Word; He only needs a willing vessel to carry out his work; keep in mind anointing knows no age.

"Then, after doing all those things, I will pour out my Spirit upon all people. Your sons and daughters will prophesy. Your old men will dream dreams, and your young men will see visions In those days I will pour out my Spirit even on servants—men and women alike." Joel 2:28-29 NLT

In this hour God is raising up a new generation of young Prophets and dreamers. You have been destined for this purpose and for this time. He wants to use you right now at the age that you are to show a generation the power of God and that He has no limits. Do not be afraid. He is the one who will train and affirm you. Just like He did with Jeremiah. He will teach you all you need to know and put you in the company of those you can watch over you and help to groom you. He knows that you are young and knows how much you can handle. He won't give you more than you can bear. God can use young people to do great things in the earth! Take the story of Elisha, where he sent the young Prophet to go and anoint Jehu to be king (**2 Kings 9:1**). This was no small task, one that was usually given to more seasoned Prophets, but God saw fit to use that young man to do big things and so can you! All He needs is a willing vessel and He will take care of the rest.

Advanced in years

To the older Prophets, I want to encourage you as well. Do not despise your age. You may just be coming into the realization of your call. You may have just started this journey of the prophetic or even fairly new in your walk with God. Maybe you have been in a place of not understanding your call. Or maybe you are one that knew you had a call from a young age but have been in a place of running from it. God has used people who were advanced in years to do great things, Moses and Aaron being just few. Moses too was on the run. He was 40 years old when he ran away as a fugitive from Egypt. It wasn't until 40 years later that Moses encountered the Lord at the burning bush and God declared to him that he would be used to deliver God's people out of bondage.

> *"And when he was full forty years old, it came into his heart to visit his brethren the children of Israel. And seeing one of them suffer wrong, he defended him, and avenged him that was oppressed, and smote the Egyptian: And when forty years were expired, there appeared to him in the wilderness of mount Sinai an angel of the Lord in a flame of fire in a bush." Acts 7:23-24, 30 KJV*

If God could use Moses at the age of 80 to do great and mighty exploits, I want to say to you, you are not too old. God still wants to use you. He needs your voice. He can give you supernatural strength even in this time. Just like the young Prophet all He needs is an available vessel. Be teachable, willing to hear and see God's grace transform your life!

References

1. Charisma definition acquired from Thayer Bible concordance (G5483) and Strong's Bible concordance

2. Edify definition acquired from Thayer Bible concordance (G3619)

3. Exhortation definition acquired from Strong's Bible concordance (G3874)

4. Comfort definition acquired from Strong's Bible concordance (G3889)

5. Ordination definition acquired from Wikipedia

6. Vocation definition acquired from Oxford Languages in collaboration with Google

7. Prophet definition acquired from Thayer Bible concordance

8. Ear definition acquired from Thayer Bible concordance

9. Role definition acquired from Oxford Languages in collaboration with Google

10. Prepare definition acquired from Oxford Languages in collaboration with Google

11. Commission definition acquired from Meriam webster dictionary

12. Mantle definition acquired from dictionary.com and

13. Consecration definition acquired from dictionary.com

14. Knowledge definition acquired from Oxford Languages in collaboration with Google

15. Omniscience definition acquired from yourdictionary.com

16. Discretion definition acquired from Oxford Languages in collaboration with Google

17. Wisdom definition acquired from Oxford Languages in collaboration with Google

18. Insight definition acquired from Dictionary.Cambridge.org

19. Discernment definition acquired from dictionary.com

20. Wield definition acquired from Oxford Languages in collaboration with Google

21. Gossip definition acquired from Oxford Languages in collaboration with Google
22. Suspicion definition acquired from dictionary.com
23. Honor definition acquired from Meriam-Webster dictionary
24. Value definition acquired from Oxford Languages in collaboration with Google
25. Appraisal definition acquired from Oxford Languages in collaboration with Google
26. Neglect definition acquired from Meriam-Webster dictionary
27. To serve definition acquired from Oxford Languages in collaboration with Google
28. Stewardship definition acquired from Oxford Languages in collaboration with Google
29. Faithfulness definition acquired from vocabulary.com
30. Integrity definition acquired from Oxford Languages in collaboration with Google
31. Covetousness definition acquired from dictionary.com
32. Divination definition acquired from Oxford Languages in collaboration with Google
33. Presume definition acquired from Meriam-Webster dictionary
34. Diligence definition acquired from Oxford Languages in collaboration with Google
35. Bigotry definition acquired from Vocablulary.com
36. Denominationalism definition acquired from definitions.net
37. "Differences of opinion" quoted from excerpt in Holman Everyday Study Bible copyright 2018
38. Coerce definition acquired from Oxford Languages in collaboration with Google
39. Disobedience definition acquired from Oxford Languages in collaboration with Google
40. Protection definition acquired from Wikapedia.org
41. Pride definition acquired for yourdictionary.com

42. Phrase "Contingencies in Prophecy" acquired from You Version Bible plan: He gave us Prophets: The   purpose of predictions

43. Influence definition acquired from Oxford Languages in collaboration with Google

44. Vaunting definition acquired from Merriam-Webster dictionary

45. Minister definition acquired from the free dictionary.com

46. Discouragement definition acquired from Oxford Languages in collaboration with Google

47. Disappointment definition acquired from Oxford Languages in collaboration with Google.

About the Author

Janell Edmondson is a dynamic prophetess, revelatory teacher, effective preacher, and enthusiastic worshipper. Most importantly, she is a devoted wife to her husband Jermaine Edmondson and loving mother to her four beautiful children. If there was one word to exemplify this gift from God, that would be altruistic! She has the inborn ability to show compassion and nobly care for the needs of others.

Prophetess Janell was ordained a minister in 2010 and then again into the five-fold office of the Prophet in 2015. She loves serving in her local youth department and is a worshipper at heart. Prophetess Janell's multifaceted approach to life, affords her the opportunity to carry many different roles well. She finished her studies as a nurse and graduated with her associates in nursing in 2017. She also started an online crafting business which she still manages today. In 2020, the Lord birthed her into her prophetic ministry, and she started The Voice of the Prophet YouTube channel where she releases the word of the Lord to the body of Christ, nations, and the world.

Even with all her accomplishments, she believes it is her calling to not only be a prophetic voice and intercessor to the nations, but also to help guide an up-and-coming generation of prophets. To help them know they are not crazy, but rather chosen by God to do a great work in the Earth! She currently resides in her birth city of Tampa, Florida, and continues to serve faithfully in her local Ministry (Truth Outreach Global Ministries) under the leadership of Elder Rosby Kelly and Apostle Michelle Kelly, as a prophet, teacher, intercessor, praise and worship leader, and youth leader.

Contact info

To purchase products visit www.TheVoiceoftheprophet.org

Or feel free to follow her through social media

Facebook

@TheVoiceoftheProphet1

YouTube

@Thevoiceoftheprophet

You can contact Prophetess Janell through email

Thevoiceoftheprophet@outlook.com

By mail: 2424 W. Brandon Blvd #1254 Brandon , Fl 33511

Made in the USA
Middletown, DE
21 April 2025

74249222R00170